D0457770

Lee Anne:

Best wishes
and
Warm Wishes,

Jane Herman

Double Lives

ALSO *by David Heenan*

Co-Leaders
WITH WARREN BENNIS

The New Corporate Frontier

The Re-United States of America

Multinational Organization Development
WITH HOWARD PERLMUTTER

Double Lives

CRAFTING YOUR LIFE *of* WORK

and PASSION *for* UNTOLD SUCCESS

DAVID HEENAN

DAVIES-BLACK PUBLISHING
Palo Alto, California

Published by Davies-Black Publishing, a division of CPP, Inc., 3803 East Bayshore Road, Palo Alto, CA 94303; 800-624-1765.

Special discounts on bulk quantities of Davies-Black books are available to corporations, professional associations, and other organizations. For details, contact the Director of Book Marketing and Sales at Davies-Black Publishing, 3803 East Bayshore Road, Palo Alto, CA 94303; 650-691-9123; fax 650-623-9271.

06 05 04 03 02   10 9 8 7 6 5 4 3 2 1
Printed in the United States of America

Library of Congress Cataloging-in-Publication Data
Heenan, David A.
    Double lives: crafting your life of work and passion for untold success / David Heenan—1st ed.
    p. cm.
    Includes bibliographical references and index.
    ISBN 0-89106-167-3
    1. Success—Psychological aspects. 2. Self-actualization (Psychology) 3. Work—Psychological aspects. 4. Recreation—Psychological aspects. I. Title.
    BF637.S8 H363 2002
    158.6—dc21   2002023780

FIRST EDITION
First printing 2002

*Go confidently in the direction
of your dreams. Live
the life you've imagined.*

—HENRY DAVID THOREAU

To our sons, Marc and Eric,
and especially to Nery

Contents

Foreword

*E*ver since I learned that Wallace Stevens, arguably the greatest American poet, spent much of his time at a day job with an insurance company in Hartford, Connecticut, I've been interested in individuals with healthy and surprising dual selves. David Heenan takes us way beyond this gentle fascination as he chronicles the double and triple lives of ten fascinating personalities.

As I got further into this unique book, I had what the French call an *apercu*, an insight, something like an epiphanic moment. I was startled to realize that *Double Lives* is a virtual guide for twenty-first-century careers. In light of the prediction that most Americans in the contemporary workforce will have nine jobs by the time they are in their mid-thirties, we can expect double lives to become a natural part of what we consider everyday living. Heenan's book, then, is not just about a few incredibly gifted individuals but about how most of us, certainly the readers of this book, will live our lives in the twenty-first century.

What Heenan has up his intellectual sleeve is invention. Self-invention. Imagination. That's basically how we get to know ourselves. People who cannot invent and reinvent themselves must not be content with borrowed postures, secondhand ideas, fitting in instead of standing out. Inventing oneself is the opposite of accepting the single role we were brought up to play.

All of us have problems inventing ourselves. I used to think I wanted to be a university president. And for seven godforsaken years, I did just that. The problem was I wanted to *be* a university president, but I didn't want to *do* what a university president does. I realized that what gave me satisfaction and happiness was being able to play multiple roles—leading, thinking, and doing. Consequently, I shucked the brass ring for opportunities that allowed me to write, teach, and lecture on a wide variety of topics.

Consider Richard Feynman. A Nobel laureate, best-selling author, and wildly popular lecturer, he was perhaps the greatest physicist of the second half of the twentieth century. A true polymath, Feynman was equally comfortable slapping the skins of his bongo drums or storytelling in New Age hot tubs. Anything that puzzled him became a challenge. As a youngster, rather than study trigonometry from textbooks, he reinvented all the formulas himself. Working summers as a busboy, he discovered new methods for stacking as many dishes as possible. While developing the atomic bomb at Los Alamos, he plied his uncanny mathematical powers picking locks in his spare time.

In the New Mexico highlands, Feynman witnessed firsthand the dangers of overspecialization. Highly trained engineers from Cal Tech and MIT were confined to cranking out rote calculations. It was pre-computer days. Boring work. Morale was low. The spunky Feynman prevailed on J. Robert Oppenheimer to explain the Manhattan Project to them and their vital role in its success. According to Feynman, staffers were transformed. Thinking beyond their narrow specialties, they invented new programs, often working through the night. That's what versatility and balance can do.

Renaissance types like Feynman are never realists. They're optimists, convinced they can do anything. They don't simply solve problems. For them, the process of self-discovery is its own reward. They have hungry, urgent minds. Over the years, I have repeatedly found these multitalented people to be pragmatic dreamers—men and women who are able to get things done while taking personal risks. They don't stand on the sidelines. They get involved in new projects, new ideas, and challenging assignments.

David Heenan knows this subject. A well-respected corporate executive, he has led his own double life as a successful writer (we recently coauthored *Co-Leaders: The Power of Great Partnerships*). It is this authenticity that allows him to lay out an intellectual road map—a set of directions any of us can follow to shape a second or third identity. While *Double Lives* offers no magic formula, no quick cure, it does provide a framework for thinking about balancing work and life in clear, unemotional terms. You'll find this insightful book full of the sort of sensible advice that seems obvious—after you've read it.

Read this book and you'll discover some simple truths that will make you happier and infinitely more interesting to yourself and others. And just wait—you may find leading several parallel lives a passport to living the life you want to lead.

Warren Bennis
Santa Monica, California

Preface

*I*t's an ethos as sacred as apple pie: Specialize when you're young and you'll acquire the skills necessary for a lifetime of success. In the past, the rising complexities of postindustrial society demanded and rewarded undivided attention and effort—nothing less. Even today the dogma persists: Doctors, lawyers, and accountants specialize; scientists, engineers, and academics specialize; even teenagers seeking admission to top-tier universities specialize in a single field, sport, or musical instrument.

Yet, in our hearts, we know that choices shape a person's life. As John F. Kennedy said, "Success has many fathers." Increasingly, people are seeking to reinvent themselves in new and exciting ways. Those living a "double life" include CNBC president Pamela Thomas-Graham, who doubles as a popular mystery writer; Mike Reid, the former NFL All-Pro tackle, now a Grammy-winning songwriter; and singer-songwriter Joni Mitchell, whose prowess as a painter has won kudos. There are many others. As poet–insurance executive Wallace Stevens put it, these adventurers yearn to live "in the world, but outside of existing conceptions of it."

The virtues of a double life come to us at different stages in our lives. My good friend Dr. Samuel Wong remembers Harvard president Derek Bok's advice at his freshman orientation: "Don't confine yourself to the narrow corridors of one profession." The idea took. After his undergraduate studies, Wong attended and graduated from the Royal Conservatory of Music in Toronto and Harvard Medical School—eventually choosing music over medicine. Today, he directs the Honolulu Symphony and the Hong Kong Philharmonic.

My own epiphany came thirty-two years ago. I had just finished reading Michael Crichton's *The Andromeda Strain* and was flabbergasted to discover that the author had penned the novel while studying at Harvard Medical School. Knowing that medical students probably have less than twenty minutes discretionary time in the day, I wondered how this twenty-six-year-old could have cranked out not only a best-seller, but one that launched the medical-thriller genre. Crichton didn't stop there. Today he wears many hats: He is the author of twenty-two novels, a science and art critic, a film producer, and a computer games entrepreneur.

Over the years, I studied other Renaissance personalities, who—like Crichton—not only defied classification, but destroyed the myth that specialization was the only path to success and happiness. In the process of my research, I assumed my own double life: For three decades, I shuffled between positions in academia (Wharton, Columbia, and Hawai'i) and business (Citicorp, Jardine Matheson, and the Campbell Estate). The constant in both lives was my writing, including books like this that question the old bromides.

Double Lives offers an alternative to the restrictions of a single focus. By examining the lives of versatile contemporary and historical figures, you will discover how to benefit from your various passions. My subjects are as different as day and night; however, they all are committed to fostering greater balance among their varying interests.

Mitch Albom, author of the best-selling *Tuesdays with Morrie*, learned life's lessons from a dying man. "So many people walk around with a meaningless life," his former college professor, Morrie Schwartz, told him. "The way to get meaning in your life is to devote yourself to loving others, devote yourself to the community around you, and devote yourself to creating something that gives you purpose and meaning." I hope my stories will galvanize you to create purpose and meaning in your life.

David Heenan
Honolulu, Hawai'i
April 2002

Acknowledgments

*M*any friends and colleagues contributed to this book. The earliest version of my manuscript was critiqued in part by Kristin Hohenadel, who brought a journalist's eye to the process. Brett Uprichard gave my ideas flight and elegance. He read and critiqued the book's overall presentation. Marie MacCord and Melissa Casumbal assisted on selected research assignments.

I also owe special thanks to Bill Hamilton, Jerry Porras, Warren Bennis, Spencer Johnson, Ed Perkins, Dan Boylan, Kent Keith, and Phil Norris, who reviewed various segments of my work. Belinda Aquino, Roger Jellinek, Samuel Wong, and Joanne Grimes also offered invaluable insights.

Many thanks to those who encouraged me to tell their stories: Norio Ohga, Sally Ride, Ron Kent, Chuck Watson, Larry Small, Jim Wolfensohn, Tess Gerritsen, and Tom Lynch. Others who gave me a better understanding of their lives include Kei Sakaguchi, Ree Sakai, Taisuke Ohnishi, Gerald Cavanagh, Hiroshi Yasuda, Tadanobu Kashiwa, Bill Bailey, Brian Powers, Jeffrey Goldstein, Poni Watson, Cathi Watson Sanders, Ken Sanders, Bill Wilson, Bob Sutton, Amy Tucker, Robert Witt, David Mas Masumoto, Myra Kent, Cy Gillette, John Barr, Suzanne Haskew, and Pastor John Harris.

My efforts were also influenced by a number of excellent writers who are duly cited in the notes. They include William Manchester, Walter Gilbert, Lady Mary Soames, Walter Graebner, Lord Moran, John Nathan, Reiji Asakura, David Stashower, Austin Coates, Onofre Corpuz, Cord Cooper, Linda Stockman-Vines, and Amy Reynolds Alexander. My heartfelt thanks go to this special group of people.

At Davies-Black, I had the pleasure of working with a talented team of wonderful professionals—especially my editor, Lee Langhammer Law. This book benefited tremendously from her wisdom and rigor.

Jill Anderson-Wilson also supplied exceptional editorial skill and wonderful enthusiasm. Laura Ackerman-Shaw, Laura Simonds, and Anita Halton offered special assistance in bringing *Double Lives* to market.

Caroline O'Connell, my agent in Los Angeles, saw the project through—guiding, helping, and inspiring me every step of the way. She clarified my earlier ideas on the subject and handled all negotiations. Martha Miller's competence, diligence, and unfailing good cheer through successive versions of the manuscript contributed greatly to its completion. She was assisted by Jenny Okano and Debbie Miyagi.

Finally, my wife, Nery, has been at my side throughout this project. She read and commented on the entire manuscript and helped shape its principal arguments. To this loving and most constructive critic goes a very special *Mahalo*.

About the Author

*D*avid Heenan is a trustee of the Estate of James Campbell, one of the nation's largest landowners with assets valued at over $2 billion. Formerly, he served as chairman and CEO of Theo. H. Davies & Co, the North American holding company for the Hong Kong–based multinational Jardine Matheson. Earlier, he was vice president for academic affairs at the University of Hawai'i and, before that, dean of its business school.

Heenan holds an A.B. degree in economics from the College of William and Mary, an M.B.A. degree in international business from Columbia University, and a Ph.D. degree in international business and applied economics from the Wharton School of the University of Pennsylvania. He has served on the faculties of the Wharton School and the Columbia Graduate School of Business. His articles have appeared in such diverse publications as the *Harvard Business Review*, the *Sloan Management Review*, the *Wall Street Journal*, the *New York Times*, and the *Christian Science Monitor*. He is author or coauthor of *Co-Leaders*, *The New Corporate Frontier*, *The Re-United States of America*, and *Multinational Organization Development*.

Heenan lives in Honolulu, Hawai'i. He can be reached at dave-hee@aol.com.

1

The Case *for* *a* Double Life

My object in living is to unite
   My avocation with my vocation
As my two eyes make one in sight.

—ROBERT FROST

S ometimes we are lucky enough to know that our lives have been changed, to discard the old, embrace the new, and run headlong down an immutable course," wrote the late Jacques-Yves Cousteau, arguably the twentieth century's best-known Frenchman. As a youth, he dreamed of a career as a naval aviator. However, a near-fatal automobile crash pointed him in a new direction. To strengthen his broken arms, Cousteau, at age twenty-six, took up swimming and thereby began his love affair with the sea. Over the years, the self-taught oceanographer assumed many identities: sailor, explorer, inventor, best-selling author, prize-winning filmmaker, staunch environmentalist, and astute businessman.

Even now, Cousteau's multiple lives seem like an anomaly in a world that still promotes focus on one—and only one—calling. But for every Bill Gates or Warren Buffett, whose single focus attracts fortune and fame, there is a Jacques Cousteau or Michael Crichton as evidence that sticking to one pursuit is not the only path to success. In this new millennium, F. Scott Fitzgerald's observation that there are no second acts in life no longer applies. The old one-act myth is giving way to the view that a career is but one among many experiences. Some wise human beings may have always known that work and life are not mutually exclusive, but finding ways to balance competing demands is the topic of countless magazine articles, talk show discussions, and self-help books.

Double Lives reflects the growing conviction that the demarcation between profession and passion—between vocation and avocation—is being blurred to the point of obliteration. The twin goals of satisfying work and multiple interests go hand in hand. The challenge is to make choices that convert the opportunities the twenty-first century provides into more diverse and fulfilling lives. People today are seeking their own personal renaissance. Above all, they want to experience the liberating effects of branching out.

This first comprehensive study of double lives challenges the time-honored advocacy of total commitment to a single profession, a position that dies hard. But everything changed on September 11, 2001. People around the world began to revisit their priorities; "balance" finally came into its own.

As the idea of balance pervades the culture, more and more people are shunning the narrow confines of conventional careers, shedding their workplace skin to feed their souls. The day job, for some, remains the primary job; but, away from work, they squeeze in as much as they can—early mornings, nights, weekends, vacations—to unleash their hidden dreams: writing, painting, acting, creating a side business. Eventually, some break away permanently. Expertly trained doctors and scientists, eager to capitalize on their skills, are plunging into e-health and biotech start-ups in record numbers. At the same time, disaffected dot-comers in their twenties and thirties are looking to reboot themselves in less harried environs. Ambitious attorneys, intent on becoming the next John Grisham or Scott Turow, are sending manuscripts to agents and publishers. Plucky teachers, suffocated by the tedium of the classroom, are entering new fields ranging from entertainment to health care. In every profession, people find themselves wanting to trade in their business cards for a second identity.

Why are these adventurous souls willing to subordinate their primary careers, a shift that seems all the more remarkable in an age obsessed with traditional success? Some see it as a way to escape the pressures of corporate bureaucracy or to fill voids in their careers. Others hope to regain control of their lives. Some want riches or fame. But, in every instance, these enterprising men and women want to eliminate the nagging feeling that their lives could be more fulfilling.

After eighteen years as a practicing attorney, Ron Bass turned to screenwriting, penning the Oscar-winning *Rain Man* and such films as *The Joy Luck Club*, *My Best Friend's Wedding*, *Snow Falling on Cedars*, and *Memoirs of a Geisha*. "I was a good lawyer, a negotiator. It was interesting and challenging," the Harvard Law School grad said in an interview. "But for me, the pinnacle was something allowing me to make the business of living—the business of what I do all day— exploring the meaning of life." Many of us, before we slip off to sleep at night, half dream of performing on stage, of making the best-seller list, of exploring a new field. People like Ron Bass give life to those dreams. In many respects, they are modern-day da Vincis.

Leonardo da Vinci, of course, was the ultimate Renaissance man. Many people would be content to excel in painting, science, architecture, engineering, or sculpture. Da Vinci excelled in all five. In his world, anything was possible. Born in Italy in 1452, this transcendent genius designed bridges, fortresses, armored tanks, flying machines, and parachutes. He was a keen observer of biology, anatomy, plant life, and the motion of water. His paintings (the *Mona Lisa*, *The Last Supper*, and others) created powerful images that persist today.

Renaissance thinkers such as da Vinci, Michelangelo, Cellini, and Galileo defied classification and inspired future generations of multi-faceted artists, scientists, and scholars, including Mozart, Goethe, Picasso, Benjamin Franklin, and Thomas Jefferson. In researching this book, I scrutinized dozens of contemporary Renaissance men and women, analyzing how they juggled various interests. Because personal stories are a lively and effective way to illustrate important points, I chose to make the case for double lives through biographical sketches of outstanding individuals, from statesman Winston Churchill to Sony chairman Norio Ohga to astronaut Sally Ride and the other men and women profiled in this book.

Double Lives looks at these extraordinary individuals to demonstrate that pursuing multiple interests contributes to happiness and personal fulfillment. Perhaps no one illustrates this better than Winston Churchill, one of the greatest figures of the twentieth century. A Nobel Prize–winning author, a mesmerizing orator, and an accomplished artist, Churchill was the quintessential Renaissance man. Balancing affairs of state with his many other roles, he made it his life's mission to reinvent himself.

But let's be clear. *Double Lives* is not confined to high-profile geniuses. This book has one overriding point of view: *Anyone* can craft a double life—all he or she needs to scale new heights are imagination and drive and some helpful tools to aid the process. As you see in the chart, I've identified twenty key themes to a successful second life— keys we will explore in the profiles.

In the course of studying those with double lives, I was constantly reminded that crafting a second identity is a process, not a destiny. Because each person is unique, I hesitate to categorize these eclectic types. The social world isn't nearly as orderly as the physical world. People—unlike solids, fluids, and gases—are anything but uniform and predictable.

As you will see, each of these subjects had or has a distinctive, often colorful, personality. Although Britain's Churchill and the Philippines' José Rizal both led their nations at critical stages—while achieving world-class honors as writers, orators, and painters—they were as different from each other as chalk and cheese. Others, although not always players on the world stage, have distinguished themselves in different fields of endeavor: Construction executive Chuck Watson sculpted gigantic ground-hugging metal pieces; stockbroker Ron Kent chisels hunks of Norfolk pine into translucent bowls; Tess Gerritsen traded her medical career for mystery writing; and Smithsonian chief Larry Small juggles flamenco guitar and Amazonian art with his day job. In the course of my research, I found that, however they differed, each of these individuals had taken one of three distinctive paths to another life. Each followed a parallel, a convergent, or a divergent track.

Parallel paths are those followed by people who give separate but equal treatment to both lives. They don't give up their day jobs, although they are drawn to another activity or pastime. Famed poet

20 Keys

TO A DOUBLE LIFE

1   *LISTEN TO YOUR HEART*

2   *DEFINE SUCCESS IN YOUR OWN TERMS*

3   *AIM HIGH*

4   *TAKE ONE STEP AT A TIME*

5   *DELIVER DAILY*

6   *LEARN FROM FAILURE*

7   *IGNORE THE NAYSAYERS*

8   *MAINTAIN A MAVERICK MIND-SET*

9   *FOCUS, FOCUS, FOCUS*

10   *AVOID DISTRACTIONS*

11   *NEVER STOP LEARNING*

12   *PLAN AND PERSEVERE*

13   *BUILD A BRAIN TRUST*

14   *RECHARGE YOUR CREATIVITY*

15   *REINVENT YOURSELF*

16   *SELL YOURSELF*

17   *KNOW THY EMPLOYER*

18   *SEEK COMPATIBLE GOALS*

19   *SAVOR SERENDIPITY*

20   *START NOW*

Wallace Stevens and pioneering composer Charles Ives both were committed to the insurance industry. Stevens was a surety claims lawyer and Ives a salesman and agency executive. Called "the Matisse among poets," Stevens turned down numerous offers to teach poetry that would have meant jettisoning his vice presidency at Hartford Accident & Indemnity Company.

Similarly, composer Ives viewed his musical achievements (a Pulitzer Prize for Symphony No. 3) as secondary to his insurance practice. Though often hailed as the founding father of American music, Ives was a weekend composer whose primary love was business, which incidentally made him a very rich man.

Those who pursue parallel paths identify most strongly with their core calling. Some actually attempt to camouflage their second lives (pseudonyms are a favorite technique). Nevertheless, they understand, in the most visceral way, the value of developing collateral interests.

Convergent tracks link both lives at the hip. Both activities are mutually dependent and feed off each other. Consider Dr. John Schott, the Freudian speculator, who, at sixty-one, doubles as a money manager and a psychiatrist. The Harvard-trained physician lectures at Tufts and Harvard medical schools and enjoys a clinical practice. In addition, he runs funds at the Boston-based Steinberg Global Asset Management, Ltd., and edits a well-regarded investment monthly, the *Schott Letter*. Specializing in the psychodynamics of investing, Schott helps investors cope with emotional hang-ups that can cause them to make mistakes in the stock market. As Father Confessor to shaken day traders, Schott finds that his vocations are completely intertwined.

For three decades, John Barr has been both a top-flight investment banker on Wall Street and an oft-published poet. He was the first businessman-poet to serve as president of the Poetry Society of America, the country's oldest poetry association. "Business and poetry aren't odd bedfellows," he says of his co-equal lives. "They both draw their water out of the same well. They are both concerned with making order out of chaos. I see myself as someone who wanders the world turning what I see into money and poetry. I can't imagine doing one without the other."

Divergent routes are the roads taken by double lifers who eventually turn their backs on their day jobs. Though trained as a physician, Michael Crichton abandoned medicine shortly after graduating from Harvard. His subsequent métiers have ranged from science-fiction writing to film producing to computer games creation. Other nonpracticing doctor-writers include Robin Cook (*Coma*), Ethan Canin (*Carry Me Across the Water*), Deepak Chopra (*The Seven Spiritual Laws of Success*), and Spencer Johnson (*Who Moved My Cheese?*).

For similar reasons, John Grisham (*The Firm*), Richard North Patterson (*Degree of Guilt*), David Baldacci (*The Simple Truth*), Jeffrey Deaver (*The Empty Chair*), and Brad Meltzer (*The Tenth Justice*) traded law for fiction. "Most lawyers would rather be doing something else," megaseller Grisham once noted of his former life. "There is tremendous dissatisfaction with the profession, and almost every lawyer I know is looking for a way out."

Whether abandoning their stethoscopes or legal briefs, these defectors chose a risky path to a new self. Some keep modest links to the past (Grisham, for instance, still takes on the occasional client). But most are on a continuous quest for a personal makeover.

For all its warts, the New Economy is both the cause and the effect of this recent renaissance. On the plus side, it has provided the technology-inspired bursts of innovation that have enriched the lives of many. Every day, Bill Gates makes people wealthy by getting them to work hard, and the number of Microsoft millionaires is legendary. But the Information Age also has its downside: We are a society obsessed with work. Harvard economist Juliet B. Schor's 1992 bestseller *The Overworked American: The Unexpected Decline of Leisure* described the corrosive effects of our long-hours culture.

If anything, the problem has worsened in the past several years— all work and no play has become the maxim for the Treadmill

Economy. Being overworked and stressed out is part of our national self-image. According to a recent Exec-U-Net poll of 800 senior managers who report working an average of 56.2 hours a week, nearly one-quarter consider themselves workaholics, and more than 40 percent admit they are exhausted at day's end.

We now put in more hours at work than any of our counterparts in the industrialized world, clocking roughly 2,000 hours a year—almost 3.5 weeks more than the Japanese. Since 1990, the average American has added about 36 hours—almost a full week—to his or her annual workload. We live in an already frantic world, yet the pace gets faster and faster, with no letup in sight. As historian Stephen Kern puts it, "Human beings have never opted for slower." Burnout, however enigmatic it may seem, is nearing epidemic proportions. How bad is it? It's probably not chronic yet, but it could be by the end of the decade.

The mounting disloyalty of the institutions that once provided lifetime security for employees is yet another example of workplace angst. If laboring in corporate America was once about what you could do for the company, today a bad day at the office means looking for a new job—or a new life. We are witnessing a populist backlash against the high-tech rat race. Except for those whose sole passion is their job, most of us crave greater balance between work and life outside the office. But how do we achieve it?

For some, the answer means postponing the problem. They are entering what the *Wall Street Journal*'s Sue Shellenbarger calls "the tomorrow trap"—a kind of mirage that people chase, while in reality they are burying themselves deeper in work and other pursuits. "An exploding array of new media and consumer goods," she argues, encourages people to neglect things and relationships that are important, thereby "depriving themselves of emotionally rewarding experiences." Rather than forging close companionships, Shellenbarger's "tomorrow trappers" let high-tech gadgets control their lives.

Sharing this almost Luddite perspective is novelist Kurt Vonnegut, who contends that, among the other ill effects of our technology-driven society, "people are getting cheated out of a whole lot of human experience and are becoming uninteresting themselves." Loneliness and loss of fellowship are endemic throughout the digital economy. Technology, while a good servant, can become a bad master.

Those most heavily ensnared in the tomorrow trap sacrifice everything else in pursuit of delayed gratification. The clearest sign is their disengagement: They lose touch with their spouses. They become strangers to their children. Friends drop away. In extreme cases, parents are barely mourned. The community that supports and cares for them begins to shrink. Worst of all, these frantic isolationists fail to scrutinize their own lives, to consider who they are and what they really need, and to make changes that will prepare them for the future.

Other Americans troubled by the wear and tear of contemporary life seek solace in the familiar. Rather than explore new directions, they cling to safe, risk-free environments that can become "intricately designed, self-constructed prisons," noted leadership expert John W. Gardner, the author of *Self-Renewal*. Eventually, these people atrophy and lose their capacity for self-renewal, costing them soul and substance.

Yet, despite the upheaval it has wrought, the New Economy has also provided a renewed sense of opportunity. "America, no longer a nation of sheep, has entered the age of autonomy," writes Professor Alan Wolfe of Boston College's Boisi Center for Religion and American Life. "People may not have a clue about how to survive on the prairie in front of an open campfire, but they are pretty much on their own when it comes to finding a mate, choosing a career, or planning retirement. Deep inside, Americans are exploring a new frontier."

In today's environment, Americans want to jump-start their search for this frontier. And they are confident they can do so. The insightful young French nobleman Alexis de Tocqueville spotted the nation's ebullient personality in 1835. "No natural boundary seems to be set to the effort of man," he wrote to describe the everyday American. "And in his eyes what is not yet done, is only what he has not yet attempted to do."

In the post–September 11ᵗʰ world, the country remains doggedly optimistic. Two-thirds of Americans believe it is possible to be who you want to be. They dream of unlimited self-realization. "So long as we believe there is no ceiling, there will be no end to the effort we'll expend on the way to self-making," writes Richard Powers, author of *Plowing the Dark*. Despite its faults, the twenty-first century is nurturing a "new spirit of nonconformity," adds Michael Lewis in his book *The New New Thing*. "We are pursuing an endless quest for originality."

No one has been more articulate on this values shift than management expert Peter Drucker, who challenges people to find individuality and excitement in a double life. He suggests developing new interests long before burnout or boredom infect your career. Many creative skills—writing, painting, sculpting—are self-generating, learned by sitting alone in a room and wrenching out a paragraph or a piece of art. Conversely, other avocations—flying, for instance—require rigorous training, and the benefits pay off over time. Therefore, those interested in a more elastic lifestyle should nurture their hidden dreams as soon as possible.

This notion of cradle-to-grave experimentation violates some of the time-honored maxims of life planning. Typically, we have encouraged those in their twenties and early thirties to swim in several ponds before committing to a chosen vocation. Those nearing retirement age also have been urged to strike out anew while they are still hale enough to face new challenges. But those in their late thirties, forties, and fifties have been told to hunker down, thereby avoiding the slings and arrows of midlife. In short, put your dreams on hold until you retire.

The old rules no longer fit. Exploring new trails is not a function of longevity. A double life is not age bound. Creative output does not crest and ebb at any predetermined time. Furthermore, technology and genetic enhancements are propelling individuals toward the upper range of our life span. Life expectancy today is thirty years longer than it was at the beginning of the last century: In 1900 it was forty-seven;

today it is seventy-seven. Scientists predict that, barring accidents or disease, today's newborns will live 109 to 120 years. Therefore, a long, healthy, and productive life (or two) is beckoning—if we plan for it.

Life's prolonged course offers everyone an opportunity to chart new horizons. This means setting your priorities early and putting in place the building blocks to achieve them. Especially challenged are the 79 million baby boomers born in the euphoria that followed World War II. As this gigantic demographic bulge of Americans moves into middle age, its members must reassess their professional situation and ask themselves what else they can, should, or want to be doing. No longer can they tell themselves "I'm too old to live my dream, but too young to do the things I really want to do when I retire."

As even the most accomplished boomers move deeper into middle age, they often feel they are entering a vacuum. No matter how many mountains they may have climbed, many feel they are not learning or deriving satisfaction from work. They no longer understand who they are or what the future holds, despite having twenty to thirty years until retirement. This is precisely why "second adulthood," a concept coined by author Gail Sheehy, should be about finding new value in life and customizing one's future years to reflect changing interests and abilities. Therefore, midlife can be an ideal point from which to launch a double life. For many, second lives mean change, and such transitions, of course, are never easy. "Often they're frightening and painful," writes Martin Groder, a Chapel Hill, North Carolina, psychiatrist and business consultant. "But on the other side of the struggle is a sense of rebirth and renewal."

"First secure an independent income, then practice virtue," goes an old Greek proverb. Many seniors wait to rebalance their lives until after their working careers have ended and they are secure financially. Even those who have stockpiled a tidy nest egg may have trouble branching out after years of single-mindedness, but steady doses of golf or bridge aren't as satisfying as their work-for-pay days. Not content to passively watch their golden years go by, smart retirees are discarding the rocking chair and taking their dreams for a brisk walk around the block. Getting their second wind, they quickly find new interests that add zest to their remaining years. Grandma Moses first picked up a paintbrush at seventy-six and was still painting when she was a hundred. Alex Haley's Pulitzer Prize–winning *Roots* was published when he was fifty-five and had retired from the U.S. Coast Guard. Martha Graham was a working choreographer well into her nineties. Frank Lloyd Wright completed the Guggenheim Museum in New York at ninety-one. Furthermore, a growing body of research suggests that cognitive ills can be delayed or prevented by taking on new mental challenges, such as learning a new language, reading a difficult book, or tackling a new pursuit.

Painters, writers, composers, and sculptors—the gamut of creative types—work until they die. They often find life's best rewards late in the game. "Don't retire, retread!" advises Robert Otterbourg, author of *Retire & Thrive*. He tells late bloomers to shun the forbidding signposts "should have," "would have," and "could have." Retirement is not life's final chapter but simply the end of one phase of adulthood and the beginning of another. Take Ed Koch, the former congressman and mayor of New York. Since leaving Gracie Mansion in 1989, the peripatetic seventy-seven-year-old has had several lives: lawyer, talk-show host, columnist, movie reviewer, university lecturer, author (*Citizen Koch*), and TV judge on *The People's Court*.

"It suits an old workaholic like me just fine," Koch has written of his many roles. Polymaths like Koch forge highways of their own choosing. "God writes straight with crooked lines" goes a Portuguese proverb—meaning the oddest happenings often make sense if only in the long run. People pursuing multiple interests recognize that the topology of life is ever changing. For them, the whole-life experience is an exploration, a journey of self-discovery. They would agree with the late novelist, poet, and composer Paul Bowles, who said, "The point of life is to have fun if there is any point at all. Enjoyment is what life should provide."

Our explorers have a clear sense of what makes life enjoyable: Joy comes from unleashing hidden dreams. Life explorers ache for time to pursue other passions, whether acting, writing, composing music, or working in a different field. "If we leave a dream, it doesn't go away," writes jack-of-all-trades Julia Cameron, a professor, film and TV writer, director, producer, and award-winning journalist. "It goes underground." Hence, the persistent theme for every pliable person: Don't let your dreams fizzle!

What, then, does it take to mold a double life? For starters, it requires tremendous drive and confidence to jettison a conventional lifestyle and head into uncharted waters. People seeking self-renewal are highly motivated. With a degree from Boston's Berklee College of Music, stockbroker-musician Douglas Lees felt a void in his Wall Street career until he formed his rock band, The Wingnuts. "I didn't know why business success was not as fulfilling to me as it was to other people," he said. "The dreams of your youth are so strong that if you try to deny them or leave them for too long, you could end up in psychic peril." But his return to the keyboard changed all that.

James Benham, founder of the highly successful mutual fund family bearing his name, also discovered that music was something he could not put aside. A first-rate jazz trumpeter, Benham insists that the perils of corporate burnout are far less for the musically inclined; performing allows him to forget a hard day at the office.

"Don't get me wrong, I really do enjoy my job," Enzo Gugliuzza, a Brooklyn-based UPS delivery driver and trumpet player, told the *New York Times*. "But we don't have to be buried by our duties. The trumpet is my outlet to express myself, to let the world know that I'm not a cockroach, even if I wear a brown uniform."

That kind of spunk pays off. "People who have something other than their work have a way of reducing stress and of assuming that they're not so bound up in the power games of life that they're highly vulnerable to disappointments and setbacks," Abraham Zaleznik, psychoanalyst and professor emeritus at Harvard Business School, noted in *Fortune*. "They have something more going for them."

An old axiom—"If you want something done right away, ask a busy person"—still rings true. The idea that more roles, rather than fewer, make people happier is well documented. For instance, research conducted at Wellesley College indicates that men and women who have more than one identity or role are mentally healthier and enjoy more marital stability. Rather than being depressed or burned out, dualists are "blessedly stressed," says University of Washington sociologist Pepper Schwartz.

"Man cannot discover new oceans unless he has the courage to lose sight of the shore," wrote André Gide. Those contemplating a second life are undaunted risk-takers. Harvard-trained Ethan Canin had the grit to leave the medical profession after only seven years. At the time, he confessed, "It makes me understand that it's the idea of writing a great book that propels me now, whereas it used to be the idea of success." Redefining success on his own terms had an immediate effect on the now highly acclaimed author: "I remember the morning of walking out of the hospital and into this shining day and just feeling this flood of relief."

Determination is another trait of these intrepid adventurers. Above all, they want to stretch their limits. They are on a never-ending search for higher mountains to climb. Take, for example, the late Gardner McKay. Though success eludes most people, it seemed to pursue McKay. As Capt. Adam Troy, skipper of the schooner *Tiki*, in the popular TV series *Adventures in Paradise*, he saw his acting career skyrocket. Yet, in his thirties, he walked away from success in television and films for his first love—writing. "Acting is pretending, and I wanted to be taken seriously," the author of *Toyer* and three other books recalled in a *Honolulu* magazine interview. With the desire so characteristic of other dualists, McKay said, "You don't want to trade life for success—it will just chew you up all the time."

Curiosity is almost as important an attribute as grit. Art historian Kenneth Clark called Leonardo da Vinci "undoubtedly the most curious man who ever lived." Thomas Jefferson also possessed a voracious appetite for knowledge. As a student, he spent as many as fifteen hours a day at his books and practicing the violin. As an adult, the author of the Declaration of Independence was among the leading thinkers of his day in a truly amazing number of fields: politics, science, agriculture, art, architecture, literature, and history. Today, doctor-inventor Harry Gruber rages with the same protean curiosity. At age twenty-seven, he secured his first patent for a class of compounds that regulate andenosin, a building block of DNA. Now forty-nine, the biotech expert and serial entrepreneur recently founded San Diego–based Kintera, Inc., an Internet marketing provider for non-profit organizations. "Harry has just amazing range. His mind is like a Web page with about sixty-two links," said J. William Grimes, a long-time colleague and former chief executive of ESPN.

High energy is another critical characteristic shared by those with chameleonlike lives. We wonder where some of them find the time to be all the people they are. Consider, for example, America's sixth president, John Quincy Adams. The consummate public servant—secretary of state, ambassador, U.S. senator and representative, as well as the nation's commander-in chief—Adams was also a connoisseur of the arts, an exponent of the sciences, and a professor of rhetoric and oratory at Harvard. "Old Man Eloquent," as Northern newspapers called him, woke up every day at 5 A.M., read the Bible, swam naked in the Potomac River, and wrote religiously. One of his brothers called him "the most exhaustless" man he ever knew.

Active lifestyles also characterize contemporary crossover artists. With an adrenaline rush, James Cramer begins his action-filled day at 3:30 A.M. after only four hours of sleep. Wall Street's so-called Pied Piper of Capitalism has been an active writer, TV commentator, hedge-fund manager, and entrepreneur. He cofounded The-Street.com, the financial news Web site where he serves as a director. But don't wait for the mile-a-minute Cramer to abandon his television career for writing. "I think I do the two jobs," he said, "because I'd be bored if I only did one."

In addition to being hyperkinetic, these people have a well-developed ability to concentrate while leading two lives. Poet-pediatrician William Carlos Williams wrote in his car while parked outside patients' homes after he made his house calls. With more than ten million books in print, David Baldacci also knows how to focus. Cranking out a thriller a year, the lawyer-turned-writer says he "zones out a lot." "I can write with a crying child on my lap," he told *USA Today*. "I have. Often."

Perhaps no one could zone out better than Peter Paul Rubens. For many years after he had become the most acclaimed artist in Antwerp, Rubens worked as an effective ambassador, frequently participating in peace negotiations on behalf of his homeland, the Spanish Netherlands. The master painter–diplomat's renowned powers of concentration were vividly described by a visitor to his studio in 1621: "While still painting, [Rubens] was having Tacitus read aloud to him and at the same time dictating a letter. When we kept silent so as not to disturb him with our talk, he himself began to talk to us while still continuing to work, to listen to the reading, and to dictate his letter, answering our questions, and thus displaying his astonishing powers."

One of Steve Jobs's mantras at Apple Computer, Inc., is "Real artists ship." Curiosity, energy, and concentration don't mean beans unless the product goes out the door—unless it leads to action. Those pursuing double lives are men and women of action, not reflection. Rubens designed and executed more than three hundred paintings, engravings, and woodcuts. Mozart produced more than six hundred pieces of music. And Benjamin Franklin definitely shipped. The master of versatility—inventor, writer, diplomat, and politician—demonstrated incredible output. Whether inventing bifocals, swimming flippers, cast-iron stoves, or lightning rods, Franklin was immensely productive. He felt compelled to fully exploit his potential. "Hide not your talents," he said. "They for use were made. What's a sundial in the shade?"[35]

Many people launch a double life from their day jobs—which can benefit the employer as much as the employee. In our Darwinian economy, talent is what matters most, and smart leaders help create a corporate culture that unleashes, not stifles, human creativity. Savvy organizations like Microsoft, General Electric, and Cisco Systems recognize that a serious avocation can enable people to escape creeping corporate ennui and boredom. James A. Autry, management philosopher, poet, and business executive—now a consultant and public speaker—describes the value of his varied lifestyle. "I started writing because I needed to," the former senior vice president of Fortune 500 Meredith Corporation told the *New York Times*. "It lets me express my anger and fear and grief about my business experience."

Besides allowing staffers to vent their frustrations, a second life can enhance on-the-job performance. A case in point is James Patterson, top-selling novelist (*Suzanne's Diary for Nicholas*) and former chairman of J. Walter Thompson–North America, one of the world's largest advertising agencies, where he serves as a consultant. For decades, Patterson penned his thrillers before dawn and ads by day. He believes his double life made him better at both jobs: "I always went to the Thompson offices in a relatively celebratory mood, with the knowledge that I had accomplished something even before I got to work."

Another oft-cited benefit is the many spin-offs these multitalented people bring to the workplace. Olaf Olafsson, forty, a high-level multimedia executive and acclaimed novelist (*The Journey Home*), contends his writing skills have been of infinite value in business. "A good writer needs to have some insights into human personalities—what makes people tick and what people are composed of," he noted in *Fortune*. "In business that comes in handy every day." Olafsson uses these special insights as vice chairman of Time Warner Digital Media, which focuses on interactivity and opportunities for high-density video products. Investment banker–bard Lindsay Hill sees similarities between poetry and problem solving in business. "In writing poetry," he said, "you're looking at relationships that don't fall together obviously or as a matter of habit."

One of the greatest rewards any organization gets from da Vincian personalities is their diverse perspectives and points of view. These nonconforming thinkers aren't shrinking violets. Fiercely independent, they are able to speak truth to power, even when it hurts. As such, they are vital checks on executive hubris. Vanguard companies don't need yes-men.

No one has been more outspoken on this than J. B. Fuqua, founder and chairman of the board of The Fuqua Companies, who urges his peers to endure occasional discomfort in order to find out what they really need to know. Today's leaders, he contends, must be more curious and open to constructive criticism. Himself a double lifer (having served four terms in the Georgia legislature), Fuqua also advises America's business bigwigs to explore parallel careers. "Becoming a CEO is not the end of the learning curve," he said in an interview in *Chief Executive*. "It's more like a new beginning."

In the final analysis, organizations inevitably benefit from ample stores of complex, well-rounded human beings. For years, Sony Corporation's chairman and former chief executive officer Norio Ohga has had a rich life outside the company as a jet pilot, an operatic tenor, and an orchestra conductor. Instead of haunting Sony's offices in Tokyo, he chooses to fly around the world pursuing his musical interests. Not your average salaryman, this managerial maestro has tapped his baton in leading symphonies on almost every continent and chairs the Tokyo Philharmonic. Whether in business or in concert, Ohga has convinced his players that they are free to express themselves, while still getting them to follow his vision and direction. When he assumed the top slot at Sony, Ohga brought not just his demonstrated talent and experience but a panoply of less obvious assets, such as self-awareness and independence, that serve both him and the company. That kind of self-possession and personal equilibrium guarantee good leadership, regardless of the title an individual may hold.

Still, people may pay a price to break the mold. Eclectic men and women have often been subjected to taunt and ridicule. In fifth-century Egypt, Hypatia's extraordinary accomplishments led to her death at the hands of a Christian mob. The first woman to have a profound effect on mathematics, Hypatia was also the world's leading astronomer, as well as a philosopher, religious thinker, and orator. Unfortunately, her public prominence as a truly exceptional female made her a target of criticism and envy. One day in Alexandria's public square, a band of thugs attacked, stripped, and killed her with pieces of broken pottery.

Even now, those contemplating a double life walk a tightrope of personal and institutional needs and obligations. Organizations supportive for a time may grow uneasy as their best and brightest become more accomplished away from work. Even the highly regarded attorney-author Louis Auchincloss found it difficult to convince his colleagues and clients that he was giving his job full attention. "There wasn't anything I could do about it, but I lost a great deal of practice," he said, recalling the false perception that he was less than totally dedicated to the law. Every organization has a distinctive culture, a set of mutual assumptions, that governs how it operates, and Renaissance individuals must learn to master them.

Of course, not everyone was meant to have a second life. What is an escape route for some can be a bumpy road for others. A double life, writes Hal Lancaster of the *Wall Street Journal*, "requires abundant energy, extraordinary time-management skills and lots of 'self' skills: self-discipline, self-sacrifice, self-marketing, and enough self-awareness to know your own limits."

"Don't give up your day job," warned the late Steve Allen, reflecting on his own paradoxical career. The actor, TV show host, jazz pianist, composer of more than six thousand songs, and writer of forty-eight books as well as countless short stories, poems, and films, understood the downside of branching out. "We ought not to make a firm commitment to a new cultural field," he said, "unless we have an actual aptitude for it."

Not everyone has the natural ability, independent of drive and intelligence, to act, write, paint, or launch a new venture. An inborn knack for storytelling, a good ear for music, a good eye for the visual arts, a flair for entrepreneurship—these gifts are unevenly distributed. Pipe dreams can lead to disappointment.

However, the wise person defines success not in terms of being famous, but in terms of happiness and personal fulfillment. To accept any other definition is to lose the control we have over our destinies. You can't necessarily make yourself into the next da Vinci or Jefferson. But you can convert your talents into a craft that can be practiced in your own unique way.

"'How can I find balance between my life and my work?' is the wrong question," writes business executive–philosopher Jim Autry. "The right one, is, 'How can I find balance *within* my life and work?'" Joyful souls like Autry find ways to savor life, often in the most unconventional ways. They realize that experimentation is one of the litmus tests of happiness. If, in the end, they become as rich and famous as Jacques Cousteau or Michael Crichton, so be it. But even if they reach only modest heights, they have found a way to live well.

2

Winston Churchill

His Finest Hour

*The creation of a hobby and new
forms of interest are a policy of
first importance to a public man.*

—WINSTON CHURCHILL

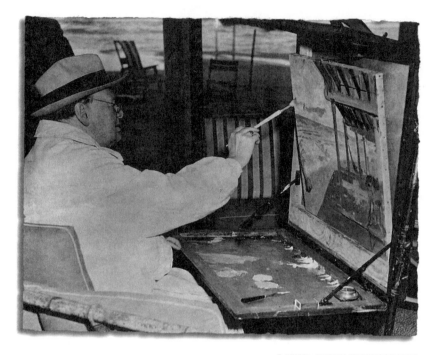

Painting offered the British prime minister
relief from political life.

*A*uthor, artist, orator, soldier, statesman—Winston Churchill was all of these and more. Puffing a cigar, giving his famous "V" sign, flashing an impish smile, this dominant figure of the twentieth century was a versatile genius who defied classification. "The Last Lion," as William Manchester called him, crafted numerous identities of almost mythical proportions: This dapper, doughy man was an unequaled voice of a nation under siege, a Nobel Prize–winning author, a prolific painter, and a towering leader whose decisions changed the course of history.

In many respects, Churchill's is the ideal personality to illustrate the successful coexistence of work and outside interests. In the course of his amazing life, he developed a broad array of talents that enriched his career in government. Each activity contributed to his success in its own way: From writing, he procured fame and fortune; from public speaking, he gained influence at home and abroad; and from painting, he obtained relief from the pressures of public service. As we will see, Churchill's inspiring tale demonstrates that varied interests need not necessarily tug us in opposite directions. And it underscores one of the axioms of double lives: that vocation and avocation can flourish to their mutual benefit.

Winston Leonard Spencer Churchill was born on November 30, 1874, at Bleinheim Palace. His father, Lord Randolph Churchill, a descendant of the first Duke of Marlborough, was a brilliant but uneven Tory politician. He was also afflicted with syphilis. Churchill's mother, Jennie Jerome, was the breathtakingly beautiful socialite daughter of a tough, successful New York financier and newspaper owner.

Young Winston was often left on his own, and his childhood was one of unhappiness and emotional neglect, redeemed only by the affection of his devoted nanny, Mrs. Anne Everest. But it seems that Churchill's isolation spawned a strain of willpower, self-sufficiency, and resilience that would last his entire life. After spotty preparatory schooling, he entered Harrow, where he was considered to be a slow developer and not very bright. High spirited and rebellious, the stocky redhead found his studies boring. "When my reason, imagination, or interest were not engaged," he later wrote of his Harrow days, "I would not or I could not learn."

The restless youngster left school having passed no written exam of any kind and, after three attempts, barely scraped into the Royal Military College, now the Royal Academy, at Sandhurst. After graduating from Sandhurst—where his academics improved somewhat—he entered the 4TH Hussars as a cavalry subaltern. Using his society hostess mother's influence, Churchill mapped out a military career that combined soldiering with writing—a dual role that British authorities permitted at the time. By the age of twenty-five, he had been a daring officer and war correspondent in Cuba, India, and the Sudan. Later, in the South African conflict, he was captured by the Boers and, with a price on his head, made a spectacular escape across three hundred miles of enemy territory. Then he led British troops in action and returned home a war hero.

"Twenty to twenty-five," he later wrote. "Those are the years! Don't be content with things as they are." During this formative period, Churchill's interest in letters blossomed. Bored by the humdrum of army life, he undertook an aggressive reading program—Plato, Aristotle, Darwin, Gibbon, Macaulay, and, on the lighter side, Conan Doyle—to make up for his shortcomings at Harrow and Sandhurst.

His re-education paid off. Slowly he developed a flair for language, and the part-time journalist's zestful dispatches from the front began to generate a popular following in England. His commissions grew, and, for the first time, Churchill sensed he could earn serious money writing newspaper and magazine articles and books. Unlike his fellow officers, young Churchill gave himself to his avocation. In 1898, working five hours a day for two months, he completed his first book, *The*

Story of the Malakand Field Force, a description of the conflict in northwest India. "The most noteworthy act of my life," he told his mother of his tome,which received an enthusiastic reception and sold 8,500 copies in nine months. Four other books dealing with his early military days followed. By age twenty-six, he had accumulated a handsome nest egg of £10,000 from writing, enough to finance a lifelong dream to follow in his father's footsteps in politics. So, in 1899, he resigned his military commission. The next year, Churchill was elected to the House of Commons on the Conservative Party ticket.

For the next six decades, he devoted himself to public service. At different times, Sir Winston held his country's greatest portfolios: home secretary, colonial secretary, chancellor of the Exchequer, president of the London Board of Trade, and secretary of war. Unique among British prime ministers, Churchill changed his party allegiance twice.

Early in his life, Churchill's political career appeared to be finished. During the first days of World War I, as first lord of the Admiralty, he took the fall for the costly failure of the Gallipoli expedition. He argued unsuccessfully that opening the Dardanelles straits between the Turkish mainland and the Gallipoli peninsula would end the stalled trench warfare campaign quickly. His plan was undermined by incompetent commanders, forcing Churchill to resign his post. Though he was later exonerated, his political career remained in jeopardy.

The next twenty years saw him in and out of office, often serving as a backbencher in the House of Commons. During his convalescence after the war, Churchill looked for new outlets to remove the undeserved stain of the Dardanelles debacle. "To improve is to change," he wrote in his memoirs, *Thoughts and Adventures*. "To be perfect is to change often. . . . It is only when new cells are called into activity, when new stars become the lords of ascendant, that relief, repose, refreshment are afforded."

As if preparing for the profound challenges that would test his mettle in another great war, Churchill had an epiphany. He turned again to letters, launching into massive writing and speaking projects.

His incredibly facile pen and love of his native tongue came to his rescue. "The English language," he wrote, "is one of the great sources of inspiration and strength, and no country, or combination or power so fertile and so vivid exists anywhere else in the world."

To convert his lifelong interest in language into books was a great opportunity for Churchill. "Books in all their variety," he noted, "are often the means by which civilizations may be carried triumphantly forward." Besides offering weighty messages, his writings kept him in the public eye during his many years in political exile, particularly from 1922 to 1939. As William Manchester argued, Churchill's literary pursuits were "necessary to fuel his [political] power." To be sure, Churchill also enjoyed writing and was invigorated by it. "Writing a long and substantial book," he said, "is like having a friend and companion at your side to whom you can always turn for comfort and amusement, and whose company becomes more attractive as a new and widening field of interest is lighted in your mind."

> ### REINVENT YOURSELF
>
> "TO IMPROVE IS TO CHANGE. . . . IT IS ONLY WHEN NEW CELLS ARE CALLED INTO ACTIVITY, WHEN NEW STARS BECOME THE LORDS OF ASCENDANT, THAT RELIEF, REPOSE, REFRESHMENT ARE AFFORDED."

Sir Winston's unrivaled energy and drive, as well as his skill in organizing major writing projects, boosted his productivity. Later he would add that writing a book is an adventure: "To begin with it is a toy, an amusement; then it becomes a mistress, and then a master and then a tyrant." Churchill understood his need to choreograph carefully any significant literary undertaking. "I write a book the way they built the Canadian Pacific Railway," he told biographer Walter Graebner. "First I lay the track from coast to coast, and after that I put in all the stations."

Longtime lead researcher Bill Deakin witnessed his master's literary formula: "He was totally organized, almost like a clock. He set himself a ruthless timetable every day and would get agitated, even cross, if it was broken." Churchill worked from 8 A.M. until 2 or 3 A.M., breaking for meals and the mandatory mid-afternoon siesta (a habit he had acquired in Cuba) sandwiched between two daily baths.

Shortly after 8 A.M., he would start the writing process from his bed. Propped up on a pyramid of pillows, he would summon a platoon of secretaries and research assistants who worked in relays around the clock. Occasionally he would take a break to visit his library, but, for the most part, his mornings were spent "writing"—that is, dictating and revising galleys in red ink (in his words, "playing with the proofs"), for only rarely did Churchill actually put pen to paper.

> **TAKE ONE STEP AT A TIME**
>
> "I WRITE A BOOK THE WAY THEY BUILT THE CANADIAN PACIFIC RAILWAY. FIRST, I LAY THE TRACK FROM COAST TO COAST, AND AFTER THAT I PUT IN ALL THE STATIONS."

In the afternoon, except during his siesta, he dictated furiously and pushed himself and his secretaries to the limit. "A very hard taskmaster," one aide called him. Churchill paused in the late afternoon for a game of cards before dinner. Around 11 P.M., he gathered a new crew together for the final writing surge that lasted until the wee hours of the morning. Then, while he slept, a team of secretaries worked through the night to type his prodigious output.

On a typical day, Churchill dictated up to 5,000 words, and on weekends, 10,000. Even when he was on vacation, he managed to crank out at least 1,500 words a day. His twin vices—alcohol and tobacco—sustained him through these backbreaking days. He always had some alcohol in his bloodstream, beginning with a weak scotch after rising and concluding with a nightcap of his favorite Napoléon brandy, named after the historical figure who most fascinated him. "No one can ever say that I failed to display a neat and proper appreciation of the virtues of alcohol," he often confessed. Even greater, though, was his dependence on Cuban cigars, a taste he had acquired during his early travels. From his cache of 3,000 Romeo and Juliets, Churchill would devour ten to twelve Havanas a day, always preferring the longest and the strongest. "Smoking cigars is like falling in love," he wrote.

"First you are attracted to its shape; you stay with it for its flavor; and you must always remember: Never, never, let the flame go out."

Despite these diversions and his political responsibilities, Churchill's devotion to the pen never faltered. Although he never experienced writer's block, Churchill did suffer from depression or, as he put it, "the black dog that comes periodically, leaving a trail of gloom in its wake." Fortunately, these dark moods were short-lived. Driven by financial pressures and the need to create something profound, Churchill never lost sight of his objective. William James once wrote that men of genius differ from ordinary men not in any innate quality of the brain, but in the aims and the purposes on which they concentrate and in the degree of concentration they manage to sustain. Like every Renaissance personality we'll study, Churchill had a phenomenal ability to concentrate on a given task.

"When his mind was occupied with a particular problem, however detailed, he focused upon it relentlessly," said Sir Ian Jacob. This resulted in a massive number of books, articles, and speeches. In the 1930s alone, this human kaleidoscope of ideas published an astonishing one million words, including eleven volumes and more than four hundred magazine and newspaper articles on various subjects. After reading one of his "Marlborough" volumes, Maxine Elliot wrote, "It is incredible that one man can possess the genius to write a book like this and at the same time pursue his ordinary life, which is a thousand times fuller of grave duties and obligations than that of lesser men."

Undoubtedly, pocketbook concerns were a part of his inspiration. Unlike most upper-class British politicians, Churchill was not a rich man. He needed to earn large sums of money to support his lavish lifestyle, sustain his family, and allow his pursuit of a career in politics. Maintaining Chartwell, his much-loved eighty-acre estate in Kent (which he purchased in 1922 and largely rebuilt), plus a London flat, foreign travel, secretaries, researchers, and extravagant tastes, constantly taxed his resources. To worsen matters, he had been heavily invested in the U.S. stock market and lost everything in the crash of

1929. Consequently, Churchill was always short of funds. "Money," he lamented, "how it melts!"

Sir Winston's second life as a scribe saved him financially. During his lifetime, Churchill was one of the world's highest paid writers. His volumes of memoirs of the First World War, published in the 1920s, were best-sellers, as were those he later wrote about World War II. His four-volume biography of his great ancestor John, Duke of Marlborough, which came out in the 1930s, also sold well, as did his crowning literary achievement, A History of the English-Speaking People, published in four volumes from 1956 to 1958. Book royalties and advances, movie and screenplay rights, newspaper and magazine sales, and lecture fees poured in, producing an annual income of almost $200,000—a significant amount for the time.

Given these economic incentives, it is easy to see why Churchill devoted much of his spare time to writing. "It is impossible to imagine him employing a ghost writer," wrote Manchester. "No one but Churchill could write Churchillian prose." Simplicity was his watchword. "All great things are simple," he said, "and many can be expressed in a single word: freedom, justice, honor, duty, mercy, and hope." Churchill the writer avoided the tendency to become "sententious" (one of his favorite words). "Short words are best," he added, "and old words when short are best of all." Consequently, his books were immensely readable and always incorporated a personal angle.

His style bothered some professional historians. "Churchill was not a great historian," scholars Robert Blake and William Roger Louis contend in their joint assessment, "though he was an intelligent and readable one. He was more interested in war and politics than in social, economic, and scientific change, or in the history of ideas, literature, and art. He saw history as a pageant, a colorful drama. This is not to denigrate Churchill, merely to point out that he, like all mortals, was not infallible."

In Churchill's defense, the British philosopher Sir Isaiah Berlin argued that it would be unfair to criticize the brilliant politician for not possessing the gifts of the professional historian. Proper perspective,

Churchill believed, was the key to historical reporting. "The further backward you can look," he once said, "the further forward you are likely to see." Putting aside the occasional criticism, Churchill's formidable skills did not go unnoticed. In 1953, after the publication of fourteen books over fifty years, the part-time writer was awarded the Nobel Prize for literature and, with it, a handsome tax-free honorarium ("a little bit of sugar for the bird," the impecunious author called it).

Even more than he felt compelled to write, Sir Winston longed for yet another life as a public speaker. "It was my ambition all my life to be master of the spoken word," he said. As a young man, Churchill dreamed of the day when his speech would captivate the masses and, like his writing, complement his political life. He recognized that powerful words could sway others to his viewpoint. "Of all the talents bestowed upon man, none is so precious as the gift of oratory," he wrote. "He who enjoys it wields a power more durable than that of a great king." Although he became an accomplished writer over time, he was far from being a natural speaker. His physician and biographer, Lord Moran, noted, "To the end of his working days he would be on edge until he was satisfied that a speech had not misfired."

Churchill freely admitted that without the most careful preparation, he could not speak at all. Part of his problem grew from a slight lisp, which he never wholly lost. But Churchill also felt inhibited speaking without a script. "I never had the practice which comes to young men at university of speaking in small debating societies on all sorts of subjects," he later wrote. Then, in a rare self-deprecating burst, he added, "I am not an orator. An orator must be spontaneous."

Because Churchill considered himself inexpert at off-the-cuff remarks, he tried never to be trapped into making them. To overcome his speech impediment and fear of improvising, Sir Winston drew on his prodigious memory and extraordinary command of the English language. During his military days, the young officer used long periods of idleness to memorize the masters. He could recite 1,200 lines of Macaulay and several Shakespearean scenes without missing a word. Moreover, he spent hour after hour practicing in front of mirrors, delivering speeches he had committed to memory. In fact, he devoted far more time to organizing an upcoming address than to working on an article, typically spending between six and eight hours polishing a thirty-minute talk.

Several days before a scheduled speech, an edgy Churchill would hunker down, fine-tuning his thoughts. He "toiled with passionate care," his daughter Lady Mary Soames recalled in her memoirs. "'Be quiet: your father is with speech' was a frequent injunction from my mother." Facts, figures, piles of background materials were brought to him for review. As with his writing, Sir Winston dictated his first draft of a speech to the phalanx of secretaries who operated around the clock. Typing, editing, and retyping interspersed with more rounds of dictation were intended to yield just the right word or phrase. Every composition took many strenuous hours with revision right up to the moment before he appeared in public. Nothing was extemporaneous, including his carefully planned pauses.

"Those pauses are just part of my trade," he said in Walter Graebner's *My Dear Mr. Churchill*. "I always—well, most of the time—know exactly what I am going to say, but I make believe, by hesitating a little, that a word or phrase has just come to me." Though Churchill's delivery gave an illusion of spontaneity, several of his contemporaries chided their programmed effect. "Winston has spent the best years of his life writing impromptu speeches," said one former colleague, F. E. Smith. Arthur Balfour, the Conservative prime minister from 1902 to 1905, added that Churchill's "artillery" was impressive, "but not very mobile." Despite these lively broadsides, Churchill's bumptious eloquence had the desired effect: He gave every appearance of winging it.

Describing a typical speech of "the consummate performer," Manchester wrote, "Winston had assumed an almost biblical pose, his feet planted apart, his body immobile save for his head, which slowly toiled back and forth as his eyes swept the chamber." Churchill's presentations were always short and punchy, littered with knockabout humor. Wit, flash, and sting peppered his patois. From the start, his richly expressive language mesmerized listeners. His maiden speech to the House of Commons on February 28, 1901—six weeks in preparation—denounced his government's decision to increase the size of the army. Using his boyish charm to full advantage, Churchill was "spellbinding," reported the *Daily Express*. The other London dailies joined in to herald the young parliamentarian's ability to seduce an audience. Like his father before him, Sir Winston spoke without a note—again trying to project an image of spontaneity.

Three years later, however, Churchill abandoned his unscripted style. Pretending to make an impromptu speech at the House of Commons, he forgot what he was going to say. Speechless and embarrassed, he retreated to the bench and buried his head in his hands. Never again would he speak in public without copious notes. "I don't know much about oratory," Churchill once wrote, "but I do know what is in people's minds and how to speak to them." Indeed, he often likened himself to a one-man English-speaking Union. His "feeling for the English tongue was sensual, almost erotic," Manchester noted. "When he coined a phrase, he would suck it, rolling it around his palate to extract its full flavor."

His was an unwanted voice in the isolationist wilderness of the late 1930s, as Adolf Hitler's Nazis terrorized the European continent. On May 13, 1940, the newly elected prime minister's "blood, toil, tears, and sweat" passage galvanized the House of Commons and a once dispirited nation into action. A month later, after the fall of France, he urged his fellow Brits to rally to "their finest hour." That August, Churchill said of the heroic effort of British airmen to defeat the massive German Luftwaffe, "Never in the field of human conflict was so much owed by so many to so few." Six years later, at Fulton, Missouri, he coined the phrase "iron curtain" to describe the growing menace of Soviet communism. And Russia, he once said, "is a riddle wrapped in a mystery inside an enigma."

Not only did Churchill have a flair for language, but his talents emerged in still another new and exciting venue. One pleasant Sunday afternoon in the summer of 1915, at age forty-one, he stumbled on the Muse of Painting. At a small country house he had been renting in Surrey, the then out-of-favor politician saw his sister-in-law Lady Gwendeline ("Goonie") painting watercolors. Intrigued, Churchill borrowed her six-year-old son's watercolors and set to work. The next morning, he dispatched his wife, Clementine, to the village for an easel, palette, paints, brushes, and turpentine. He now had the proper tools, but he was unsure of where to begin. His untrained eye "seemed arrested by a silent veto," he later wrote. Fortuitously, Hazel Lavery, a gifted painter and the wife of the famous artist Sir John Lavery, arrived at Churchill's home. "What are you hesitating about?" she asked him. "Let me have a brush—the big one." She proceeded to dive into the turpentine and, with large, fierce strokes, splashed colors across the canvas. "The spell was broken," Churchill remembered. "His cares seemed to evaporate," wrote biographer Walter Gilbert. "He had found a release for his tension and depression."

"Painting came to my rescue in a most trying time," Sir Winston said of his first experiment with the brush and the palette. "I had great anxiety and no means of relieving it; I had vehement convictions and small power to give effect to them. . . . The Muse of Painting came to my rescue." With his inhibitions conquered, Churchill courted the Muse for almost fifty years, producing more than five hundred pictures. Many of

> **LISTEN TO YOUR HEART**
>
> "I HAD GREAT ANXIETY AND NO MEANS OF RELIEVING IT; I HAD VEHEMENT CONVICTIONS AND SMALL POWER TO GIVE EFFECT TO THEM. . . . THE MUSE OF PAINTING CAME TO MY RESCUE."

them are on display at his Chartwell studio and in collections around the world. What began as the therapeutic hobby of "Sunday painter" became a serious avocation.

"We must not be too ambitious," he wrote in his monograph, *Painting As a Pastime*. "We cannot aspire to masterpieces. We must content ourselves with a joy ride in a paint-box." Yet Churchill the perfectionist was never content to be dismissed as a mere dabbler. To capture the nuances that would bring his compositions to life, he forged close alliances with professional masters who gave him practical help, technical advice, and critical guidance. Besides Sir John Lavery, the distinguished leader of the Glasgow School, William Nicholson, another highly esteemed British artist, gave him countless pointers. Swiss painter Carl Montage taught him the proper selection of oils and canvases. The well-known French artist Paul Maze advised him to "paint like you speak," while Simon-Lévy, André Dunoyer de Segonzac, and Jacques Majorelle, three of France's best, tutored him on technique. British impressionist Walter Sickert offered him many helpful tips, such as how to use photographs for reference indoors and grids to develop a sense of scale. "Put on the paint as though you were scraping your feet on a doormat," Sickert also told him. (Mystery writer Patricia Cornwell recently fingered Sickert as the infamous Jack the Ripper.)

Besides heeding the advice of his top-flight tutors, Churchill devoured Ruskin's *Elements of Drawing* and many other books on painting; he visited numerous galleries; copied pictures (especially the work of John Singer Sargent) in friends' collections; and corresponded with celebrated artists, from Pablo Picasso to Anna Mary Robertson ("Grandma") Moses. To further develop his new passion, Sir Winston brought his exceptional organizational skills to bear. "Painting a picture," he said, "is like fighting a battle; and trying to paint a picture, I suppose, is like trying to fight a battle. It is, if anything, more exciting than fighting it successfully."

Commenting on this battlefield analogy, Lady Soames wrote in her memoirs, "Winston Churchill ably carried his historic sense of battle into his world of art. He seemed to have no hesitations and no inhibitions." Simple, beautiful, and bold describe Churchill's style. His first advice to every budding artist was to paint with a spirit of "audacity." Unlike most painters, he never used drawings or sketches. He went immediately to canvas using broad, vigorous strokes, experimenting along the way with texture. Fearless and free from convention, his joyous brush yielded honest, natural output.

Churchill loved the richness of oils, preferring them to watercolors. He especially favored lush hues. "I cannot pretend to feel impartial about colours," he noted. "I rejoice with the brilliant ones and am genuinely sorry for the poor browns." Painting places that carried special meaning, Churchill always remained direct and clear in his relation to the scene before him. Like most successful artists, he focused on scenes he knew, things he liked. His principal genre was landscapes. "A tree doesn't complain that I haven't done it justice," he wrote.

Over the years, he painted many exotic vistas, from the ruins of Pompeii to Amsterdam's canals to the Italian Alps. Many of his landscapes were English, as were his still lifes, flowers, and interiors. But he also enjoyed capturing foreign scenes, because "every country where the sun shines and every district in it has a theme of its own." Whenever foreign travel beckoned, Sir Winston put his work worries aside to search for the ideal subject for his brush. He would spend hours outside studying everything meticulously: the setting, time of day, proportions, and tones. To ensure that he had the right tools, he always brought along a movable studio, well-stocked with canvases, easels, palettes, paints, brushes, and parasol—plus the ever-present box of Havanas and bucket of chilled champagne. With his kit properly installed, Churchill focused on the simple beauties of nature: a Jamaican sunset, the Canadian Rockies, a Madeiran fishing port, the Egyptian pyramids, the French Riviera. Painting in sunlight, preferably at its most intense, he poured himself into a world where time stood respectfully aside.

Unlike with his writing or speaking, Sir Winston did not paint to enhance his political career or to make money. Over the years, he donated or gave away many of his pieces. He used his art to cheer up himself and others. "Painting is a friend," he said of his favorite Muse, "who makes no undue demands, excites no exhausting pursuits, keeps faithful pace even with feeble steps, and holds her canvas on a screen between us and the envious eye of Time or the surly advance of Decrepitude."

In this parallel life, Churchill found a respite from crowding events and pulsating politics. "Painting dissolved the frustrations and times of bitterness at being cast in the role of a voice crying in the wilderness," daughter Mary observed. "Despite all [his] duties and occupations, he still found and made time for painting." Whenever there was a "paintatious" (a favorite Churchillian adjective) target of opportunity, he arrived with his easel, and nothing shattered his concentration until he was finished. "He painted busily away with sublime disregard for the bustle going on behind him," Graebner noted, adding that Churchill was "completely oblivious to everything except the scene in front of him."

During World War I, Churchill rejoined the army as a colonel and was dispatched quickly to the Low Countries. In Belgium, he amazed his young officers by setting up his painting paraphernalia in the midst of battle, where he turned out several scenes of the desolate countryside. Not even shell bursts in the immediate area could shatter his deep concentration. Painting was Churchill's escape valve, sought under any and every circumstance. Before the 1945 Pottsdam Conference, Prime Minister Churchill was tired and depressed. "But," wrote Lady Soames, "the magic of painting soon laid hold of him, absorbing him for hours on end, and banishing disturbing thoughts of either the present or the future."

Some thirty-three years after his first dabble, Churchill told a friend, "If it weren't for painting, I couldn't live. I couldn't bear the

AVOID DISTRACTIONS

"[CHURCHILL] PAINTED BUSILY AWAY WITH SUBLIME DISREGARD FOR THE BUSTLE GOING ON BEHIND HIM. . . . COMPLETELY OBLIVIOUS TO EVERYTHING EXCEPT THE SCENE IN FRONT OF HIM."

strain of things." In *Painting As a Pastime*, Churchill encouraged every prospective dualist to discover the lure of the brush and palette "even at the advanced age of 40! Just to paint is great fun," he wrote. "The colours are lovely to look at and delicious to squeeze out. Matching them, however crudely, with what you see is fascinating and absolutely absorbing. Try it if you have not done so—before you die." Finding tranquility in art, Sir Winston continued painting well into his eighties.

Churchill put painting aside only during World War II when, because of his ministerial responsibilities, he completed just one picture. In January 1943, after the Casablanca Conference with President Franklin Roosevelt, he traveled 150 miles inland to Marrakech, where he

START NOW

"JUST TO PAINT IS GREAT FUN. . . . TRY IT IF YOU HAVE NOT DONE SO—BEFORE YOU DIE."

painted Morocco's snowcapped Atlas Mountains—"the most lovely spot in the world." He later gave the picture to General George C. Marshall, whom he deeply admired.

After the war, Churchill renewed his romance with the brush, creating some of his most memorable works. Like many instinctive artists who never took a painting lesson, he was filled with self-doubt. "Although confident and self-assured in his fields of politics and oratory and writing," Lady Soames wrote, "Winston Churchill was always truly modest about his achievements as a painter." He felt he never transcended amateur status. "When I get to heaven," he said, reflecting on his artistic career, "I mean to spend a considerable portion of my first million years in painting and so get to the bottom of the subject."

Actually, the self-effacing "amateur" often stole the show. Using various pseudonyms to shield himself from possible rejection, Churchill reluctantly sent his pictures to major exhibits. In 1921, under the name "Charles Morin," he sold four of five pieces at a Paris show. Later, in London, his "Winter Sunshine, Chartwell," won first prize in an amateur competition. As his underlying natural abilities matured, so did his artistic success. In 1947, using the name "Mr. Winter," he had two pictures accepted by London's prestigious Royal Academy of Art. A few years later, Sir Winston received the academy's distinction as Honorary Academician Extraordinary, and the Society of British Artists made him an honorary member as well.

Meanwhile, his "little dabs" were being shown regularly at the Royal Academy, the Tate Gallery, and other leading exhibition spaces around the world. "His rise from gifted amateur to academician was no easy flight," wrote art critic Ron Cynewulf Robbins. "But, with the twinkling mischief which charmed even his enemies, Churchill could be dismissive of his painting skills." Notwithstanding the generally high praise bestowed on him, he constantly yearned for reassurance. At his Chartwell studio, he paraded visitors through his collection over and over again. "He loved showing it to his friends," Graebner observed, "particularly if they left him in no doubt of their high regard for his skill."

How good was this untutored artist? Churchill was certainly no less a painter than many of the professionals of his time. "His skill as an artist had reached the point," wrote Robert Lewis Taylor, "where any word except 'professional' would be an unjustified description of his success." Sir John Rothenstein, director of the Tate Gallery and one of England's eminent art critics, judged Churchill's works to be "of real merit which bear a direct and intimate relationship to his outlook on life. In these pictures there comes bubbling irrepressibility of his sheer enjoyment of the simple beauties of nature." To many, his bold, uninhibited style was fresh and exciting.

The undisciplined vigor and spontaneity of his canvases signaled greatness—greatness perhaps prejudiced by his fame as a statesman. Picasso said of Churchill, "If that man were a painter by profession, he'd have no trouble earning a good living." In Sir John Lavery's opinion, "Had he chosen painting instead of statesmanship,

> **NEVER STOP LEARNING**
>
> "WHEN I GET TO HEAVEN, I MEAN TO SPEND A CONSIDERABLE PORTION OF MY FIRST MILLION YEARS IN PAINTING AND SO GET TO THE BOTTOM OF THE SUBJECT."

I believe he would have been a great master with the brush." Renowned painter Sir Oswald Birley argued even more vehemently that "had Churchill given the time to art that he has given to politics, he would have been by all odds the world's greatest painter." Strong words, indeed!

"I have had a wonderful life, full of many achievements," Sir Winston told Clementine, his wife of fifty-seven years, reflecting on his multifaceted career. "Every ambition I've ever had has been fulfilled—save one . . . I am not a great painter." Lady Soames speculates that painting was the only alternative profession to politics that her father would have ever contemplated seriously. "Painting is a companion with whom one may hope to walk a great part of life's journey," Churchill noted. But in 1960, the journey ended: Sir Winston put down his brush and bid farewell to the Muse.

"Happy are the painters," he once said, "for they shall not be lonely. Light and colour, peace and hope, will keep them company to the end, or almost to the end of the day."

"The creation of a hobby and new forms of interest," Churchill recalled in his memoirs, "is a policy of the first importance to a public man." He called idleness "a dangerous breeding ground," something to be avoided at all costs. "To be really happy and really safe," he reminded us, "one ought to have at least two or three hobbies and they must be real." The Victorian adventurer found sanctuary in everything from polo to gambling, hunting, foreign travel, and even bricklaying. To him, change was paramount, "the master key." "The tired parts of the mind can be restored, using other parts," he wrote. "It is not enough merely to switch off the lights which play upon the main and ordinary field of interest; a new field of interest must be illuminated."

Flying was another of Churchill's many interests. Though fearful of flying, Sir Winston took up aviation in his late thirties and managed up to ten flights a day. "A very fair pilot once in the air," his flight instructor called him. But, he added, Churchill was "altogether too impatient [to be] a good pupil." Against his wife's wishes and his own instincts, Churchill continued to fly until a crash at Croydon ten years later convinced him to stay on terra firma. "The air is an extremely dangerous mistress," he conceded. "Once under the spell, most lovers are faithful to the end, which is not always old age."

"The vistas of possibility are limited only by the shortness of life," Churchill once wrote. He sampled virtually every possible vista until old age and ill health slowed him down. Undoubtedly, his longstanding passion for alcohol and stogies, plus his ample girth (a roly-poly 210 pounds on a 5′ 8″ frame) and a complete disdain for exercise ("Energy of mind does not depend on energy of body," he said), contributed to his lifelong battle against stroke, hypertension, pneumonia, and other maladies. Nevertheless, his "energy and stamina were prodigious," wrote historian Arthur Marder. Indeed, the most serious accident of his life occurred in December 1931 when he looked the wrong way as he stepped off a New York sidewalk and was knocked down by an automobile on his way to visit a friend, financier Bernard Baruch. Churchill's indomitable spirit, iron constitution, and inexhaustible energy enabled him to bounce back from such a life-threatening episode, as well as from illness and enfeeblement. To a large degree, his eclectic interests contributed to his longevity. But in his late eighties, his powers were visibly failing. For the first time, Sir Winston complained that it was "difficult to find new interests."

On January 24, 1965, at age ninety, the legendary icon died after a massive stroke. Following a state funeral at which almost every nation paid tribute, he was buried in the family grave in Bladon churchyard, Oxfordshire.

In a career marked by many distinguished roles, Winston Churchill was the quintessential Renaissance man. In him "the triumphal accomplishments of the well-rounded celebrity have found their most felicitous meaning," historian Robert Lewis Taylor wrote, proclaiming Britain's wartime hero "the liveliest personality yet produced by the upper vertebrates." He was a man, in the words of his wife, "tingling with life to the tips of [his] fingers." Indeed, it is easy to ascribe Churchill's success in balancing multiple lives to his personal genius. Yet, in many respects, he personified the everyday man or woman. He was afflicted with the same limitations that affect us all, from self-doubts to career setbacks. What set him apart was his incredible grit. To Churchill, anything was possible; victory was always at hand. "Never give in!" he told students at Harrow in 1941. "Never give in, never, never, never, never!"

3

Norio Ohga
Managerial Maestro

Music is spiritual.
The music business is not.

—VAN MORRISON, SINGER AND SONGWRITER

*Sony chairman Ohga regularly taps his baton
while leading orchestras around the world.*

*P*rofessional opera singer, licensed jet pilot, symphony conductor, and chairman of the board of Sony Corporation, Norio Ohga is a Renaissance man of the East who, by every measure, shatters the image of the stereotypical Japanese businessman.

Ohga has found a sanctuary in music—in his words, "my closest friend in life." He spent his career balancing musical scales with the corporate ladder. With Sony's celebrated cofounders, Masaru Ibuka and Akio Morita, he helped change Japan's image from the junkman of Asia to the archetypal postwar success by transforming a fledgling company into a global entertainment colossus.

Under Ohga's leadership, Sony ushered in the digital audio age with the compact disc and the minidisc systems. He facilitated the company's acquisition of CBS Records (now Sony Music Entertainment) and Columbia Pictures Entertainment (now Sony Pictures Entertainment). He was also instrumental in developing many signature products, including the phenomenally popular PlayStation® game machines. Thanks in part to his versatility, Sony today stands as the world's leading maker of high-tech playthings.

> **SAVOR SERENDIPITY**
>
> "THE UNIQUE THING ABOUT MY LIFE IS THE EXTENT TO WHICH IT TOOK ME ON A PATH—BUSINESS—I HAD NO DESIRE TO WALK."

For one of life's high achievers, Ohga comes off as surprisingly serene. With the polished elegance of a world leader, he speaks slowly, methodically, as if pondering life's true meaning. In Tokyo, on a brilliant autumn day in 2000, he discussed his unconventional career. Music, he explained, has always been his primary passion. "The unique thing about my life," he said, "is the extent to which it took me on a path—business—I had no desire to walk."

Fast forward to January 17, 2001. Tuxedo-clad Ohga strides from the wings to the center stage of Blaisdell Concert Hall to lead the Honolulu Symphony Orchestra in an all-Beethoven program. His sculpted features, shiny black hair, and intense eyes create a commanding presence. After accepting introductory applause, the maestro pivots to face an orchestra of eighty professional musicians. Raising his baton, Ohga begins tonight's performance. From the start, his approach is majestic and stately. He shows a true gift for making an orchestra sing; his precise rendition of Beethoven's Symphony no. 3—*Eroica*—is without reference to a printed score. The guest conductor conquers Beethoven's dramatic and witty innovations, his awkward extensions, irregular repetitions, and abrupt shifts. At the end, the near-capacity crowd leaps to its feet, clapping enthusiastically.

> ## *FOCUS, FOCUS, FOCUS*
> "IT'S MY NATURE TO CONCENTRATE ON ONLY ONE THING AT A TIME AND PURSUE IT TO ITS FULLEST."

Over lunch the next day, the seventy-one-year-old maestro is beaming. Since arriving in Honolulu two days earlier, he has conducted a full round of six-hour rehearsals, followed by meetings with business and government leaders. Yet this survivor of several heart attacks—like the Energizer Bunny®—just keeps going. But then nothing about Norio Ohga is conventional. For instance, in his thirties, he set out not simply to learn to fly but to acquire the skills of a major airline pilot. Over the years, he taught himself to fly six different types of aircraft, including multiengine jets. To maintain his proficiency, he flies Sony's Falcon 900s on business trips, logging up to 300 hours a year. His logbook reveals 2,300 hours, impressive for any private pilot.

How did Ohga pilot himself from professional singer and symphony conductor into Sony's top slot? He credits his ability to completely shift gears at any time. He professes never to think about music at work. "It's my nature to concentrate on only one thing at a time and pursue it to its fullest," he told historian John Nathan. "When I fly my jet, I'm a pilot, and all I think about is flying safely. When I land, I remember I must be prepared to negotiate a contract. Then I remember I must conduct and pore over a score."

Keeping his various lives separate, Ohga was at his corporate desk every day and on the symphony rostrum whenever opportunities arose. In Japan, where workaholism abounds, Ohga's beyond-the-job accomplishments seem all the more amazing. Sony, an unconventional company, provided the space in which this high-flyer could soar. Ohga, in turn, helped make the $58-billion company one of the planet's best-known names.

Born in 1930, the fourth of seven children of a wealthy timber importer, Ohga grew up in Numazu in the Bay of Suruga, eighty miles southwest of Tokyo. Since his father spent much of his time in Southeast Asia, his mother and siblings raised him. As a youngster, Ohga had taught himself flute and piano, and, later, calligraphy, which became a lifetime interest. At thirteen, bedridden with pleurisy, he missed a year of school. However, Ichiro Iwai, a thirty-year-old electrical engineer and family friend living in the neighborhood, tutored Ohga in music and the arts and also in math and science—including how to read oscillograms and musical scores. To this day, Ohga follows Iwai's example, counseling music students on the importance of acquiring a broad education, including heavy doses of science and engineering.

At the end of World War II, Japan was in ruins. Tokyo was a ravaged, war-torn city, where homeless veterans and street urchins vied for handouts. There were few job openings in traditional heavy industry. Consequently, Ohga lost his enthusiasm for engineering and decided he would be "a better artist than engineer." In 1946, the sixteen-year-old began an intense program of voice and operatic studies. For four years, he commuted once a week, three hours each way, to Tokyo for individual lessons in lieder—German songs—with the distinguished voice instructor and opera singer Teiichi Nakayama. In 1949, Ohga applied to the Tokyo National University of Fine Arts and Music and was one of thirteen students admitted to its highly competitive voice program.

While at university, the young baritone was introduced to his future employer. Through a neighborhood contact, Ohga met Masaru Ibuka, cofounder of Tokyo Telecommunications Engineering (renamed Sony Corporation in 1958). Ibuka showed Ohga the company's recently produced G-type tape recorder. Tape recorders had been developed in Germany in the mid-1930s, but they were cumbersome and expensive. The Japanese machine was adequate for recording speeches and ordinary conversations, but the outspoken music student told Ibuka that its sound quality was deficient. The biggest problem was that transient sounds like those made by a piano became blurred when recorded and played back. At first, Ibuka regarded Ohga as just another music school student; but, in time, he became impressed with Ohga's grasp of technology and told his partner, Akio Morita, that Ohga's "knowledge of tape recorders would put a professional to shame."

A few months later, a Tokyo Telecommunications representative made a sales call on Tokyo National University of Fine Arts and Music with the G-type recorder. During his demonstration, he encountered Ohga, who was convinced that tape recorders offered the music world great promise. "Like a ballerina uses a mirror to learn her trade," he often says, "so a musician should learn with a recorder." The self-confident sophomore convinced the faculty to purchase the machine, provided appropriate modifications were made. Ohga then prepared a detailed list of specifications, along with a sketch and wiring diagram. Among other things, he proposed that an impedance roller be incorporated into the machine to minimize sound distortion, or wow and flutter.

Ibuka and Morita invited Ohga back to the company's Shinagawa head office to discuss further modifications. In no time, the precocious student's frank assessment of the company's tape recorders made him an invaluable critic. "Eventually," writes Nathan, "Ibuka directed that no prototype would be put into production before Ohga had an opportunity to test it and render an opinion." Ohga was earning more and more of the cofounders' trust.

Credit Sony's patriarchs for creating an enterprise open to free spirits like Ohga. In the company's 1946 founding prospectus, Ibuka stated that the purpose of incorporating was "creating an ideal workplace, fun, dynamic, and joyous, where dedicated engineers will be able to realize their craft and skills at the highest possible level." Master marketer Morita later said, "I consider it my job to nurture the creativity of the people I work with, because at Sony we know that a terrific idea is more likely to happen in an open, free, and trusting atmosphere than when everything is calculated, every action analyzed, and every responsibility assigned by an organization chart." In Japan's buttoned-down business world, these two leaders had the temerity to be different, particularly when it came to recognizing fresh talent.

Those same values persist today. Sony remains the protruding nail in corporate Japan that refuses to be hammered down. "We've never been constrained by stereotyped convention," boasts Ohga. "When a new person joins our company, we start everything on a zero basis, meaning we do not care which university a person graduated from, or what major that person studied. From the first day, we try to look at what the person excels in and what the person can contribute to the company. That's our basic philosophy: 'To recognize, develop and promote people.' In that sense, I think Sony is unique among Japanese companies."

After graduating from university in 1953, Ohga was asked by Ibuka and Morita to join Sony "informally" as an adviser. "Frankly, I had no interest at all in being involved in the company," says Ohga.

Nonetheless, the young artist recognized that such an association would allow him to combine his two loves, music and electronics. He also sensed tremendous opportunity in this unusual Japanese company that rewarded unconventional types like himself. So he accepted a part-time consultancy, while continuing postgraduate studies under his voice instructor, Teiichi Nakayama.

Ohga's talents as an operatic baritone soared as his range improved, and he appeared in broad repertoires that featured German and Italian operas, cantatas, and recitals, many of which were broadcast nationally on the radio. Frequently, his accompanist was his girlfriend and future wife, pianist Midori Matsubara.

During his not-so-free time, Ohga continued to provide advice—typically in the form of stinging critiques—to Sony's engineers. Even as a student, he never had much trouble getting people's attention. But, to the chagrin of Ibuka and Morita, the ambitious baritone and his fiancée set off for Germany for further instruction in 1954. "At the time it was difficult to obtain a visa for occupied Germany, but Professor Gerhard Hüsch of the music college in Munich vouched for me," Ohga recalls. For the next three years, he studied in Munich and Berlin, where he graduated first in his class from Berlin's Hochschule für Musik. In 1956, he won an award for his singing at Austria's Salzburg Festival.

Despite the distance, Morita continued to woo his future protégé, writing him weekly and sending him new products to review. Sony also paid Ohga with scarce foreign exchange. The artist, in turn, kept close tabs on the latest European technology, providing Morita with lengthy letters on industry leaders Telefunken and Philips.

After returning to Japan in 1957, Ohga resumed his operatic career and married Miss Matsubara. The two were committed to lives in music. But Morita wouldn't give up. "He kept telling me how talented I was," Ohga remembers, "and asked that I spend one or two days a week at the company doing nothing in particular." So Ohga resumed his part-time consultancy with the company—making the occasional visit to Shinagawa—while enjoying growing success as an opera star.

In 1958, Morita pleaded with the talented Ohga to accompany him to Europe to develop a regional strategy for the company. After their six-week trip, Morita's lobbying campaign intensified. Even his wife, Yoshiko, pitched in. The cofounder told Ohga that he could wear "two hats"—one in music, the other in business—and held out the possibility of his being Sony's president one day. "Again, I told him I didn't want to be a businessman," says Ohga. "But when he presented the 'two hat' concept, I finally gave in."

In April 1959, after six years of courtship, the twenty-nine-year-old Ohga began his full-time career with Sony as *buchō*, or general manager, an unusually high entry level in Japanese industry. He headed the Second Manufacturing Group, which directed the company's three-hundred-person broadcast-equipment unit. After putting in long days at the Atsugi plant and hawking equipment across the country, Ohga continued his operatic career in the evenings. "For the first few years, I had two hats," he says. "Sometimes I was singing, sometimes I was in the laboratory making new inventions." But by 1961, the combination of a heavy workload and musical bookings began to take its toll.

"I had just finished a successful sales trip in Hiroshima," he told me. "We had won a big contract, and our junior people were overjoyed. They all went out to celebrate, but I was scheduled to perform Count Almaviva in *The Marriage of Figaro* that night. I arrived at the theater very tired with just enough time to get into my costume and makeup. I performed effectively through the first three acts. But with act four about to begin, I sat down on a wardrobe box and fell asleep. All of a sudden, I heard a familiar melody, signaling my turn! I was supposed to enter from the other side of the stage, but I had no time. Figaro and Susanna were waiting for my appearance and were, no doubt, a bit perplexed. Fortunately, the performance concluded satisfactorily. Apparently the Hiroshima audience didn't spot the irregularities. After the performance, I went to the conductor and explained my day. I thought he would be angry, but he just laughed."

Nevertheless, Ohga the perfectionist realized that wearing two hats was no longer possible. Gradually, he scaled back his concert appearances, completing his singing obligations in 1964. From then on, he concentrated on business, deploying his musical and engineering abilities to help make Sony an entertainment giant.

Looking back on his earlier decision to defer his double life, Ohga has no regrets. "I was doing such a big job," he recalls. "I was prohibitively busy. The daily tasks were too demanding, too burdensome to continue singing." Yet he promised himself that when he reached age sixty, he would resume his musical career by conducting symphony orchestras.

Meanwhile, Ohga's corporate responsibilities were expanding rapidly. As head of Sony's tape recorder division, he had a staff of more than a thousand employees. He also directed the entire company's product planning, industrial design, and advertising functions. In no time, he was revolutionizing the firm's profile and its product line, and his career sky rocketed. In 1964, Ohga was appointed to Sony's board, an unprecedented achievement—given his age, thirty-four, and limited tenure with the company.

In the following years, Ohga's musical abilities and experience became a continuing strength. His artistic background and astonishing attention to detail proved invaluable in developing the cassette recorder with Philips Electronics of the Netherlands, condemning reel-to-reel tapes to oblivion. Sensing numerous limitations in reel-to-reels, Ohga declared, "We want to create a worldwide standard for encased magnetic tape products. My goal is to make easy-to-use tape recorders available to everyone." At the time, Philips, Grundig, and Telefunken were engaged in a heated battle to develop compact cassettes. Each needed low-cost Japanese production to crack the world market. Sony, in turn, lusted for the Europeans' state-of-the-art technology.

Despite the allure of a global alliance, Sony's cofounders always had preferred an independent, go-it-alone strategy. From day one, "the elevation of Japanese national culture" was one of their principal objectives. They set out both to change the national mind-set from imitation to innovation and to push Japanese cultural values toward proprietary technology and entrepreneurship. On several occasions, the fledgling gadget-makers shunned overtures from foreign investors to collaborate. For example, in 1955, the board—at Morita's insistence— turned down an order for 100,000 radios from Bulova Watch Company, a deal worth more than Sony's entire market capitalization at the time. Bulova insisted on selling radios under its own brand name, but Morita had his eye on building the Sony brand globally. Later, he called his rejection of Bulova's offer the best business decision of his career.

Understandably, Sony was reluctant to team up with a European multinational. But eventually, Ohga convinced Ibuka and Morita that joining forces with his preferred choice, Philips, would accelerate Sony's global ambitions. In 1966, Ohga concluded a cross-licensing agreement with the Dutch electronics giant that allowed both companies to use each other's manufacturing and technology at no charge.

Philips, for its part, received highly efficient Japanese manufacturing and access to a future stream of exciting products. Sony, in return, catapulted onto the world stage, while avoiding the onerous licensing fees it had previously paid the Dutch. Ohga's deal-making skills and partnering prowess so impressed Morita that the following year he entrusted Ohga with one of the most significant events in the company's history: a joint venture with CBS Records.

For years, Morita viewed the U.S. market as the linchpin in a global strategy. In 1960, he established Sony's American subsidiary— moving himself and his family to New York to more fully understand Western consumers. Although a technology buff, the consummate salesman recognized that building a worldwide brand required "content"—music, films, and games—to complement the delivery side of the business, everything from TVs and audio gear to movie theaters. In October 1967, Morita dispatched his talented protégé to New York to negotiate a deal with CBS for its records division. In return for naming rights, Ohga extracted lucrative concessions on royalties, which, over the ensuing years, cost CBS hundreds of millions of dollars.

Under his leadership, the partnership grew to become the most profitable division of both parent companies. Ohga also played a central role in the decision to acquire CBS Records outright. Negotiations continued for more than a year, culminating in Sony's purchase of the record company in November 1987 for $2 billion—at the time, the largest overseas acquisition by a Japanese business. Ohga installed himself as president of the new company, which he later renamed Sony Music Entertainment.

While building what would become one of the world's largest and most profitable record companies, Ohga also helped coordinate the development of Morita's marketing triumph, the Walkman®. Earlier, in the 1970s, his principal interests shifted to the compact disc and optical-laser technology. Sony and its partner, Philips, were trying to move into the digital age by establishing the compact-disc format. Teams of optical and audio engineers on both continents raced to develop an optical-laser disc, visiting each other periodically in Tokyo and Eindhoven.

By 1979, Philips produced a 14-bit format with 11.5-centimeter audio digital disc with a recording capacity of 60 minutes. Ohga, however, felt that the format was too limited and insisted on a 12-centimeter, 16-bit format that offered 74 minutes of music. He argued that the longer length could accommodate Beethoven's Ninth Symphony, his favorite piece of music. The modification could be accomplished by expanding the disc's size from 11.5 to 12 centimeters and still maintain Ohga's mandate of "portability"—that the CD fit in a suit pocket. Philips consented, and the appropriate changes were made.

Two years later, Sony developed an affordable CD player to match the disc's potential. In October 1982, the company launched the CDP-101, which was immediately greeted with fierce industry opposition. Professional musicians, in particular, spurned the new technology, considering it "too expensive and hollow." To stem the criticism, Ohga dispatched one of his top lieutenants and a team of thirty audio engineers to Hollywood with the company's $150,000 digital recorder. At the same time, CBS/Sony launched the world's first fifty CD titles, starting with Billy Joel's *52nd Street*. Famous artists like Stevie Wonder and jazz pianist Herbie Hancock waxed faborably over the new equipment's benefits. Endorsements poured in, and, by 1984, Sony commanded a whopping 90 percent share of the CD market.

Since its inception, Sony has sought to create new markets and provide exciting lifestyle concepts to consumers. "We are committed to remaining close to our customers and bring new meaning to the word 'fun' in electronics and entertainment," says Ohga. To that end, Sony's easy-to-use compact disc brought a whole new dimension to the enjoyment of music. Yet audiophiles continued to complain that the sound from conventional CDs couldn't match the warmth and body of vinyl records. Evidently the problem related to the fact that CDs—to save storage space—often cancel high-frequency sounds. Though sound waves at frequencies higher than 22 kilohertz can't be heard by the human ear, they can become audible as they ricochet around the room when the frequency drops.

Sensitive to these complaints, Ohga the artist resolved to create a better sound. Working once again with Philips, Sony created the MiniDisc, a small recordable compact disc that incorporated a speedier way to measure sound waves, thereby eliminating the earlier glitches. In 1992, the new generation of discs would replace audio compact cassettes and captivate consumers in Japan, Western Europe, and the primary market, the United States.

Driven by personality and gut feeling as much as by formal strategy, company executives remained convinced that the twenty-first century was the century of content. "What was most important was that Sony have the most extensive library of programs," says Ohga. Shortly after finalizing the purchase of CBS Records, he and Morita targeted Hollywood for their next acquisition. Following their successful gambit with records, a foray into movies and television seemed like a natural.

"I always thought that music revitalized our audio hardware business, and that buying a studio would strengthen our TV business," says Ohga. In 1989, while in a hospital recovering from open-heart surgery, he proposed the purchase of Columbia Pictures Entertainment with its two studios and vast library of movie and television titles. The acquisition did not come cheaply. The purchase price was $3.2 billion plus the assumption of $1.6 billion in debt. Morita delegated responsibility for the new purchase to Ohga, who later transferred power to his protégé at the time, Michael P. Schulhof, president of Sony Corporation of America.

The decision to buy Columbia Pictures, later called Sony Pictures Entertainment, generated special challenges for Sony. Ohga had consistently believed that its U.S. affiliates were best run with a decentralized, hands-off management style. He was wrong. The abrasive American business style clashed with Sony's Japanese sensibilities. Columbia Pictures produced a string of flops and began hemorrhaging badly. Costs skyrocketed as a result of lavish office renovations, expensive parties, and overly generous production deals. One executive used the corporate jet to send flowers to his girlfriend. In retrospect, Ohga had given Schulhof too much freedom.

In 1994, the embarrassed Sony president wrote off $2.7 billion and assumed a loss of $510 million for the Hollywood experiment. Some felt that Ohga would resign from the company. But the cofounders, both in failing health, refused to throw their heir-apparent to the wolves. They desperately needed him to lead Sony into the new century.

Besides coping with the company's first loss in its history, Ohga was confronted with a full-blown recession at home and a surging yen inhibiting the firm's exports. Japan's economic miracle was stalling, leaving Sony somewhat tarnished. When Akio Morita resigned as chairman in 1994, Ohga turned to his last and perhaps most important mission for the company: a succession plan. In March 1995, he announced the appointment of fifty-seven-year-old Nobuyuki Idei as his replacement. An audiophile with a penchant for marketing and a love of artfully designed gadgets, the thirty-five-year-veteran's selection came as a surprise to the business community. Idei's overseas assignments had kept him out of the corporate spotlight. Also, he had been in his present job as director of advertising, public relations, and product design functions only a year.

In explaining his choice, Ohga said, "Sony needs someone who is not necessarily an engineer but appreciates technology; someone who recognizes the latest technological developments and has foresight to see future technology trends; someone who understands the software business; and someone who has a global perspective. All these indicators led to Idei-san."

By every benchmark, Ohga succeeded. Under Idei's leadership, the company has been able to ride out Japan's prolonged economic slump. Shortly after assuming command, the hard-nosed executive began the most ambitious restructuring since Sony's founding in 1946—closing factories, laying off workers, slashing costs, and trimming the board of directors. He installed a new management team at Sony Pictures that cranked out a string of box office hits—*Jerry Maguire, My Best Friend's Wedding, Air Force One, Men in Black*, and *Crouching Tiger, Hidden Dragon*. Diversifying away from its traditional, stand-alone electronic-device business, under Idei's direction the company has entered the digital and broadband era through networked products and services.

Keeping his earlier promise to himself, Ohga, at age sixty, returned to his first love, music. Years before, to prepare himself for the podium, the retired opera star had founded and led Sony's award-winning brass ensemble. On February 4, 1990, he made his debut conducting the Tokyo Philharmonic, Japan's oldest orchestra, at the Orchard Hall. At first, he restricted his performances to two a year. Later, with his successor, Idei, in place, he began conducting five or six times a year, leading such orchestras as the Boston Symphony, the Metropolitan Opera, the Berlin Philharmonic, the Israel Philharmonic, and the Pittsburgh Symphony. By 2000, he had doubled the number of engagements, with visits to St. Petersburg, Montreal, and several other cities.

Between appearances, Ohga puts all his energy into practicing and rehearsing. He studies composition, poring over orchestral scores and striving for technical accuracy. He dissects the works of the great composers to understand them as best he can. He attends concerts and visits musicians. His encyclopedic grasp of repertoire is constantly on display. When conducting, Ohga is able to rely exclusively on his memory, with no score before him. Even when performing Beethoven's lengthy and complicated Ninth Symphony, he shuns the printed copy.

LISTEN TO YOUR HEART

KEEPING HIS EARLIER PROMISE TO HIMSELF, OHGA, AT AGE SIXTY, RETURNED TO HIS FIRST LOVE, MUSIC. ON FEBRUARY 4, 1990, HE MADE HIS DEBUT CONDUCTING THE TOKYO PHILHARMONIC, JAPAN'S OLDEST ORCHESTRA.

Though not as well known for his music talent as for his business skills, the maestro has won converts in professional circles. "He can indeed conduct," wrote Canadian music critic Douglas Hughes, after observing Ohga's Vancouver program of works by Mozart, Beethoven, and the Japanese composer Yasushi Akutagawa. "He used his baton in the same way I imagine an artist would use brush and pen to create those delicate shades characteristic of Japanese prints. Ohga delivered a searing and richly colored performance." Another critic, Honolulu-based Ruth Bingham, applauded his "controlled, reserved conducting style" after an evening of Beethoven.

Indeed, Ohga the conductor transcends amateur status in much the same way as did Churchill the artist. "This is not a hobby," insists Tom Todd, president and CEO of the Pittsburgh Symphony Society, in evaluating Ohga's orchestral contributions. "To be a conductor at this level is a vocation." Clearly, Ohga would like to be accepted by the musical community, to whom he has always been a bit of an outsider. "Because I am chairman of Sony, I am called an 'amateur' when conducting a symphony," he says dryly. "But in light of my schooling, I think I am an amateur businessman." As for his skills on the stage, Ohga is content to leave the matter to those listening: "Who can decide if this particular man is a professional conductor or not? It's best left to the audience. If the audience thinks that someone is a great conductor, then, from that point on, that person is a professional."

The man who has spent his career integrating his musical and corporate skills believes in the cross-fertilization of both lives. He claims that symphony conducting, like business, implies a series of balancing acts. "Great conductors don't just beat time," San Francisco–based composer Bob Greenberg points out. "They inspire their players." A successful performance happens only when the players are accountable to, not constrained by, the score. Effective conductors—the

> **DEFINE SUCCESS IN YOUR OWN TERMS**
> "BECAUSE I AM CHAIRMAN OF SONY, I AM CALLED AN 'AMATEUR' WHEN CONDUCTING A SYMPHONY. BUT IN LIGHT OF MY SCHOOLING, I THINK I AM AN AMATEUR BUSINESSMAN."

Bernsteins, Soltis, Toscaninis—literally orchestrate the energies of those around them. Like leaders everywhere, they allow individuals to feel they have the power to express themselves, without ever surrendering their own power, their vision, or their responsibility.

Ohga has always tried to unleash Sony's free thinkers. "For me, a successful company is one whose engineers create products that have never been conceived before," he says. "The development of the PlayStation project is a prime example." A decade ago, video games were considered to be a notoriously perilous business, entirely foreign to Sony and dominated by Nintendo Company and Sega Corporation. Many inside and outside the company opposed Sony's entry into the market. Ohga, however, consistently supported game-making, wanting "to establish a core business other than audiovisual equipment." He viewed video games as a high-risk, high-reward segment, but felt that Sony could buffer the downside by making both hardware and software.

In October 1989, Ken Kutaragi—an extraordinary engineer and genuine maverick—began the PlayStation project. In 1992, he boldly recommended that Sony develop and market game machines on a proprietary basis. Against the wishes of most of his fellow executives, Ohga handed down the critical decision to proceed with the PlayStation. "Do it!" he commanded. "Let's chart our own course," although he later acknowledged that "to make a success of a proprietary format is extremely difficult."

Nonconformist Kutaragi—now president and CEO of Sony Computer Entertainment—would often clash with his more traditional colleagues in Tokyo and New York. But Ohga stood by him. "I wanted to be Kutaragi's strongest supporter," he told journalist Reiji Asakura. "I was tremendously impressed with his ideas and unyielding spirit." The Sony president carefully monitored every stage of the PlayStation's progress, incorporating several modifications of his own. When he reviewed the first prototype in the early 1990s, the notorious nitpicker conceded, "It was rather good. Very Sony!"

After the console's introduction, Ohga warned the PlayStation team not to enter a mindless price war with rival Sega. "Lowering the price of a Sony product without accompanying product modifications is out of the question," he told Kutaragi. "There has never been an instance in the history of the company of reducing the price of a product once it's on sale. There is no way to justify it to stores selling the current product, not to mention those who bought it."

Though the two men frequently disagreed over pricing and other strategies, Ohga calls Kutaragi "a true genius" and credits him with the product's mind-boggling popularity. The red-hot PlayStation has become the world's top-selling game platform and a tremendous financial boon for the company. At its peak in 1998, it was responsible for nearly 40 percent of Sony's entire operating profits. (Since its Japanese launch in March 2000, the company has shipped more than twenty million PlayStation 2 systems.)

Just as a conductor's passion and knowledge of music generate players' respect, so, too, has Ohga's understanding of Sony's products and people allowed him to succeed. In his role as chairman of the Tokyo Philharmonic Orchestra, he constantly finds himself coping with the same inner tensions and political maneuvering found in the corporate world. Far from producing sounds of harmony, orchestras often are amalgams of cliques, competing interests, petty rivalries, and personality clashes. "Beasts with a hundred heads," composer Greenberg calls them.

> **SEEK COMPATIBLE GOALS**
>
> "AS LONG AS SOMEONE'S PERFORMING WELL AT WORK, DEVELOPING ANOTHER INTEREST IS ENCOURAGED."

On April 1, 1999, To-Phil, as the Tokyo Philharmonic is known, summoned the managerial maestro to chart its future course—no easy task, since Tokyo houses nine full-time professional orchestras, more than any other city in the world. Given these competing interests and the stagnant Japanese economy, Ohga's first move has been to put the orchestra on firm financial footing. How successful he will be "is really a question of whether you're skillful or lousy at getting donations," says Ohga. Then, he confidently adds, "But I do know a lot of people."

Throughout his career, Sony's musical beacon has endeavored to nurture future generations of artists and performers. Fifteen years ago, he founded the Sony Music Foundation, which promotes young talent in Japan; he also serves as honorary chairman of the Sony Symphony Orchestra, staffed by employees. When asked if there are any junior Ohgas in the company, he says, "Perhaps. A number of our people are performing in professional symphonies. And it's Sony's culture not to tie anyone's hands. As long as someone's performing well at work, developing another interest is encouraged."

How does Sony's super-active chairman find the time to balance his various interests? By programming carefully. Typically, he goes to bed early—between 9 P.M. and 10 P.M. But around 1 A.M., he awakens for an hour or two of rigorous study. Then, it's back to bed for a few more hours' sleep, before departing for Sony's Tokyo headquarters at 8:30 A.M. On the weekends, he returns to his latest pursuit.

However, last November, while conducting the To-Phil in Beijing, Ohga collapsed with a minor brain hemorrhage that has restricted his double life. Reflecting on his mortality, he still insists, "We have only one life to live and I intend to live it to the fullest." But unlike many Japanese executives, Ohga has no plans to work in his eighties or nineties. As for his countrymen who choose to do so, he says, "They're crazy."

"Like the traveler in Aesop's fable *The North Wind and the Sun*, the Japanese in general are very reluctant to take off their overcoats," Ohga concedes. By contrast, this rugged individualist stands alone in a nation that for decades denounced individualism as a threat to society. Ignoring conventional wisdom, he brought a fresh dimension to corporate Japan; his strategic insights and tactical daring revolutionized consumer electronics and popular culture.

"There's not much I haven't done," says Sony's elder statesman, assessing his many contributions. "Life is full of good dreams and bad dreams. But so far in my life, the bad dreams have been few."

4

Sally Ride

Outer Space to Web Space

*In the Space Age, the most
important space is between the ears.*

—ANNE ARMSTRONG, PRESIDENT,
CENTER FOR INNOVATIVE TECHNOLOGY

*Sally Ride, the nation's first woman astronaut,
brings space technology down to Earth.*

S ally Ride never planned to be an astronaut. Nor did she ever expect to see her name splashed across the media. "My personality was that of a physicist," she recalls, "not the personality of someone who wanted to be a public figure." That changed on June 18, 1983.

Twenty-two years after the first spaceflight, Ride rocketed to fame as the first American woman in space. Proving she had the "right stuff," the unassuming thirty-two-year-old scientist made one giant step for womankind. Since her historic flight, more than thirty other women—including Air Force Lt. Col. Pamela Melroy, who piloted the one-hundredth space shuttle in October 2000—have made chauvinist mincemeat of the Old Boys' Space Club.

The adventures of the shuttle fleet have long dominated the U.S. space program—thanks, in part, to the multitalented Ride. In the years following her epic journey, only one mission—the ill-fated *Challenger* mission in 1986—ended in disaster. Today, the novelty of space flight has worn off. Most Americans take for granted the technical marvels of floating around the cosmos. The current hot topic is commercialization of space, which includes sending tourists into orbit. We tend to forget the bravery of Ride and other first-generation astronauts, who voyaged into the dangerous unknown. In their day, space was an even more hostile environment: Liftoff was a controlled explosion, and landing a controlled crash.

Ride's courage and achievements have led her along many paths—physicist, professor, astronaut, author, tennis player, and entrepreneur. However, "science has always been a constant for me. It's always been at the core of my motivation," she says. "I see myself as a scientist as opposed to an ex-astronaut or something else. That's really how I define myself."

Changing skins comes easily for the self-confident scientist. In fact, she reinvents herself every few years. "I have a tendency to be fascinated and totally involved in something for five or six years—and then find something else to do," she says, insisting that it's not because she gets bored easily. "It's just that I find myself looking around for other new, interesting opportunities to dive into."

Ride's latest project is running Imaginary Lines, Inc., a San Diego–based start-up that provides training and career opportunities for young women interested in science and math. "Those skill sets," she argues, "are appropriate to lots of different things. If you have a good understanding of them, there are lots of different directions you can take." By opening up the male-dominated world of science and math, America's space heroine has high hopes of instilling in girls "the importance of learning new things throughout their lives"—in other words, preparing them for the possibility of multiple lives.

Sally Kristen Ride was born in Encino, California, on May 26, 1951. Her father, Dale, taught political science at Santa Monica Community College, where he went on to serve as an administrator. Her mother, Joyce, was a volunteer teacher and, later, a volunteer counselor at a nearby women's prison. Both parents encouraged Sally and her younger sister, Karen, to explore their own interests. The only pressure the family put on their children was to do their best or, as Ride puts it, "to bring home the right kind of grades."

REINVENT YOURSELF

"I FIND MYSELF LOOKING AROUND FOR OTHER NEW, INTERESTING OPPORTUNITIES TO DIVE INTO."

A gifted and competitive athlete, Ride played football, baseball, and soccer with the boys in the neighborhood. "When they chose up sides, Sally was always the first to be selected," her sister recalls. Her dream was to play shortstop someday for the Los Angeles Dodgers.

An avid reader, Ride particularly enjoyed the sports pages and could rattle off the batting averages of her favorite players. Science fiction also held special appeal. Ride remembers, "When I was growing up, I was always fascinated by the planets, stars, and galaxies." Conversely, she showed an aversion to music. When her mother encouraged her to learn to play the piano, she refused. "The main thing was that if Sally was interested in a subject, she'd give it all her attention," her mother recalls. "If she wasn't interested, she wouldn't give it any attention. She set her own goals."

At age ten, Ride discovered tennis. She practiced for hours on end, hitting balls against the garage door, trying to target a particular spot. The next year, her mother arranged for her to have lessons with Alice Marble, a four-time national women's champion. By the time she was twelve, Ride was competing on the national junior tennis circuit, spending her weekends crisscrossing the country to play in tournaments. Her athletic prowess landed her a scholarship at Westlake School for Girls, an elite private school in Los Angeles.

NEVER STOP LEARNING

"ONE OF THE THINGS THAT ALWAYS FASCINATED ME ABOUT SCIENCE WAS THAT I WANTED TO UNDERSTAND HOW THINGS WORK. THERE ARE SO MANY MYSTERIES OUT THERE THAT ARE FUN TO SOLVE."

While polishing her tennis strokes, Ride developed a keen interest in science and math. Her favorite teacher and mentor, Dr. Elizabeth Mommaerts, introduced her to the scientific method and how it was used to solve difficult problems. The approach appealed to Ride's orderly mind. "She was obviously intelligent, clear thinking, and extremely logical," according to Mommaerts. "I have never seen logic so personified."

Science also tweaked Ride's curious side. "One of the things that always fascinated me about science was that I wanted to understand how things work," she remembers. "There are so many mysteries out there that are fun to solve. That's what really led me into science."

Ride graduated from Westlake with honors in 1968. That fall, she entered Swarthmore College in Pennsylvania, where she studied physics and played on the school's tennis team. She won the Eastern Intercollegiate Women's Tennis Championship, and one sportswriter called her "the best female college player in the East." Ride decided that she wanted more from tennis: a professional career. In 1969, after only three semesters at Swarthmore, she returned home to southern California to improve her game.

For the next few months, Ride practiced hours each day against some of the country's most talented players. In spite of concerted effort, she decided that the professional circuit was not for her. "I wasn't that good," she confided.

The next year, Ride transferred to Stanford University in Palo Alto. While studying math and science, she continued to play competitive tennis. She was the top-ranked player on the Cardinal women's nationally ranked team. But science became her first love.

In 1973, she graduated from Stanford with bachelor's degrees in physics and English. She went on to earn a master's degree in physics two years later. Ride was enrolled in the doctoral program in astrophysics in 1977 when she saw an advertisement in the school newspaper.

NASA was looking for a new breed of astronauts. Previously, military test pilots had represented the agency. But, in the period after the *Apollo* flights and moon landings, money for space projects decreased sharply. NASA decided to go for a new generation of reusable launch vehicles with the idea of later using them to build a space station. To win support for the shuttle, the agency made what later proved to be inflated claims about what a shuttle fleet would accomplish and how it would greatly reduce the cost of sending payloads into space. To justify the program economically, NASA began to develop projects with private industry, where the skills of scientists and technicians were just as important as those of pilots. The agency began soliciting applications from nonaviators to serve as "mission specialists" on future spaceflights.

Ride answered the ad the same day. "I don't know why I wanted to do it," she recalled. "I never had any burning ambition to be in the space program. I never even thought about how they recruited astronauts. When I saw them on TV, they all seemed to be Navy or Air Force test pilots. I suppose I just took it for granted that it was pretty much a closed club." But Ride believed she could crack the club.

More than eight thousand men and women applied. Two hundred and eight finalists, including Ride, were selected and summoned to Johnson Space Center in Houston for a week-long battery of physical and mental tests. Ride returned to Stanford reinvigorated. The NASA competition had given her "a lot of motivation" to finish her thesis work. She completed her doctoral studies, mastering specialized subjects such as X-ray astronomy and free-electron lasers.

On January 16, 1978, Ride received the long-awaited call from George Abbey, director of flight operations at the Johnson Center. "Well, we've got a job here for you, if you're still interested in taking it," he said. "Yes, sir," she immediately responded. Dr. Sally Ride was one of thirty-five selected for the astronaut class of 1978. Also included were five other women: a surgeon, a biochemist, a geologist, a physicist, and an electrical engineer. Despite its mixed composition, the group was known as the Thirty-Five New Guys—TFNG.

Ride joined her fellow astronaut candidates at Johnson Space Center in July. During the first year, TFNG'ers were expected to master the Space Transportation System (STS) program. Ride and her colleagues spent much of their time in the classroom studying basic shuttle systems. They also took courses in mathematics, meteorology, astronomy, navigation, and computers. Although they would not fly the shuttle, they needed to know how it worked, including how to operate its payload bay doors, computers, environmental control systems, and remote manipulators. Shuttle simulators, run by computers, gave the prospective astronauts a sense of actual flight. "They turn you on your back and shake and vibrate you and pump noise in," she recalls. "It's very realistic."

Besides spending numerous hours in the simulators, Ride and her cohorts flew about fifteen hours a week in the backseat of a T-38 training jet. The experience helped them master radio communications and navigation and sensitized them to higher-level g-forces. Ride so enjoyed her flight training that she went on to get her private pilot's license. Today, when she can squeeze a few minutes into her busy schedule, she flies a Grumman Tiger.

In the 1970s, NASA had no special fitness program for astronaut candidates. It was the responsibility of each trainee to prepare for the physical demands of spaceflight. Ride stayed fit by running four or five miles a day during the week and eight to ten miles on weekends; she continued to play tennis and volleyball—and she lifted weights, because every would-be astronaut had to be able to lug around the forty-five-pound parachute used in the training jets. Scuba diving and parachute training were part of NASA's survival course. In one sequence, Ride was dropped from a helicopter, four hundred feet above the water. She then had to make her way to a small raft in rough seas and paddle to safety.

Also demanding were the sessions on adapting to the change from Earth's gravitational pull to the weightlessness of space. Ride was introduced to NASA's infamous flying lab, aptly called the "Vomit Comet." Flying at carefully controlled high-speed arcs, this specially outfitted KC-135 aircraft can produce the sensation of stomach-churning weightlessness for nearly half a minute. Astronaut candidates float inside the jet, practicing activities such as eating, drinking, putting on space suits, and using shuttle equipment. For many trainees, even veteran pilots, the sensory mix-up brings temporary nausea.

In 1979, at the age of twenty-eight, Ride became a full-fledged astronaut. For the next two years, she was assigned to an engineering team that worked with a Canadian manufacturer to design a remote mechanical arm to be used in deploying and retrieving space satellites. This equipment proved to be invaluable in subsequent shuttle missions.

During the second and third flights of the space shuttle *Columbia*, Ride served as a "capcom," or capsule communicator, at Mission Control. As the indispensable backseat drivers of the space program, capcoms are the only people allowed to talk to the shuttle crew during flight and are responsible for landing and bringing the astronauts home safely. Failure on their part means a lost or marooned spacecraft and a dead crew. As the first woman to occupy this critical position, Ride had to understand everything about the mission from liftoff to landing.

In April 1982, NASA announced the names of the four crew members for the seventh STS mission: Robert Crippen, commander; Rick Hauck, copilot; John Fabian and Sally Ride, mission specialists. (Dr. Norman Thagard was added the following December.) Three months later, the first American woman chosen to fly in space married fellow astronaut and TFNG'er Steven Hawley in a small, informal wedding, which took place in Hawley's parents' home in Salina, Kansas. The ceremony was performed by two ministers—Hawley's father and Ride's sister, Karen. Ride kept her maiden name, and the couple settled into a three-bedroom house in Clear Lake City, Texas, near the Johnson Space Center.

After the wedding, Ride plunged back into training for her first flight into outer space. She had to master the voluminous crew training manual, which covered emergency procedures, use of in-flight equipment, maintenance requirements, and countless other details. During a typical week, she might fly her jet to the East or West coast for meetings, spend a day in the simulator, train for a space walk in NASA's water tank, engage in rigorous computer-based courses, or devote countless hours to administrative duties. Invariably, her crew training for STS-7 involved press interviews. One reporter asked her if she'd wear a bra in space. "There's no sag in zero-g," she answered, revealing a dry sense of humor. Most of the queries from the press revolved around how she would perform normal bodily functions. Ride patiently explained that she would be using the specially designed zero-gravity potty, refitted to include a curtain and a wide cuplike attachment between the legs to collect urine.

As the country's first female space cadet, Ride, now thirty-two, eschewed her celebrity status, constantly shunning the limelight. "It's too bad that society isn't yet to the point where the country could just send up a woman astronaut and nobody would think twice about it," she remarked. Downplaying the historical importance of her first trip in space, she said, "I'm not historical material. I did not come to NASA to make history."

Why was Ride selected? She speculates that it was her strengths: "A good educational background and one that showed I could learn new things readily." NASA's Abbey, who was on the selection panel, offers another explanation: Ride is a team player. Those who are determined to do their own thing, he said, "probably wouldn't be happy here."

As commander of STS-7, Captain Crippen had veto power over all crew choices. He told reporters why he wanted Ride on his team, "You like people who stay calm under duress. And Sally can do that. She hit all the squares . . . and will fit in well with the group." Ride's husband, Hawley, chimed in, "If they hadn't picked her, I'd be mad, because she deserved it."

On June 18, 1983, Hawley, Ride's parents, and her sister Karen were at Kennedy Space Center in Cape Canaveral to watch the historic launch. Among those cheering her on were several hundred thousand spectators, many wearing T-shirts on which "Ride, Sally Ride" was printed. Also gathered in the early morning hours were numerous feminists, including Jane Fonda and Gloria Steinem. Despite the doyenne of America's space program's earlier re-

> **IGNORE THE NAYSAYERS**
>
> "IT'S TOO BAD THAT SOCIETY ISN'T YET TO THE POINT WHERE THE COUNTRY COULD JUST SEND UP A WOMAN ASTRONAUT AND NOBODY WOULD THINK TWICE ABOUT IT."

marks, Ride's supporters trumpeted the significance of STS-7. "It's an important first," said Steinem, "because it means millions of little girls are going to sit in front of the television and know they can become astronauts after this." Whether Ride liked it or not, she was making history.

The moment had finally come. After five years of training, Ride was perched 195 feet above the ground in the nose of the *Challenger*. Anticipation and expectations were running high. At seven minutes to launch, the walkway was removed and the power units started. The five-person crew, the largest ever to be put in space, closed the visors of their helmets. The space shuttle quivered as its engines slowly moved into position for blast-off. Seven seconds before launch, the engines ignited. At T-0, the solid rockets fired up, and the shuttle leaped off the launch pad. At precisely 7:33 A.M., the *Challenger* zoomed into space.

"All we can see of the trail of fire behind us is a faint, pulsating glow through the top window," Ride later wrote. As flight engineer, she was responsible for monitoring the flood of data on the instrument panel and reporting to the pilot and commander. Forty-four minutes and twenty-seven seconds after liftoff, the spaceship reached its final orbit, two hundred miles above Earth. After twenty-two years, fifty-seven astronauts, and thirty-six "manned" missions, an American woman was finally in space.

Traveling at five miles a second and circling Earth every ninety minutes, Ride felt no motion. But she soon noticed that virtually every system in her body was affected by weightlessness. Body fluids surged to her head and chest, causing her face to puff up and her legs to constrict. Her neck veins bulged, her heart enlarged a bit to support the other organs and her spinal disks expanded. Yet, surprisingly, Ride never experienced the temporary nausea that often affects astronauts.

Ride quickly adjusted to zero gravity and came to enjoy it. "The best part of being in space is being weightless," she said. "It feels wonderful to be able to float without effort; to slither up, down, and around the inside of the shuttle just like a seal." Enjoying the freedom of her zero-g environment, she engaged in a contest to see which of the astronauts could travel fastest in the cabin. John Fabian won; Ride finished second. With her shuttle mates, she also helped retrieve jellybeans provided by President Ronald Reagan that were floating around the spaceship.

Most of her time, however, was devoted to hard work, performing a variety of complex tasks. After reaching orbit, she and others deployed *Anik-C*, the Canadian communications satellite. The next day, she helped launch *Palapa B*, an Indonesian satellite that provided

LISTEN TO YOUR HEART

"THE THING I'LL REMEMBER MOST ABOUT THE FLIGHT IS THAT IT WAS FUN. . . . I'M SURE IT'S THE MOST FUN I'LL EVER HAVE IN MY LIFE."

telephone signals to one million people in Southeast Asia. The mission's highlight occurred on the fifth day, when Ride and Fabian used the shuttle's finicky fifty-foot-long, remote-controlled mechanical arm to deploy and retrieve a self-contained 3,300-pound space laboratory built in West Germany. The scientists needed to know if the shuttle could recapture malfunctioning satellites, make onboard repairs, and return the satellites to orbit.

Mission accomplished, the close-knit crew prepared *Challenger* for reentry, or "de-orbit." They immediately began to experience the effects of increasing weight. After a week in the cosmos, the spacelings would again become earthlings. Wearing specially designed "g-suits," pants lined with inflatable pressure tubes, the astronauts were able to redirect the flow of blood from legs to brain, allowing their bodies to readjust to gravity.

As the crew orbited about two hundred miles above ground, Captain Crippen initiated a tail-first, then nose-first, descent into Earth's atmosphere. During the reentry, temperatures outside the spacecraft reached 2,700 degrees, causing a twelve-minute blackout with Mission Control in Houston. At lower altitudes, the commander maneuvered the shuttle like a glider. The landing gear came down, and after a week in space and ninety-eight orbits around Earth, the hundred-ton *Challenger* made a perfect landing at California's sprawling Edwards Air Force Base.

During a homecoming reception at Johnson Space Center, where the crew was later flown, Ride insisted on being treated as one of the guys. Yet she could not hide the adrenaline high of her first journey in space. Said Ride, "The thing I'll remember most about the flight is that it was fun. In fact, I'm sure it's the most fun I'll ever have in my life."

But, after three weeks of debriefing, the fun began again as Ride prepared for another *Challenger* flight. In October 1984, she flew on her second and final shuttle mission. The seven-person crew included another woman, Kathryn Sullivan, a classmate of Ride's in elementary school. Unfortunately, the mission encountered a series of mechanical mishaps, from solar panels that wouldn't open to radar panels that wouldn't close. With Ride's deft assistance, the crew was able to resolve these problems. When she discovered that the hinges on the solar panels of the satellite had frozen in storage, Ride and a crewmate asked Commander Crippen (the leader of her first flight) to reposition the *Challenger* so that the sun's rays could melt the ice. Their suggestion worked, and the satellite was launched successfully.

After eight days in orbit, the astronauts landed safely at Kennedy Space Center. Later, technicians discovered that four thousand tiles in the shuttle's protective heat shield needed to be replaced—an indication that similar glitches might occur on future missions.

Following her second spaceflight, Ride traveled the country promoting America's space efforts. Royally feted, she received the Lindbergh Eagle Award from Anne Morrow Lindbergh and the Jefferson Award from the American Institute for Public Service. In the meantime, she prepared for her third flight in space. But, on January 28, 1986, the unthinkable happened. On its next mission, the *Challenger* exploded seventy-three seconds after liftoff, killing all seven crew members, including teacher Christa McAuliffe and Judith Resnick, who had been the second American woman in space and Ride's fellow TFNG'er. The accident had a devastating effect on Ride, and her faith in NASA waned.

Within days of the disaster, she was assigned to a presidential commission, led by former Secretary of State William Rogers, to investigate the tragedy. The panel found that the explosion was caused by faulty O-rings on one of the solid rocket boosters. More disturbing, however, were the panel's findings of a general lack of attention to safety and the need for sweeping management reforms at the agency. The Rogers Report virtually grounded the U.S. space program.

The following September, NASA head James Fletcher summoned Ride to the agency's Washington headquarters, where she was named acting head of a new Office of Space Exploration. She became one of several working astronauts to be tapped for a managerial position. Her brief, said Fletcher, was to produce "a blueprint to guide the United States to a position of leadership among the spacefaring nations of earth." The real questions were simple, Ride said, "We must ask ourselves, 'Where do we want to be at the end of the century?' and 'What do we have to do now to get there?'"

Over the next eleven months, Ride and her task force of space experts authored a comprehensive study of America's long-term role in space. The effort, known as the Ride Report, focused on four "leadership initiatives": Mission Earth, a calculated look at Earth sciences with the aid of satellite sensors; exploration of the remote reaches of the solar system with a new generation of robot probes; a return to the moon to establish a permanent lunar base; and a piloted expedition to Mars.

In attempting to set NASA back on track, Ride pulled no punches about some of its shortcomings. She argued for an "evolutionary" policy with diverse objectives, rather than one splashy, signature project. "It would not be good strategy, good science, or good policy," according to Ride, "for the United States to select a single initiative, then pursue it single-mindedly." The report recommended that the country establish a lunar outpost that could serve as a research laboratory and enable scientists to exploit the moon's resources. "While exploring the moon," Ride reasoned, "we would learn to live and work on a hostile world beyond Earth." Mars would logically come next. As Ride put it, "Settling Mars should be our eventual goal, but it should not be our next goal."

In recommending a cautious, stepwise approach, Ride disappointed some in NASA's tight-knit community who believed the moon had been explored sufficiently and preferred a direct shot at Mars. However, agency head Fletcher endorsed the Ride report. Ride later testified before Congress on the report and presented it to then-Vice President Bush and the National Academy of Sciences.

In 1987, on her thirty-sixth birthday, Ride retired from NASA to become a senior fellow at Stanford's Center for International Security and Arms Control. "The change is something I have been thinking about for quite a while," she said. "I always wanted to go back to Stanford in some capacity. I just got the right offer." That same year, she also divorced Hawley.

At Stanford, Ride discovered life after NASA. She helped train scientists in national security and arms control affairs. In 1989, she accepted a position as a physics professor at the University of California, San Diego (UCSD), where she also directed the La Jolla–based California Space Institute. In her professorial duties, Ride continued to conduct her own research, specializing in the theory of free-electron lasers and the interaction between relativistic electron beams and radiation. Her assignment at the institute involved coordinating space research among the University of California's eight campuses and assisting California companies interested in the promise and potential of space.

In addition, Ride began a personal crusade to help girls and young women acquire an interest in math and science. Though she claims to have never run into any real obstacles in pursuing her own space and scientific dreams, Ride said she "had enough people tell me about their problems. So it was very important for me to help break down some of the stereotypes."

As director of the California Space Institute, Ride developed "KidSat," kids' satellite, an innovative program for students of all ages. With a $3 million grant from NASA and a boost from the agency's Jet Propulsion Laboratory in Pasadena, the program directly involves students in the space-shuttle effort. Launched in April 1996, youngsters from several states are required to plan, coordinate, and direct an Earth-looking camera aboard the shuttle. Typically, a camera onboard the spacecraft beams a steady stream of information over the Internet to interested students. A campus lab at UCSD acts as control center, mimicking some of the activities at the Johnson Space Center.

"It's a new way to promote science education," says Frank C. Owens, director of NASA's educational program. "As students study math and science, they will see there are real-world applications." Ride and NASA view the kids' satellite as a creative way to boost America's scientific brainpower.

To spread the word further on the merits of science, Ride has authored four children's books. *To Space and Back* describes her first *Challenger* flight. In *Voyager: An Adventure to the Edge of the Solar System*, she examines the travels and discoveries of the *Voyager I* and *II* spacecrafts. *The Third Planet: Exploring the Earth from Space* considers Earth's fragile environment from afar, and *The Mystery of Mars* offers insights into the mysterious red planet, including a discussion of the possibilities of life on Mars.

In early 1999, the ex-astronaut undertook another reincarnation when she joined the board of directors of SPACE.com, a Web site that provides news and information about space exploration and the space industry. The company was launched by prodigal CNN financial news anchorman Lou Dobbs, who was chairman and CEO. Its board included space luminaries such as former NASA astronauts Neil Armstrong and Eugene Cernan and ex-cosmonaut Alexey Leonov, along with high-powered financiers Donald Marron, then chairman of PaineWebber, and Ray Rothrock, general partner at Venrock Associates. Ride served as executive vice president of strategic planning, while continuing to hold her academic post at UCSD.

When SPACE.com's cofounder, Rich Zahradnik, unexpectedly quit in August, the board asked Ride to become president. "Sally's depth of experience, strategic approach and proven record of success are exactly the right mix of skills necessary to lead this company as we continue on a path of accelerated, focused growth," Dobbs said at the time of her appointment.

Ride clearly brought many skills to the job: "I have a lot of contacts in the world of space and I bring expertise in space programs and space science," she said. "I'm really trying to help build the vision of the company, based on that experience."

One thing Ride wouldn't do was pull up stakes in San Diego and move to New York, where SPACE.com is headquartered. Taking a leave of absence from UCSD, she shuttled back and forth between the East and West coasts. For the next year, the former space mariner threw herself into her new role. The company grew from ten to more than a hundred employees, attracted 502,000 visitors a month to its Web site, and unveiled *Space Illustrated* magazine. In addition, Ride helped the fledgling enterprise secure its second round of financing in March 2000.

> **AIM HIGH**
>
> IN FOUNDING IMAGINARY LINES, INC., RIDE HOPES TO CONNECT "HUNDREDS OF THOUSANDS OF GIRLS TO COLLABORATIVE TOOLS, RESOURCES, AND ROLE MODELS AT A CRITICAL TIME IN THEIR LIVES."

With the company's vision in place and its finances assured, Ride decided it was time to move on. "I had watched this company grow from a small dot-com start-up to a major cross-media player," she says. No doubt the steady diet of cross-country travel had taken its toll—"a killer," she called it. In September 2000, she resigned from SPACE.com to pursue yet another life.

In January 2001, Ride founded Imaginary Lines, Inc., to encourage girls and young women to take up careers in math, science, and engineering. Based in San Diego, the venture creates communities, develops branded products, and offers services for young women, their parents, teachers, and future employers.

"We will initially focus on upper elementary and middle school girls through the creation of The Sally Ride Science Club—a 'cool,' interactive natural club designed to resonate with a broad cross-section of girls," Ride said at its inception. "The club will link girls to each other, to female scientists, to mentors, and to their own source of interactive science content. Members can chat with an astronaut, follow the adventures of a science 'soap' and join online 'invention conventions.' The club will connect hundreds of thousands of girls to collaborative tools, resources, and role models at a critical time in their lives."

In many respects, Imaginary Lines seems like a metaphor for Ride's multiple lives. Combining science and space in an interactive learning environment underscores her special interests. For years, she has crusaded for greater scientific literacy for America's children, particularly young women. "In elementary school, roughly the same number of girls and boys are interested in science and math," she says. "But beginning in about sixth grade, more girls than boys begin to disengage from these subjects. One consequence of this leaking pipeline is that women remain underrepresented in most technical professions— while the nation's need for scientists and engineers remains unmet."

Ironically, technology—Internet technology—is helping restore gender balance in science and engineering. "I see the Internet as an equalizing force," says Ride. "As a professor of physics, I watched undergraduate students of both sexes and in all majors and how they interacted with computers and the Internet. They are on the Web all the time, and you can really see the equalizing effect of the Internet just by watching the way they use it."

As Ride presses ahead with Imaginary Lines, she continues to be an active spokesperson for U.S. space exploration. In addition to her business and academic responsibilities, she maintains an intensive speaking schedule and sits on a variety of boards, from Mitre Corporation to the President's Committee of Advisors on Science and Technology.

RECHARGE YOUR CREATIVITY

"IN TWENTY OR SO YEARS FROM NOW, I MAY CALL NASA TO SEE IF THEY'LL GIVE ME A ROCKET TRIP TO MARS."

Asked if the United States is maintaining its edge in space, the woman who has logged 343 hours of space flight responds, "The baseline commitment is there, and it cuts across both political parties. But having said that, it's probably impossible to generate another major space effort like sending a human to Mars." Ride reckons that the Mars journey will probably take at least fifteen years.

"It's an enormous logistical effort," she explains. "Depending on how much fuel and which propulsion system you decide to use, it could take eight or ten months to get there. And because of orbital mechanics, you have to stay on the planet for three months. Then, when you come back, it's another eight to ten months. So you're talking about a round-trip travel time of well over two years."

For Ride, any return to space might be anticlimactic. Nevertheless, she likes the John Glenn model. "In twenty or so years from now, I may call NASA to see if they'll give me a rocket trip to Mars," she says. But for now, her space-flying days are over.

Ride still downplays her fame and guards her privacy. However, in recent years, she has displayed her athletic good looks in television ads for U.S. Robotics and in a cameo appearance on CBS's *Touched by an Angel*. "It's not so much that I don't like attention," says the down-to-earth ex-astronaut. "It's just that I want to have a life."

For Ride, at age fifty, that life revolves around giving young Americans the same panoply of lifestyle options that she has sampled. "One of the most important things in preparing kids for the future," she says, "is instilling in them the flexibility of constantly exploring new horizons." A staunch advocate of straddling new worlds, Ride contends, "One thing that comes through loud and clear is that you can head in different directions. You can have a second, a third, a fourth life. You can do it relatively often and quite successfully."

> **REINVENT YOURSELF**
>
> "YOU CAN HAVE A SECOND, A THIRD, A FOURTH LIFE. YOU CAN DO IT RELATIVELY OFTEN AND QUITE SUCCESSFULLY."

5

Ron Kent *and* Chuck Watson

The Art of Paradise

*Don't let making a living
prevent you from making a life.*

— JOHN WOODEN, BASKETBALL COACH

*Stockbroker Ron Kent coaxes delicate beauty
from rough trunks of Hawaiian timber.*

*Executive, builder, sculptor Chuck Watson focuses
on the project at hand in his Honolulu studio.*

The Hawaiian Islands may have a worldwide reputation as the ultimate place for fun in the sun, but two people who moved to the idyllic beach town of Kailua long ago have done much more than just beachcomb and sunbathe. Although their paths have never crossed, *malihinis* (newcomers) Ron Kent and Chuck Watson have both led extremely successful double lives, pursuing business and art just a mile from each other in one of the best beach towns in the world.

Kent, a well-known stockbroker in Honolulu, is even better known for his exquisite translucent wooden bowls. Watson, once the CEO of Hawai'i's premier construction company, found an equally rewarding second life as a metal and stone sculptor whose works can be seen throughout the Pacific.

Here's how two businessmen with artistic talents lead double lives in an environment better known for vacations than avocations, testimony that dual careers can be achieved anywhere in this world, even though others may suffer "Polynesian paralysis."

BALANCING BONDS AND BOWLS

In the predawn hours, Ron Kent labors over another potential masterpiece. The heat, the smells, the colors tell us that we are far away from the world's major art centers. Kent's airy studio sits within sight of one of Hawai'i's prettiest beaches on Oahu's windward coast. In his five-hundred-square-foot hutch, the stockbroker-artist toils in silence. In deference to Kent's neighbors, his three-horsepower lathe, the tool of choice for all great wood turners, rests for the night.

Kent's task is a familiar one: to coax delicate beauty from his preferred material, native Norfolk pine. With infinite patience, he oils and sands for hours on end what were once parts of nearby trees. It can take as long as six months to produce one of his signature pieces: translucent, fingernail-thin, oil-soaked vessels. Highly acclaimed for the glowing luminescence of his pine bowls, Ron Kent ranks as one of the world's master wood turners.

His graceful silhouettes, integrating the inherent properties of wood and light, can be found in the world's finest galleries and museums (the Louvre; the Metropolitan Museum of Art; the Museum of Fine Arts, Boston; the Smithsonian), in private collections (Whoopie Goldberg, the late John Denver), and in movies (*Speed, Short Cuts*). The Pope, Emperor Akihito, and former president Bill Clinton own his bowls, as do two Supreme Court justices. With more than a thousand vessels in circulation, Kent's works command up to five-figure price tags from eager clients on every continent.

Crafting a double life came easily to the self-taught artist. Chicago-born Kent grew up in Los Angeles, where his parents encouraged him to pursue multiple interests. An early aptitude test indicated that young Ron could do almost anything well—except accounting and sports. "I was the last kid who was ever chosen on any team," Kent recalls. As a result, the clumsy youngster gravitated toward solving problems. Later, it was off to UCLA to pursue a degree in engineering, the purest form of problem solving. As a struggling married student, Kent started making furniture for the family apartment.

Soon he got hooked on the beauty of wood and, in no time, began turning out pieces far superior to store-bought goods. After graduating from college in 1957, Kent began a traditional career in engineering. Eight years later, he abandoned the security of a high-paid position in southern California's booming aerospace industry for the vagaries of the stock market.

Shortly thereafter, Ron and his family left California for Hawai'i, where he worked as a stockbroker until his retirement in 1997. Kent's artistic career began in the early 1970s in a two-car garage with a small second-hand "toy lathe" his wife, Myra, bought him for Christmas. His first creations were stubby wooden bottles shaped from driftwood gathered from nearby beaches. After much trial and error, Kent's experimentation shifted to long-necked bottle forms with small but pronounced lips, which then evolved into shorter, more rounded forms with increasingly prominent tops—his "spittoon period."

Eventually, he concentrated on the shape of the top itself, tapering as it did to a narrow neck. The result was a translucent, thin-walled bowl with its edges flaring to form a delicate base. Like many people with no formal training in art, Kent didn't know what you weren't supposed to do.

His choice of the ubiquitous Norfolk pine, for example, surprised many of his formally trained colleagues, who preferred the elegant hardwoods of Hawai'i: koa, milo, and ohia. Unencumbered by orthodoxy, he chose pine because of its availability and its rich patterns and translucence when oiled. Kent soon discovered that his favorite wood, when cut, absorbs a fungus that creates an irregular and unpredictable pattern in the wood. This process, called spalting—a kind of rot—can produce dramatically different colorings depending on how long the cut wood is exposed to the Hawaiian humidity. A few weeks of exposure will yield a vessel that is golden with a few streaks of black; three months on the log pile yields a black bowl with amber markings.

But Kent also found that by freezing freshly cut wood blocks, he could modify, even halt, spalting to produce desirable colors. Plucking a coarse pine chunk from his chest-high freezer (bought for $50 at a garage sale), Kent cranks up his lathe to begin shaping his next piece.

Hardwoods are unforgiving, and carvers must be disciplined when working with them. Once the chips start flying, they cannot be added back: Wood turners are irreversibly confined to an ever-reduced block of wood. So the challenge is to visualize the design and then chip away for the desired result. If the turner is too aggressive, or too subtractive, the methods "devour themselves": the wood will crack as easily as an eggshell, and weeks of work will be lost. Or if the turner fails to press the limits of the material, the piece will not produce the translucence that is Kent's special contribution.

"Properly lit, his bowls glow," says writer and curator John Perreault. "He can control the light by the thickness and thinness of the walls so that the turned bowl shapes light." Art critic Matthew Kangas adds, "Kent's union of execution and sensitivity of materials is foremost."

LEARN FROM FAILURE

"BREAKS ARE GOOD. I USE THEM AS A GAUGE OF HOW MUCH I'M PUSHING MYSELF. THE OCCASIONAL CRACK LETS ME KNOW WHAT I'M DOING IS WORTHWHILE."

The freewheeling stock-broker credits his artistic accomplishment, in part, to his lack of formal training. "I never had a lesson," he says.

Like Mark Twain, who "never let his schooling interfere with his education," Kent abhors academic constraints. He chalks up his world-class credentials largely to the fact that he is a risk taker who is prepared to make his delicate bowls so thin the shadow of one's hand can be seen through the wood. "My mission is to create and select the silhouette that best interacts with the natural characteristics of each log, highlighting the intrinsic beauties that nature has provided and seeking a harmonious blend," says Kent.

Outstanding turners, he warns, "must be willing to make mistakes." This means every third or fourth bowl will shatter on the lathe. "This would be thoroughly depressing," he admits, "except that breaks are good. I use them as a gauge of how much I'm pushing myself. The occasional crack lets me know what I'm doing is worthwhile."

After the bowl has been properly shaped come up to sixty applications of hand-rubbed oil, alternated with sanding, to saturate the wood and seal the surface. Like resin turning to amber, the oil in the wood polymerizes and adds to the translucence. It is not just the thin walls, but also the voids that create a startling presence. As are the best potters, Kent is concerned with negative space, with the relationships between the inside and the outside of his works. The concave centers of his pieces contrast subtly with the large open rims. Every vessel is an interplay of the inherent properties of wood and light, dramatizing the whorls, grains, colors, and patterns that nature has provided.

Though many imitators have surfaced, no one has captured Ron Kent's reputation as the premier minimalist. He credits much of his success to his ability to accept limits. As famed conductor Igor Stravinsky once put it, "Every piece of music has two endings—one where it should end and one where you end it. Know the difference." Ron Kent knows where to end it. The genial, enthusiastic turner cautions against shooting for total perfection. "Good enough is good enough," he insists. "If something's worth doing at all, it's worth doing halfway. Seeking perfection in art or in life is a lesson in futility." Many people, Kent believes, would be far better off making midcourse corrections and moving on to the next challenge.

Ron Kent's work "celebrates the natural colors and grain of the wood itself," writes Deborah Shinn, assistant curator of applied arts at the Smithsonian Institution's Cooper-Hewitt National Design Museum. He has been cited for his originality, technical perfection, inspired design, and sensitivity to material. His peers include a short list of contemporary artists: David Ellsworth (Kent's personal

> **DEFINE SUCCESS IN YOUR OWN TERMS**
>
> "GOOD ENOUGH IS GOOD ENOUGH. IF SOMETHING'S WORTH DOING AT ALL, IT'S WORTH DOING HALFWAY. SEEKING PERFECTION IN ART OR IN LIFE IS A LESSON IN FUTILITY."

favorite), Dennis Elliott, Mel Lindquist, Ed Mouthrop, and Ronald Wornick. Excepting Ellsworth, all have led double lives.

Earlier in his life, Elliott was the drummer for the well-known British rock group Foreigner. In his post-rock life, he ran a craft gallery and discovered turning. An engineer for General Electric, Lindquist began exhibiting his work at craft shows. Architect Mouthrop, a part-time turner for many years, traded in his thriving Atlanta-based practice for a successful second career in art. Wornick held executive positions with United Fruit Company and Clorox; for the past twenty-six years, he has run his own food processing and packaging company in Burlingame, California, while developing an impressive record as an artist and collector. Obviously, double lifers come from all walks of life.

With his prominence in the art world, Ron Kent could have retired early and lived off the income from his vessels. But he always put his chosen profession as a stockbroker first. "I know who I am and what I am," he said, prior to his official retirement a few years ago. "I *am* a stockbroker—a conservative, traditional stockbroker—who happens to dabble in art as well as in scuba diving, gardening, acting [three appearances on *Hawaii Five-O*], and several other interests. And I love it." Nor did he ever experience a conflict between business and art. "During my professional days, work always came first," he says.

"My clients' needs in particular demanded 100 percent attention and frequently required me to put various wood-turning projects on the backburner." Despite increasing fame as an artist, Kent remained doggedly focused on business: "I always knew when and where to draw the line between brokering and art."

Unlike the second-rate attorney who constantly brags to clients about his low golf scores, Kent left his avocation out of client dealings. "This is important to understand," he explains. "Because if you were my brokerage client and things didn't go well, and they often don't, you might start wondering if I were thinking about bowls when I should have been thinking about bonds." Kent's "bonds-over-bowls" approach paid off for him and his employers, Prudential-Bache and PaineWebber.

Over the years, Kent's reputation as a savvy financial adviser flourished; though, to the chagrin of many, he often broke rank with corporate colleagues and was unconcerned about causing offense to higher-ups. For example, he steadfastly refused to make cold calls to prospective customers. Nor would he speculate on the market. At Prudential-Bache, he wouldn't recommend limited partnerships to his clients, in defiance of the firm's heavy promotional pressures.

No doubt his stubbornness cast him as a loner. "Strange" and "pig-headed" are how two former colleagues describe him. He is "a little nutty" and "not all that easy to get along with," Kent admits. "I've always been an outsider. Although I yearned to be part of the crowd, the costs—to me at least—were too high."

Early on, Kent had decided he would do things his way. This meant working only with customers he enjoyed—not an easy feat. "I was a terrible salesman," he concedes, "but a great marketer." With missionary zeal, he launched a radio call-in talk show on the stock market, complemented by a series of popular seminars and newspaper articles on personal finance and creativity. "I put myself on display so that people who liked me would eventually come to me," he says. As with his art, Kent's "nutty" approach produced handsome results.

His income soared, as did his clients' net worth. But "everything in life is subject to review," he reflects. In 1987, he abandoned the establishment and joined a national network of independent brokers. Shortly thereafter, he cofounded the successful brokerage firm of Kent/Qualthrough, which, among other things, pioneered Hawai'i's first locally owned and managed municipal bond fund.

> **MAINTAIN A MAVERICK MIND-SET**
>
> "I'VE ALWAYS BEEN AN OUTSIDER. ALTHOUGH I YEARNED TO BE PART OF THE CROWD, THE COSTS—TO ME AT LEAST—WERE TOO HIGH."

Kent still passionately pursued his avocation, confining his wood turning to weekends and the occasional afternoon when he got home early from the office. His artistic reputation began to spread nationally and internationally. No one was more surprised than Kent: "I was amazed at what my hobby had become," he recalls. "I didn't really believe I had any natural talent." Like many artists, Kent was often filled with self-doubt. What he calls "the imposter syndrome" affected his life. "A lot of people who begin to enjoy success are filled with the nagging feeling they're fooling everyone," he explains. "I even feel that way every now and then."

Renaissance types like Ron Kent often speak with some embarrassment about their artistic accomplishments. Many grew up in a world of single identities. Applying traditional values like hard work and loyalty, they prospered on the job; it was considered frivolous to dabble in outside interests. On the one hand, they want to enjoy their off-the-job recognition, but, on the other, they don't want to lose their corporate focus.

Kent credits strong family ties for his success in art and business. His wife of fifty-one years, Myra; son, Steven, a Seattle-based journalist; and daughter, Elizabeth, an attorney general and deputy director of Hawai'i's Office of Human Services, have always supported his two lives. Frequently, Myra pitches in with sanding and oiling his vessels. Like work, family has always taken precedence over wood turning. "I could always retreat from my art," says Kent. "That meant sometimes closing up shop and going off to do something together." Now he thinks nothing of taking a break (but never more than two weeks) to strengthen his family ties.

> **SEEK COMPATIBLE GOALS**
>
> "HAVING YOUR FIRST LOVE ALSO BE YOUR SOLE SOURCE OF INCOME LIMITS CREATIVITY. I DIDN'T HAVE TO CATER TO COMMERCIALISM WITH MY ARTWORK."

Throughout his working career, Kent advised full-time artists to "go out and get a job," adding that in the long run it is easier on the nerves and more fulfilling. "Having your first love also be your sole source of income limits creativity," he explains. "I didn't have to cater to commercialism with my artwork." Kent's work as a stockbroker energized his artistic accomplishments. "I need the structure of work and family to create," he says. "Also, I tend to be rather goal-oriented, and the slow process of wood turning is a particularly good discipline."

In a Zen-like way, Kent believes that control of the body is paramount to control of the mind and the effective use of one's creative impulses. For him, wood turning is therapy. But did his art make him a better stockbroker? "I don't know—maybe, maybe not," he says. "But anything that fulfills you must make you better—it makes you a more interesting person."

To maximize his artistic endeavors, Kent keeps distractions to a minimum. Even though he has turned his hobby into a second career, he has no students and shies away from exhibition openings and professional meetings. He prefers to use his time for thinking and working.

"Block out diversions," he advises those seeking a double life. Focus is the key to balancing life's competing needs. It has allowed Kent to channel his energy and enthusiasm. "You need discipline for a sense of identity," he contends. "Otherwise you're going to try to be and do everything." Energized by his dual interests, Kent practices and preaches "carpe diem." "Don't wait for lightning to strike," he tells those interested in reinventing themselves.

At seventy-one, Kent now concentrates on art. As his work has become better known, his reputation as a wood turner has spread, garnering awards and commissions at home and abroad. But, to the stockbroker-turned-artist, "Recognition is baloney. Accomplishment is real. I don't talk about what I am, but what I *do*—what I've accomplished." Crafting a second calling has been rewarding in more ways than one for Kent. "I'm like a nymphomaniac working as a Park Avenue call girl," he says. And, for all his love

> **AVOID DISTRACTIONS**
>
> "BLOCK OUT DIVERSIONS. YOU NEED DISCIPLINE FOR A SENSE OF IDENTITY. OTHERWISE YOU'RE GOING TO TRY TO BE AND DO EVERYTHING."

of brokering, he readily confesses, "It's making the bowls that became the real source of pride." Reflecting on his double life, he concludes, "You can't have everything in life. Life is a series of compromises, and success is being able to choose your compromises."

HARD-HAT SCULPTOR

Name any significant building or structure in Hawai'i, from Honolulu International Airport to Oahu Stadium, and there's a good chance

Chuck Watson had a hand in its development. Watson became the builder of choice for this rapidly growing state in the 1960s and 1970s, erecting hospitals, schools, hotels, cement plants, and flour mills. As board chairman of Hawaiian Dredging and Construction Company, Hawai'i's largest general contractor, he left an indelible imprint on the Islands.

But the hard-nosed hard-hat was more than a builder: Watson created inventive sculptures, ranging from delicate flowers to mammoth abstracts, using scrap metal. For three decades, the CEO-turned-sculptor let his imagination run wild, carving

LISTEN TO YOUR HEART

"IT HAS ALWAYS BEEN IMPORTANT TO ME TO CREATE."

thirty-foot-high artworks in steel and welding colorful works with an oxyacetylene torch.

A double life came naturally to Watson. "Engineering and construction make a good base for art," he explains. "But in the building trades there's no latitude for imagination when you're interpreting other people's designs. There's too much regimentation of energy and thinking." No one could ever accuse this remarkable man of rigid thinking.

His innovative use of geometric principles and remnant materials from job sites led to so many commissions of his massive outdoor pieces that he began to work evenings—and twelve to fifteen hours every Saturday and Sunday. Eventually, the engineer–backyard tinkerer negotiated a four-day workweek with his employer. In 1980, at age sixty-five, Watson retired, turning his hobby into a second career and "doing something I really wanted to do."

Charles W. Watson was born in 1915 on a windswept farm in Guelph, Ontario, the son of a prospector and real estate developer. An independent streak showed itself early, and as a young man he set out to sample life's many flavors, making a living as a professional boxer, carpenter, ironworker, sailor, and roustabout in the oil fields. But Watson had a goal.

"It has always been important to me to create," he says. "When I was a kid, I wanted to be an architect." After moving to California,

Watson served as a carpenter's apprentice, took engineering courses at Santa Monica City College, and went into construction. World War II altered his life. When the conflict began, Watson worked on a strategically designated magnesium plant in Nevada. At the end of the project, he served in the U.S. Navy on the aircraft carrier *Intrepid* in the Pacific.

In 1947, his employer, California-based McNeil Construction Corporation, assigned him to Hawai'i as branch manager. Three years later, when the firm closed its office due to a prolonged shipping strike in the Islands, he hired on with Hawaiian Dredging and Construction, one of Dillingham Corporation's predecessor companies. As a general building superintendent in the 1950s, Watson thrived on the challenges of the construction world, but he also felt the need to express the creative side of his personality.

At first, he dabbled in art unsuccessfully. "Painting was frustrating," he recalls. "I could never completely execute what I imagined. It always missed a little." Despite expanding work pressures and growing family responsibilities, Watson started sculpting for recreation in the mid-1960s. He built his first studio, next to his construction shack, from remnant materials at the Ala Moana Shopping Center worksite. His first creation consisted of a series of Alexander Calder-style mobiles, using discarded wire and welding rods from various job sites.

Later, he progressed to his much larger signature projects, weighing several tons, which were an ideal combination of construction, design, and energy. The 1960s and 1970s were a blur of activity. Watson's talents shone even though they were unpolished by formal training.

The earthy engineer preferred manmade objects ("permanent, forceful things") to natural ones. "Few things in nature have pure forms," he says. "But lots of manmade things have pure, simple forms, and they have a fascination for me." With a scavenger's eye, Watson constantly scoured construction projects, junkyards, and swap meets for interesting mechanical fragments.

"Tree," for instance, was fashioned from the jaws of a rock crusher, worn down into a strikingly symmetrical shape. Similarly,

"Abacus," a twelve-foot-high, two-ton parabola inset with small discs, evolved from weathered chunks of steel. His ring sculpture, "To the Nth Power," was formed by welding pieces cut from half-inch-thick slabs of Cor-Ten steel left over from the Aloha Stadium project.

Watson went at sculpting the same way he constructed a major building. Like an architect, he tried to visualize each part of his constructionist compositions and made a model mold. Working in a medium referred to as "direct metal sculpture," he welded, cut, and brazed metal into aesthetically pleasing forms.

Eventually, the tough-as-nails builder converted part of the family's magnificent 2.2-acre homesite ("Puu o Kale," or "Chuck's Hill") in Lanikai, overlooking the azure Pacific Ocean, into an artist's studio with its own living quarters. Equipped with the latest in hoists, cutters, kilns, even a minifoundry, and with a forty-foot-high ceiling, the loft gave Watson the freedom and flexibility to unleash his creative drive. He often hunkered down in his studio for days on end to see a project through its final stages. Metal sculpting, like construction, is dirty, difficult, and demanding. His massive chest, bull neck, ironworker's forearms, and two-hundred-pound frame helped Watson sweat out his complex compositions.

Burn marks scattered over Watson's arms bear testament to more than three decades of wrestling heavy metal into shape. Gnashed fingers, including one missing pinky, are another price he has paid. Bedecked in cumbersome clothing, worn to protect him from the spray of hot metal, Watson used his trusty oxyacetylene torch and welding rods to create his pieces. After completing a model, he would build a framework by welding together steel rods an eighth of an inch in diameter. To this frame, he welded a solid skin made of fused rods or other materials. Then, using various hoists and cranes, he attached, by brazing, castoff objects and jagged strips of weighty metal. Returning to the torch and welding rods, he put on the finishing touches.

For every artist, the reward is in the creating. As the late Victor Bergeron—founder of the famous Trader Vic's restaurant chain, inventor of the mai tai, and an accomplished sculptor—once said, "When you know you have results, that's exciting—you're in the pink." Watson's intuitive geometric style has been compared with those of other leading large-scale sculptors who spurn the traditional pedestal to position their work directly on the ground. Included in this gravitas school are George Sugarman, Anthony Caro, Donald Judd, and Mark di Suvero.

Despite his artistic accomplishments, Watson was first and foremost a builder. It was his extraordinary career at Hawaiian Dredging and Construction that gave him power and reach. Watson's determination to build a better Hawai'i helped change the way contractors saw themselves. He always viewed construction in a holistic light, arguing that building and development have as much effect on people's well-being as diet and health care and that builders must find solutions to thorny social and environmental problems.

"I'm sure that if some of the so-called environmentalists had been around years, even centuries, ago, a lot of interesting things never would have been built," says Watson. "The pyramids would have been deemed impractical, the

MAINTAIN A MAVERICK MIND-SET

"THE REALISTIC, I'VE FOUND, IS TOO SIMPLE, TOO EASY."

Sphinx ugly, the Leaning Tower of Pisa and the Eiffel Tower too high. It would have also been argued that the Boulder Dam would interfere with the course of the Colorado River, though it prevents erosion in several states and the irrigated lands that were once desert." With characteristic vigor, Watson staunchly defends his profession: "I think society tends to forget that when all is said and done, the building industry is an honest business. We bid on our work against tough competition, and a lot of businesses don't have to do that."

Watson, if anything, was an experimentalist. Determined to leave an artistic legacy, he found new ways to integrate manmade remnants into powerful works of art. His compositions grew larger, more complex, and more abstract over the years. "The realistic, I've found, is too simple, too easy," he said. At the same time, Watson mastered a comprehensive mélange of materials: I-beams, welding rods, Cor-Ten steel, ceramics, imported marble, indigenous volcanic rock, and basalt. Sculpture, one of the oldest arts known to man, is intensely personal. The way Watson saw it, sculpting extended his knowledge of life.

"Sculpture became my hobby because I was the designer *and* the builder," Watson says. His business career paralleled his development as an artist. Unpretentious and seemingly oblivious to social rank, he worked outside convention. Lighting out into unexplored territory, he developed revolutionary building techniques that shook the prevailing practices of the times. He championed the use of special concrete forms, prestressed fabrication, and steel erection methods. During the construction of the Ala Moana Shopping Center, for example, he insisted that the prestressed concrete piles being used to shore up the foundation be extended above ground to serve as columns for the parking structure. This technique not only saved the company considerable money but became standard industry practice for subsequent projects at home and abroad.

To be sure, Watson's double life confounded many people in the arts who often stereotype those in corporate life as anything but creative—and, conversely, business types who often categorize artists as shirkers who've never met a payroll. "Anyone [like Chuck Watson] who has participated in both worlds has got to know that they are really different manifestations of the same fundamental thing—the desire and the need to create," stated a profile in *Fortune*. Regardless of Watson's impressive accomplishments as a builder, it may have been in the artistic world that this rigorously pragmatic man made his greatest contribution.

Though art critics were never fully sympathetic to his work, commissions poured in. His first patron, John Bellinger, chairman of First Hawaiian Bank, was instantly enthusiastic about Watson's massive works. Eventually, his rugged pieces—fashioned from old boilers, sugar cane rollers, and rusted tractors—began to appear in parks, shopping malls, hotel lobbies, and college campuses throughout

Hawai'i and the Pacific, making Watson one of the most prolific public sculptors of his time.

Though a prickly personality, Watson had a gift for collaboration. His remarkable artistic feats were nourished by the close personal and working relationships he fostered with a succession of outstanding sculptors, including Thomas van Sant and Isamu Noguchi. Whenever the opportunity arose, Watson discussed sculpting with others who shared his passion. Over time, his style came to incorporate their influences.

Some professional artists did tell Watson to stick to the construction business, and a few viewed his work as shallow and "lacking in aesthetic quality." Perhaps his reputation as a serious sculptor was somewhat tainted by his executive position. Some critics found it easy to be dismissive of an artist who was such a prominent figure in the corporate world. Highly competitive, Watson displayed nearly total dedication to his art, which may have been intensified by the fact that he began sculpting at a relatively late age. No doubt his popularity and Johnny-come-lately status also aroused the envy of some fellow artists.

> **IGNORE THE NAYSAYERS**
>
> "[CRITICISM] IS NOT ALL THAT IMPORTANT TO ME. IF MY ART HAS RHYTHM AND WARMTH OF FEELING, IT DOESN'T MATTER WHETHER THERE'S AN IDEA COMMUNICATED OR NOT."

However, Watson did not kowtow to the critics. Nor did he try to convert them. He just carried on and pursued his creative urges. "It's not all that important to me," Watson said of the critics. "If my art has rhythm and warmth of feeling, it doesn't matter whether there's an idea communicated or not." Yet his family and friends tell a different story. They report that the part-time sculptor found critical reviews tough to take, and he remained confounded by them. "The critics troubled him greatly," his wife, Poni, says. "He never felt really accepted by them, that he'd made it as a sculptor."

"I am always ready to learn, although I don't always like being taught," Winston Churchill once said. Restless and impatient, Watson shared Churchill's skepticism for formal training. Unlike many of his professional counterparts, he had no real art education—and he was proud of it. What he did have was artistic passion; with fierce tenacity and unswerving ambition, he turned his lack of training into a solid reputation for accomplishment. He took heart when, in 1970, the Hawai'i Cultural Arts Foundation chose him over many big-name artists to sculpt an outdoor composition for the University of Hawai'i. That work, the twelve-foot-high, three-ton sculpture "To the Nth Power," remains one of his most powerful pieces.

Those who know Watson well describe him as a man's man, a builder's builder, a diamond-in-the-rough. Whether he was playing poker with the boys late into the night or surfing at Waikiki Beach, he lived life with gusto. Once, on an early-morning spearfishing expedition, he was attacked and bitten by a moray eel. The wound required twenty-eight stitches. Yet the indomitable Watson was back in the water right after being sutured.

Renowned for his irreverent wit and a sense of humor that could reduce friends and foes to tears of laughter, Watson became a working-class hero. While distrustful of corporate hierarchies, he was always ready to listen to those on the ground. He refused to be cast in an iconic role as company chairman. Whenever possible, he shunned the head office and took to the field, galvanizing those around him into action. At work, there was only one thing that mattered: bringing another project in on time and under budget. Despite his fiercely independent style, Watson was much revered by his soul mates, the hard-hats. As for the higher-ups, they simply tolerated "the wild Canadian who couldn't take orders."

Watson could celebrate with the best of them. When a project was finished, his topping-off parties with the troops were legend. After the completion of one Honolulu office building, the hard-drinking, hard-driving Watson led the charge late into the night, tossing empty beer cans off the top of the skyscraper. The incident, widely publicized in the national and international press, earned the feisty builder a fine and a police citation "for loud and troublesome noises by night." Wat-

son shrugged off the incident, but ensured that the
police were invited to all
future events "to kind of
repair our relations." Vin-
tage Watson.

Comfortable in his own skin, Watson says you can never go wrong
being yourself. His multifaceted life was a whirlwind of activity. Apart
from building and sculpting, he was also a scratch golfer, an accomplished sailor, a surfer, a scuba diver, and an inveterate gambler. "A real
charger," said Cy Gillette, a lifelong compatriot, who once joined
Watson, then fifty, on a run with the bulls in Pamplona. "A wild man"
is how Poni describes her husband. "My mother warned me never to
marry him." The gallivanting Chuck Watson was the exact opposite of
this petite and gracious teetotaler. Yet somehow the marriage survived.
Four children and six decades later, Poni claims that her husband's
defining trait was doing the impossible: "Whenever anyone said something couldn't be done, that set him off. That was all the inspiration he
needed."

In the mid-1960s, the Watsons purchased a large two-story home
in suburban Kailua. He visualized removing the top floor and placing
it on a hill two house-lots away, converting one homestead into two.
"No way!" said the skeptics of an undertaking known as "Watson's
folly." Yet, true to form, the builder had the last laugh, executing the
complicated makeover with minimal difficulty right under the noses of
disbelieving neighbors.

Chuck Watson was at his best when he was fully energized. But
several years ago, he began to lose some fire. On April 20, 2002, the
rags-to-riches hero, at age eighty-six, died quietly in his sleep. In the
course of his remarkable career, Watson achieved more than he ever
could have imagined as a builder. He never became an architect; he
became an artist instead. Like other crossover artists, his defining trait
was that there was no time to waste. This restless stirrer showed us a
way to live outside conventional boundaries. More than a builder-

executive-sculptor, Watson was impossible to pigeonhole. He lived through his creativity, but he was always a practical man—leading a life of action and sweeping ambitions.

Most people find it hard to believe that a person can excel in two disparate fields. The temptation persists to measure greatness by concentrated achievement. This equation often holds true, but for every Charles Schwab or Michael Eisner whose single-mindedness pays off, there is a Ron Kent or a Chuck Watson as evidence that specialization is not always the way to success.

With the energy of creation, Kent and Watson stood apart as engineers of Hawai'i's artistic dreams. Yet their real work of art was in crafting double lives: Each scaled new heights in both business and the arts. In the process, they brought new dreams to life and put old myths to rest.

6

Tess Gerritsen
Publish and Practice

I have two professions and not one.
Medicine is my lawful wife
and literature is my mistress.

—ANTON CHEKHOV, PHYSICIAN AND PLAYWRIGHT

Tess Gerritsen left a successful medical practice to raise her children and concentrate on writing.

A scalpel is a beautiful thing." So begins another spellbinding mystery by Tess Gerritsen. The reigning champion of the medical thriller, Gerritsen offers suspense as sharp as a scalpel's edge. Megaseller Stephen King calls her stories better than those of fellow doctors-turned-writers Michael Crichton, Robin Cook, and Michael Palmer.

Once a practicing physician, Gerritsen chose to pursue a second life as a full-time writer. And why not? She has penned five popular novels, each a clever combination of suspense, terror, and scientific research. Seven-figure book advances and film rights are almost routine now. As her fame and fortune grow, she has become a literary brand, one that Tess and her husband, Jacob (also a nonpracticing physician), nurture and promote with great skill. The Tess Gerritsen Enterprise demonstrates how a multitalented woman transformed her medical training into heart-stopping fiction.

Born and raised in San Diego, Terry Tom Gerritsen hardly dreamed she would become a doctor who keeps her readers up half the night. Her father, a second-generation Chinese American, enjoyed modest success as a contracts estimator in southern California's aerospace industry. Outside of her father's brief military stint in World War II, Gerritsen remembers him as "never, never taking any risks. He was the opposite of brave." Her mother, on the other hand, was "extremely brave, very bold and courageous." As a teenager, she fled Communist China and immigrated to the United States where, with little knowledge of English and meager savings, she enrolled in college in rural Arkansas, graduated, and married. "My mother was always reading to me," Gerritsen says of her formative years, "even though she could scarcely pronounce the English words." As a result, Terry Tom became a voracious reader, devouring Nancy Drew mysteries, the J.R.R. Tolkien trilogy, and Isaac Asimov's science fiction.

Mrs. Tom also instilled in her daughter a strain of inquisitiveness. "My mother was a most unconventional woman," Gerritsen says. "She was deeply into parapsychology and many other strange things. We always had a stream of crazy people coming into the house." Those exchanges, Gerritsen believes, "made me intensely curious about everything." As a child, she was fascinated by science and dissected everything in sight, especially "creepy crawly things."

Growing up as a third-generation Chinese American in California, Gerritsen never forgot that she was in the minority. "My mother constantly told us that we had to be perfect. Chinese Americans could expect to be treated 'differently,'" she says. "Therefore, we had to strive harder and perform better than anyone else to prove that we were truly worthy. For example, I can recall vividly my mother telling my father to go back inside and change into a nicer shirt because otherwise 'people will think all Chinese are sloppy dressers.' It wasn't just that he happened to be sloppy; he represented his entire race."

In their predominantly white neighborhood, Gerritsen and her younger brother (now a physician living in Texas) were called "bananas": yellow on the outside, white on the inside. "It's still a funny phenomenon," she explains. "As a child, whenever I looked into the mirror, I would be surprised that this Chinese girl was staring back at me." Even today, Gerritsen imagines white people as she visualizes her stories.

A gifted student, Gerritsen attended Stanford, graduating Phi Beta Kappa with a degree in physical anthropology, followed by medical school at the University of California, San Francisco, where she met her future husband. In 1979, the newlyweds moved to Hawai'i to begin their residencies in internal medicine.

Although she had done quite a bit of writing in college, Gerritsen put pen and paper aside during the grueling years of medical school and the hundred-plus-hour workweeks of internship. But, while on maternity leave with her first son, the young doctor renewed her longstanding desire to write fiction. "Life is made of moments strung together by forgotten pieces of time," she says. "Sometimes, moments remind us of other moments."

One such moment came in October 1983. On a whim, Gerritsen submitted a short story to *Honolulu* magazine's annual fiction competition. "It was a tough piece to write," she remembers. "I rewrote the piece many times." Her hard work paid off. Among 266 entrants, she won the $500 first prize. "It was the first time I'd ever published anything," she says. "And the award gave me my first validation of my skills as a writer." It also signaled, at age thirty, the beginning of her double life.

For the next several years, Gerritsen balanced writing and doctoring. "I wrote at night," she recalls of those early days, "usually from about 8 P.M. until 1 A.M., after the baby had gone to bed. There wasn't much time for [husband] Jacob, and it was hard on the marriage." Focusing on romance novels, Gerritsen took the pen name Tess to appeal to her readers. In 1987, her first novel, *Call After Midnight*, a romantic thriller, was published. It was followed by eight similar titles, as well as a 1993 screenplay, *Adrift*, which aired as a CBS Movie of the Week starring Kate Jackson.

On a summer vacation in northern New England, the Gerritsens fell in love with the natural beauty and solitude of Maine's midcoast. In 1990, after eleven years in Hawai'i, the couple relocated to small-town Camden, set between expansive forests of fir and bold headlands that overlook the Atlantic. Jacob plunged into private practice, but Tess chose not to apply for a Maine medical license. With motherhood came a strong belief that she needed to be home to raise her two sons, Adam and Joshua. Combining the responsibilities of doctoring, writing, and taking care of family had become exhausting. "I couldn't handle it all," she concedes. "My real problem was child care. Whenever one of the kids got sick, either Jacob or I had to

DELIVER DAILY

"I WROTE AT NIGHT, USUALLY FROM ABOUT 8 P.M. UNTIL 1 A.M., AFTER THE BABY HAD GONE TO BED."

stay home—and our patients would get mad." So, in her mid-thirties, she retired from medicine to become, in her words, "a housewife writer."

Looking back on her decision, Gerritsen believes that a "mommy track" does exist for some women. "It happens to lots of professional women," she says. "Everything temporarily goes on hold." In explaining women's difficult choices, Michele Kremen Bolton, researcher and author of *The Third Shift: Managing Hard Choices in Our Careers, Homes and Lives As Women*, suggests that working women reassess their priorities. "They need to understand their true calling in life," she writes. "For many, the material circumstances of their lives, conflicting priorities or the desire for active involvement in family life may mean that pursuing one's calling must, at times, be woven through the background, rather than the foreground, of life. That's OK, but it needs to be her choice."

But people like Gerritsen enjoy a special advantage. Having another identity, particularly in a portable craft such as writing, enables them to choose to keep their talents in the foreground, not the background. In Gerritsen's case, she has no regrets about trading in the scalpel for the pen. "Doctors just don't make that much money," she acknowledges. "And during those early years we struggled with the mortgage, car payments, retirement savings, and the thought of steep college tuitions."

LISTEN TO YOUR HEART

"PURSUING ONE'S CALLING MUST, AT TIMES, BE WOVEN THROUGH THE BACKGROUND, RATHER THAN THE FOREGROUND, OF LIFE. THAT'S OK, BUT IT NEEDS TO BE [ONE'S] CHOICE."

Gerritsen also doesn't miss her career as an internist, particularly when she recalls the mound of insurance-related paperwork that was choking her husband's practice. "Medicine's changed so much," she says. "I think I'm probably just as fulfilled writing." She also remembers the sneers of several of her professional colleagues who couldn't understand why a highly educated, successful doctor would leave medicine to crank out romance novels. Their reaction today? "ENVY!" beams the celebrity author.

Not wanting to waste her medical background and lifelong interest in science, Gerritsen eventually abandoned romance writing for bio-thrillers. Though the romance fiction market is considerably larger than that of the medical-mystery thriller, the latter category pays better. Hospitals are a particularly good setting for high drama and conflict. And medical thrillers have universal appeal; we are all patients at one time or another. "Think about it," Gerritsen explains. "People are facing the worst crises of their lives. They're either dying or giving birth. Hence, writers in this genre are literally dealing with life and death."

Gerritsen also knew there were only two doctors, Robin Cook and Michael Palmer, writing medical mysteries at the time. So she pitched the idea of a medical thriller to her agent. Initially, the response was negative. "To have any credibility as a medical suspense author," her agent said, "you have to be a doctor." "But I *am* a doctor," Gerritsen responded.

A chance dinner conversation introduced Gerritsen to the plot for her debut medical-mystery thriller. She was seated next to an ex-cop who ran a security service protecting American business executives in Russia. Local authorities told him of kidnapping rings that shipped Russian orphans overseas to serve as organ donors. The shocking story prompted Gerritsen to call her brother-in-law, a music reporter for *Newsweek*, to investigate the charges. However, he was unable to turn up any proof. Weeks later, Gerritsen still could not forget those missing Russian children, who were to serve as the inspiration for *Harvest*.

Another key moment in the doctor-turned-writer's career came in a life-changing phone call about the sale of the rights to her first bio-thriller. "Did you say it went for $50,000?" she asked. "Five *hundred* thousand dollars!" her literary agent, Meg Ruley, responded. Finally, success had arrived. *Harvest* hit the *New York Times* best-seller list in 1996 and was hailed by acclaimed mystery author-ad exec James Patterson as "the best thriller I've read since *Coma*." Paramount

Pictures bought the film rights for $500,000, and the book was translated into more than twenty languages. Since then, Gerritsen has published four more medical thrillers: *Life Support* (1997), *Bloodstream* (1998), *Gravity* (1999), and *The Surgeon* (2001)—each generating millions of dollars in royalties and subsidiary and movie rights.

Agent Ruley credits Gerritsen's success to her natural ability to tell a story: "Tess has an incredibly fertile imagination, which, with the added authenticity of her medical training, allows her to plot a story like very few authors. She's especially skilled at pacing—slowly building higher and higher levels of tension throughout her books." As for storytelling, Gerritsen prefers interesting situations to ironclad plotting. She subscribes to the dictum that writers should be able to state the premise of any book in a single sentence beginning with "What if. . . ."

This one-sentence premise works for every Gerritsen novel: What if a conspiracy of seemingly well-intentioned doctors collaborated with the Russians to create a black-market trade in donor organs (*Harvest*)? What if the illegal use of tissue exchange created a mysterious outbreak of an incurable disease in a Boston retirement home (*Life Support*)? What if some unknown force caused a small town's youths to display abnormal aggression and, for no apparent reason, go into terrifying rages (*Bloodstream*)? What if a deadly microbe invaded the International Space Station, making it impossible for NASA astronauts to return to Earth (*Gravity*)? What if a deranged man of medicine went on a killing spree (*The Surgeon*)? Gerritsen's scenarios are outrageous, even ghoulish, but plausible.

Each thriller starts with a bang: Her knotty plots and skillfully laid surprises grab readers from page one. Writing romance fiction, she claims, taught her to zero in immediately on a story. "Romance novels are put down unfairly all the time. But in romance writing, you can't afford to waste time," she contends. Developing strong emotional relationships between the hero and heroine, another key component of romance novels, also enabled her to get the human dimensions right. "I first hear their voices," she says of her characters. "But as I begin to write, they change, they evolve, as the book goes on. They have to, to make the story satisfying."

Indeed, Gerritsen's vividly rendered characters underscore fast-moving yarns, with the central players blending almost imperceptibly into her own personality. In fact, her characters seem so close to her that she speaks of them as though she had nothing to do with inventing their deadly dilemmas. "There's always something of me in my stories," she admits. All her protagonists are female doctors.

In *Harvest*, surgical residents Abby DiMatteo and Vivian Chao hope that a donated heart will save the life of a seventeen-year-old boy, only to discover that a wealthy patient who has jumped to the top of the organ recipient list will get the heart instead. The two doctors plunge into an investigation that reveals an intricate and murderous chain of deceptions—leading to a Soviet ship anchored in Boston harbor. In *Life Support*, Dr. Toby Harper, an emergency physician, investigates a mysterious outbreak of a disease in rich men and discovers that her knowledge of these events makes her expendable. *Bloodstream's* Dr. Claire Elliot has moved to Tranquility, Maine, to shelter her adolescent son from big city dangers. But she soon finds herself searching for a medical explanation for a terrifying rash of teen violence. In *Gravity*, Emma Watson, a young NASA doctor, is confronted in space with a lethal microbe that threatens Earth's population. And Dr. Catherine Cordell exposes the shocking link between those who kill and those who cure in *The Surgeon*.

> **TAKE ONE STEP AT A TIME**
>
> "I FIRST HEAR THEIR VOICES. BUT AS I BEGIN TO WRITE, THEY CHANGE, THEY EVOLVE, AS THE BOOK GOES ON. THEY HAVE TO, TO MAKE THE STORY SATISFYING."

As autobiographical as her heroines appear, Gerritsen breaks rank with these courageous crime fighters. "They're all very brave," she says. "And like all good heroes, they're always dead certain about what's right and wrong. That's not me." For a writer who instills spine-chilling fear in her readers, Gerritsen professes to being scared witless about a number of things: "pain, small planes, and being buried alive."

She also refuses to write—or read—about dangers confronting young children: "As parents, we all have a special weakness, a vulnerability, when it comes to our kids. If they're endangered, our world falls apart. And I don't want to be part of that." The closest she got to violating this principle was in *Bloodstream*, her mystery of bizarre adolescent behavior.

"When you have teenagers, you start to think about issues such as youth violence in a different sort of way," she explains. "I had two teenage boys at that time and watched them grow from sweet little creatures to sorts of aliens. They didn't talk much; they just grunted. And they became muscular. Eventually, you begin to understand why parents become fearful of their children. That's the ultimate fear. To be afraid of someone you love right under your own roof." *Bloodstream* tries to address the fears of parenthood, which, according to Gerritsen, is life's most important and challenging role.

Besides skillful plotting, credible characters, and fresh dialogue, her not-so-cozy mysteries reflect the harsh, day-to-day realities of medical life. Her work embodies the maxim "Write about what you know." Gerritsen sees writing as an opportunity to explore medical issues within the context of easy-to-read thrillers. Elegant prose woven into tightly coiled plots combine with years of medical training and scientific research. Her thrillers leave readers with chills because they are realistic. "Medicine really contributes a lot to my writing. I try to make the details vivid—for instance, the autopsies," she points out. "I've stood in on a number of them for medical training, but they were far more horrifying than you can imagine because I usually knew the patients when they were alive. It's easier when they're total strangers in a morgue."

Every Gerritsen story carries the authority of firsthand experience. For example, *Life Support* runs the gamut of medical situations— surgeries, autopsies, technical discussions among physicians. In medical school, Gerritsen learned about Creutzfeldt-Jakob disease (CJD), an incurable illness affecting the elderly that produces progressive memory loss, wild mood swings, and frightening hallucinations. She incorporated this rare and fatal condition into the book's central theme with bone-chilling results.

It is not surprising, given her scientific interests, that Gerritsen started compiling an inventory of rare or seemingly unexplainable phenomena into a newsletter called *Creepy Biological Facts*, which she distributes to bookstores and makes available on her Web site (www.tessgerritsen.com). "Science, medicine, space, engineering—they all fascinate me," she says. "I'm especially interested in the technical details." To gather material for *Gravity*, Gerritsen spent two weeks with dozens of NASA scientists, engineers, flight surgeons, and flight directors. "I had a longtime interest in space," she recalls. "I even wanted to be an astronaut—that was one of my burning dreams while growing up. Somewhere along the way I got diverted by marriage and a medical career. But I never lost my fascination with the space program."

Gerritsen says NASA was extremely cooperative, answering just about every question she asked. Besides learning the lingo of space, she wanted to gain insights into the kind of person who would volunteer to become an astronaut and face a one-in-fifty chance of death. She also was particularly interested in the way cells and a rare class of microbes called archaeons, the oldest bacteria ever found, behave in space. Could they multiply and assume lethal characteristics in microgravity? In addition, Gerritsen talked to a number of flight surgeons about the rigors of practicing medicine in orbit, and she probed NASA officials on the feasibility of bringing a contaminated spacecraft back to Earth. Among other things, she discovered that the agency maintains a team of range safety officers that is ready to destroy any shuttle that veers too close to populated areas.

Incorporating these themes into *Gravity*, Gerritsen provided the gritty realism that both terrified and delighted readers. In its review of the thriller, *Publishers Weekly* said, "Gerritsen meshes medical suspense—her specialty—and the world of space travel in another nail-biting tale of genetic misadventure. The novel's detailed descriptions of life in space consistently ring true." Stephen King also let it be known that *Gravity* was the author's best book yet. Not only did the tale woo Gerritsen's critics and colleagues, but the book enjoyed best-seller status, and film rights were snapped up for $1 million up front and another $500,000 upon production. Executives at 20TH Century-Fox see the movie as *Titanic in Space* and have commissioned Michael Goldberg, who wrote the script for the movie *Contact*, to develop the screenplay. "I view the movie deal as validation," Gerritsen says. "So often book critics will bash a novel, branding it 'written for Hollywood.' But if Hollywood likes it, I believe it means it's a good story—visual, with a great plot and strong characters. I take it as praise, not criticism."

On several occasions, the studios have approached Gerritsen to serialize her characters á la Miss Marple. For the time being, she prefers introducing fresh faces, often borrowing names for her characters from the obituaries. "When you sell film and television rights to books, you sell the rights to the characters as well," she told the *Bangor News Daily*. "So it's really a business decision to create new characters for each new book." From reading fan mail, the author observes that *Gravity* seems to be especially appealing to men. Although the protagonist is another female doctor, the setting in space and NASA insights are attracting many male readers. Gerritsen's previous novels were two to three times more popular with women, who are the greatest buyers of books. "She's only going to get bigger and bigger," her agent, Meg Ruley, predicts.

> **IGNORE THE NAYSAYERS**
>
> "SO OFTEN BOOK CRITICS WILL BASH A NOVEL, BRANDING IT 'WRITTEN FOR HOLLYWOOD.' BUT IF HOLLYWOOD LIKES IT, I BELIEVE IT MEANS IT'S A GOOD STORY. . . . I TAKE IT AS PRAISE, NOT CRITICISM."

The Gerritsens' lair sits one mile inland from breathtaking Penobscot Bay in this picture-perfect town of five thousand. The large, attractive federal-style home, set on a knoll amid leafy trees, houses the Tess Gerritsen Enterprise. Ironically for the mystery writer, many of her neighbors are former CIA agents who reportedly read about

Camden's merits in a retirement magazine. When I visited for an interview, the tall, slender author greeted me at the front door and led me past the kitchen, which was undergoing a facelift. For years, she scribbled her whodunits on the nearby dining room table. Last year, in an act of uncharacteristic self-indulgence, she converted part of their home into a working office lined with stacks of books, scientific journals, and notes for current and future writing projects. There she still writes the old-fashioned way: with pen and paper. She then goes to the computer for later drafts, constantly revising.

In her sunny studio, Gerritsen was polishing her most recent book, *The Surgeon*, about a serial killer using the latest medical technology to dispose of his patients. "I've often felt that the reason serial killers are so frightening is that, for the most part, they're so normal," she said. (*The Surgeon* hit the bookstores in August 2001 and cracked the *New York Times* best-seller list a month later.)

For many doctors, writing has opened up a parallel universe. In 1888, physician-playwright Anton Chekhov told his publisher, "I have two professions and not one. Medicine is my lawful wife and literature is my mistress." However, no one raised the bar higher for literary-minded medics than Sir Arthur Conan Doyle.

Arthur Conan Doyle: Fiction and Prescriptions

"I have had a life, which for variety and romance could hardly be exceeded," said the famous doctor-turned-writer. Blending his talents in medicine and letters, the Scottish physician introduced the double helix of science and crime fiction in his gripping Sherlock Holmes stories. Conan Doyle revolutionized the detective story and made suspense one of the most popular genres in history. While the world's most celebrated crime fighter and his faithful friend, Dr. Watson, dominated Doyle's career, he sampled, in his own words, "every kind of human experience." He wrote everything from mysteries to historical novels, science fiction to ballads. Over his lifetime, he produced more than thirty books and 150 short stories—prodigious output for a man who once confessed, "I never dreamed I could myself

produce decent prose." Besides writing, he was actively involved in numerous activities from criminology to parapsychology.

Passionately public-spirited, Dr. Doyle wrote and spoke extensively on various social and political issues of his time. He championed divorce reform, the repeal of the witchcraft laws, and the creation of the Central Court of Criminal Appeals. He invented life preservers and inflatable rafts for the navy and steel helmets for the army, and he recommended the use of armored vehicles. He developed secret codes for the Home Office and warned of the impending threat that German submarines posed to the West. He roundly criticized his nation's actions in Ireland and South Africa and twice stood unsuccessfully for Parliament. Sir Arthur portrayed the best of the Victorian spirit. He "was the perfect pattern of a gentlemen," said his son, writer Adrian Conan Doyle.

Arthur Conan Doyle frequently came to the aid of popular causes, typified by his impassioned and successful twenty-year defense of two accused criminals. He contributed to many charities and led the funding drive for Britain's Olympic athletes. An accomplished photographer and ardent sportsman, he loved boxing, golf, billiards, bicycling, and cricket. He is credited with promoting Switzerland's ski industry. A pioneering motorist, he was one of the first Brits to receive a speeding ticket. In between these efforts, the multitalented physician found time to write his numerous works.

"A diversified genius," some called him, leading Conan Doyle to concede, "My life has been dotted with adventures of all kinds." Yet it was the brilliant investigator—in the deerstalker cap and the Inverness cape, smoking a Meerschaum pipe—and his good-hearted aide—the subjects of sixty tales—who propelled an obscure physician to literary greatness. The tall, thin, angular detective and his rotund companion remain two of the world's most vivid characters. To this day, Sir Arthur's immortal pair continues to enjoy an uncanny life beyond the printed page. It is this great partnership in crime fiction that, above all, made Doyle's thrillers so largely popular in their day, and makes Holmesian loyalists of fans from London to Los Angeles today. Had it not been for the interplay of Conan

Doyle's remarkable double life, it is quite possible that neither he nor the mystery genre would have achieved their prominent place in English literature.

Doctor-poet William Carlos Williams was equally passionate about his double life. In fact, he was once sued by a patient he wrote about. More recently, Michael Crichton and Robin Cook skillfully intertwined Space Age technology and medicine into novels that make your heart skip a beat. In so doing, they now enjoy lifestyles like Jay Gatsby's. Crichton, for example, has earned between $33 million and $100 million over the past few years, according to *Forbes*.

In nonfiction, too, some doctors are parlaying physicianhood into great success. Consider Deepak Chopra. The so-called "Dr. Feelgood" gave up Western medicine, he says, because it turned him into a technician of the body; he wanted to be a healer of the soul. Translating Eastern mysticism into Western language, the Indian transplant struck a sympathetic chord with American readers. His books *Ageless Body, Timeless Mind,* and *The Seven Spiritual Secrets of Success* have sold well over 1.5 million copies each, making the self-help guru a multi-millionaire.

Dr. Spencer Johnson is another fixture on the best-seller charts. With luxurious homes in Hawai'i and New Hampshire, the Big Kahuna of management-made-easy teamed up with Ken Blanchard to author *The One-Minute Manager*, which boasts more than eleven million copies in print. The former internist's latest product, *Who Moved My Cheese?*, is a ninety-four-page parable about two mice and two small people living in a maze and how they variously respond one day when the cheese disappears. At the time of this writing, *Cheese* has sold more than five million copies and sits at the top of every business best-seller list.

These authors are among the fortunate few who have found full-time writing more successful and more profitable than doctoring. However, most physicians have chosen not to give up their day jobs. William Carlos Williams never quit his practice as a New Jersey physician, for instance. Such people are energized by juggling both lives, and many use the pen to publicize causes that are especially important to them. Take John Stone, a cardiologist and dean of admissions at Emery Medical School in Atlanta. His central mission in life is to create greater compassion in a profession increasingly dominated by bottom-line concerns. "What medicine is all about is being human," he says. Stone's popular lectures, four books of poetry, and an anthology—*On Doctoring*, which, with the support of the Robert Wood Johnson Foundation, is sent to every freshman medical student in the country—stress the importance of listening to patients and understanding their lives and their concerns at home.

Equally vocal is India-born Abraham Verghese, a professor at the Texas Tech School of Medicine in El Paso and author of the bestselling *My Own Country*, which chronicled life in a Tennessee AIDS clinic early in the epidemic, and *The Tennis Partner*, a memoir of drug abuse among physicians. Though not afflicted himself with either, the infectious-disease specialist wanted to share his patients' pain with a wider audience. Of his double life, Dr. Verghese says, "To me, they're a seamless enterprise. . . . [Writing and medicine] are very parallel disciplines. When you take a patient's clinical history, what is that but a story?"

According to some surveys, as many as 40 percent of physicians would do something else if they could. And, given the universal appeal of all things medical, it's understandable that there has been an outbreak of creative writing among medics. "Every doctor I know is writing a book," says doctor-author Ethan Canin. "They're calling me and want to show me their manuscripts."

The link between medicine and letters is even becoming institutionalized. Many medical students at Columbia University's College of Physicians and Surgeons have taken a full-credit literature course from Michael Ondaatje, author of *The English Patient*—complemented by guest lecturers Joan Didion and Paul Auster—to enhance their sensitivity to patient needs. The Association of American Medical Colleges reports that, in 1999, 74 percent of medical schools offered literature classes—and, of those, 39 percent required them.

Gerritsen often meets with doctors who want to write. Some seek to amuse, shock, and surprise; others, to inform and provoke. Last summer, Gerritsen and Michael Palmer led a conference on Cape Cod for seventy-seven physicians, young and old, with literary aspirations. "Although most doctors are very bright, they really don't know how to write, especially fiction," Gerritsen says. "They are far too objective. It's part of their training." The author also chides fellow physicians who have never written a thing but contact her for the name of a literary agent. "It makes no sense," she says. "It would be like coming up to a doctor and saying 'I want to be a brain surgeon.'"

Robin Cook, who has earned millions from the sale of his thrillers, also urges any physician looking to pursue the Big Book to do his or her homework. After disappointing sales of his first novel, *Year of the Intern*, written while serving on a navy submarine, the young ophthalmologist regrouped. "Anytime you want to do something serious, you have to go back to the literature," he told *Smart Money*. Cook scrutinized the best-seller lists and dissected the underlying themes for mysteries' success. The winners, he discovered, were "applying a pseudoscientific method to something that people don't think is amenable to it." The result: *Coma*, published in 1977, sold ten million copies.

Cook's predecessor, Michael Crichton, warns medical colleagues to be prepared for the difficulty of writing, which he describes as "excruciating." The wildly successful ex-doctor follows his own bootcamp ritual. "For seven days a week, he enters a sparsely furnished room that minimizes distractions," the *New York Times* reported. "For the duration of each book he eats the same thing for lunch each day and permits few diversions except exercise and family. As his writing progresses, he wakes up earlier and earlier each day, until he is at the computer beginning at 2 A.M."

Given the stresses and strains of authorship, Samuel Johnson once said, "Anyone who writes for anything other than money is a blockhead." Gerritsen, however, claims she doesn't write for money. "I never have," she insists. "I write because I have stories to tell and like to tell them. I also write to hear people tell me I've written the most accurate book ever on a particular subject. What's especially appealing are the doctors and nurses at various book signings who are amazed at how authentic my books are." Gerritsen feasts on positive feedback. In her case, the need may be culturally driven: "My Asian heritage, I think, demands from people: 'Will you, please, please accept me!'"

That said, the unpretentious author admits her recent riches have provided the clan with considerable financial security. Besides allowing Tess to focus even more on writing, economic success has prompted Jacob to give up his medical practice. At first, retirement was a big adjustment for Gerritsen's husband, but he has now happily accepted his new role as literary helpmate and computer assistant to the family's primary breadwinner. He is also delighted that he can now pursue a passion of his own: portrait photography. Indeed, the license plates on Jacob's new Lexus read "THXTESS."

> **RECHARGE YOUR CREATIVITY**
>
> "I WRITE BECAUSE I HAVE STORIES TO TELL AND LIKE TO TELL THEM. I ALSO WRITE TO HEAR PEOPLE TELL ME I'VE WRITTEN THE MOST ACCURATE BOOK EVER ON A PARTICULAR SUBJECT."

If anything, the down-to-earth couple is concerned that their new-found wealth may negatively affect their two boys, now twenty and seventeen. "We keep waiting for them to blossom," says Tess, revealing her strong maternal instincts. "It would be our fondest hope that our financial situation won't spoil them, that our children keep their minds open to new ideas, and that the unfamiliar will not inspire fear—but wonder."

Unspoiled by money or success, Gerritsen has never felt the sting of prejudice in Camden. Though she is often mistaken for one of the three other Asian American women in town, it doesn't bother her. "There's a special innocence about Camden," she says. "It's a wonderful place to live. Besides, women here don't have to wear makeup."

Gerritsen's priorities remain focused on writing. The sign "PER-SISTENCE" over her desk tells it all. She is prepared to drop all obligations until she finishes her next book. "She's very, very focused," says agent Ruley. "Nothing gets in her way." Maine's long, cold winters surely help. "I concentrate very well, especially when there's nothing to do outdoors," says the author. But, with the coming of spring, Gerritsen lets the Muse recharge, taking a break from her punishing thriller-a-year pace. For diversion, she turns to her two other loves: gardening and music.

Gerritsen proudly leads visitors through her backyard garden. She boasts that her prized roses are the best in town, and in agricultural zone 5—where the temperature can plummet to −20°F—that takes great skill. "The secret," she confides, "is picking the right species." From peonies to cold-weather kiwi fruit, evidence of the writer's green thumb abounds.

When she's not puttering around the garden, Gerritsen finds solace in music. "If I ever have a third life, it will be as a musician," she says. Thanks to her mother's prodding, Gerritsen became an accomplished pianist and violinist, and she continues to play both instruments. She has fiddled with various local groups, performing at nursing homes and special events. At the invitation of Tabitha King, Gerritsen was a guest musician in Stephen King's rag-tag rock band, the Rock Bottom Remainders, perhaps better known in literary than musical circles. The authors-only group includes Dave Barry, Amy Tam, Mitch Albom, Ridley Pearson, and Kathi Kamen Goldmark. Clearly, the variety that Gerritsen aspires to achieve in her fictional life is repeated in real life.

Looking back, the celebrity author, now in her late forties, attributes much of her success to her "universal interests." Understandably, she advocates multiple lives. "People today live so long they can have four or five different experiences," she says. "But," in a note of caution,

> **FOCUS, FOCUS, FOCUS**
> "SHE'S VERY, VERY FOCUSED," SAYS GERRITSEN'S AGENT, MEG RULEY. "NOTHING GETS IN HER WAY."

she warns, "when you balance two lives, you should be realistic. It may just take you twice as long to accomplish your objectives." Today, Gerritsen refers to herself as a writer and remains enamored of her second life. She has no problem dealing with the solitude that many authors find debilitating. "I'm comfortable in my own skin," she says. If anything, it is the uncertainty, the fear of failure, that bothers her most. She knows that publishing is, at best, a fickle business. "There are a lot of once-famous authors out there—basically doing nothing or not publishing," she says.

Tess Gerritsen has become something of an icon for the Renaissance woman. Reflecting on the plots and twists in her own life, she hopes her novels will continue to raise the reading temperature. Though medicine will contribute to her writing, a return to doctoring is not in the cards. "I don't think I'll ever go back to medicine," she says. For now, the former healer is content to wear just one hat: a writer's beret.

PLAN AND PERSEVERE

"WHEN YOU BALANCE TWO LIVES, YOU SHOULD BE REALISTIC. IT MAY JUST TAKE YOU TWICE AS LONG TO ACCOMPLISH YOUR OBJECTIVES."

7

Larry Small

From Finance to Feathers

*Few people do business well
who do nothing else.*

—EARL OF CHESTERFIELD, STATESMAN

*Renaissance man Small (shown with wife, Sandra)
balances flamenco with managing the Smithsonian Institution.*

*L*awrence M. Small, the eleventh secretary of the Smithsonian Institution, is a man of many interests. He is an avid collector of indigenous art, a flamenco guitarist, and a former executive of high-powered financial institutions. He speaks four languages, windsurfs, scuba dives, and bicycles marathon distances. Small is one of a growing number of private-sector executives finding fulfillment in the nonprofit world. As head of the world's largest museum complex, he can indulge his personal passions: artistic, anthropological, linguistic, and musical. "It's not work," he says of his latest assignment. "It's total enjoyment."

His second-floor suite in the Smithsonian's famous "Castle," the first building on the National Mall after the Capitol, is not only a microcosm of the megamuseum but also a reflection of its occupant's eclectic personal tastes. It once served as the bedroom of the first secretary, Joseph Henry, a scientist known for his discoveries in the field of electromagnetism. "He died in that space over there," Small tells visitors, pointing next to a panoply of borrowed objects: portraits of composer George Gershwin and writer F. Scott Fitzgerald, sculptures by Henry Moore and Frederick Hart, Kermit the Frog, and—his personal favorite—one of Chet Atkins's guitars.

"Wherever you look, there is a depth and a breadth of information about human life and human accomplishment," says Small, commenting on the Smithsonian. "It's like watching the greatest show on earth." James Smithson, a wealthy English scientist who never visited America, died 172 years ago, leaving his fortune to the United States with the understanding that it would be used to promote knowledge. Well known by generations of Americans, the Smithsonian Institution now consists of sixteen museums and galleries, the National Zoo, and eleven research centers located in the nation's capital, seven states, and Panama. Each year, some forty million people visit its exhibits, which house more than 142 million specimens and works of art. In its vast collections in "the nation's attic," as the Smithsonian is fondly called, sit the 45.5-carat Hope Diamond, the original "Star-Spangled Banner," the lap desk on which Thomas Jefferson wrote the Declaration of Independence, the Wright brothers' *Flyer*, and the *Spirit of St. Louis*.

"Ninety-two percent of Americans recognize the works in the Smithsonian and what they mean," says Small. "To many, the institution is a more meaningful representation of American life than the Statue of Liberty. Every day you come across something that is terrific."

On a chilly day in January 2000, the respected banker received a large brass key, traditionally given to a new secretary, from Chief Justice William Rehnquist, the institution's chancellor. The ceremony was held in a heated tent on the mall in front of the Castle, which opened nine years after the founding of the museum. In his remarks, Rehnquist reminded the audience of the institution's early commitment "to occupy so far as may be, ground hitherto untenanted." His message was not lost on the incoming secretary. Fortunately, blazing new trails comes easily to this Renaissance man.

> **LISTEN TO YOUR HEART**
>
> "I CAN REMEMBER THE MOMENT AS CLEAR AS A BELL. . . . IT WAS AS IF A LIGHTNING BOLT CAME DOWN. BY THE TIME I HIT THE TOP STEP, I SAID, 'I HEREBY DEDICATE MY LIFE TO BECOMING THE WORLD'S GREATEST FLAMENCO GUITARIST.'"

Born in New York City but raised in suburban New Rochelle, Small acquired some of his talents from his parents. His mother ran Walton High School in the Bronx. With eight thousand students, it was the largest girls' high school in the United States. Small's father, an architect who worked on the design of several massive projects, including the Strategic Air Command base in Greenland, died when

Larry was fifteen. His stepfather, now eighty-eight, led a double life as a financial executive and an abstract painter.

When Small was a freshman at Brown University, a fortuitous incident introduced him to the guitar, which became a source of inspiration for the next forty years. "I can remember the moment as clear as a bell," he says. "It was late August 1959. I was between the third and fourth floors of South Slater Hall when I heard a recording of Carlos Montoya playing flamenco guitar. It was as if a lightning bolt came down. By the time I hit the top step, I said, 'I hereby dedicate my life to becoming the world's greatest flamenco guitarist.' It sounds stupid now, but if you're a teenager, that's what happens."

Determined to fulfill his dream, Small studied Spanish literature at Brown, while commuting to New York City on weekends for guitar lessons. Slowly, he began to progress, but his music teacher told him that to really learn he would have to go to Spain. His college mentor, Alan S. Trueblood, a professor in the Spanish-Portuguese department, helped him talk his way into Smith College's junior year abroad program in Spain. To jumpstart his studies, Small moved to Granada a few months before classes began. He practiced the language and the instrument for hours on end. His playing got better and better, but he also became more realistic about his musical ambitions.

"After six months in Spain, I sat down and made a list of the top ten flamenco guitarists in the world," he says. "After analyzing the list, I discovered that all were prodigies who'd been on the stage before the age of twelve, all were Spanish Gypsies, all were 5'6" or shorter, and all had great-looking thick, dark, shiny black hair and bronze cheekbones. Of the ten, only a couple of them could make a living, and only a couple could read and write. Here I was, a 6'3" student from an Ivy League college in the United States trying to do this—and it was just not going to work. I went to Spain, and I failed."

But Small's failure didn't spoil his love for the instrument. He still plays every day, usually in fifteen- to twenty-minute spurts. If he's lucky, he has time to strum for an hour or two—for the sheer exhilarating pleasure of it. Although he regrets "all the time" that he's not a professional musician, his fluency in Spanish and love of living abroad pushed him in a new direction: global finance. During his senior year at Brown, Citibank/Citicorp, both now parts of Citigroup, offered him an international job at $6,136 a year.

Professor Trueblood was furious. Corporate America was robbing the academy of one of its best Spanish-lit students and a potential colleague. After a few tense weeks during which the two men didn't speak to each other, professor and protégé reconciled. Trueblood wished the Phi Beta Kappa graduate well and gave him a volume of Wallace Stevens's verses, which included the famous poem "The Man with the Blue Guitar" and an inscription from Trueblood noting that the Pulitzer Prize–winning poet had led a successful double life as an insurance executive. The gift validated Small's career move, encouraging him to balance business with his love of music and languages. To this day, Small carries a copy of Trueblood's note in his briefcase.

In 1964, Small began what would be a twenty-seven-year career with Citicorp. With his bank job as his passport, he was posted initially to Chile. There he met his future wife, Sandra Roche, an American psychology student who was born in a prison camp in China during World War II. During their travels south of the border, the young couple developed a passion for collecting and restoring tribal art. After several years in South America, Small was transferred to corporate headquarters in New York, which became his base for frequent travel as he advanced in his career. Initially, he worked with John Reed, Citicorp's future chairman, in the operating group. In 1972, he began a three-year stint overseeing the company's human resources. Then he embarked on a decade-long assignment in corporate banking, which eventually expanded to include responsibility for all the financial giant's global lending.

During his many trips abroad, Small continued to pursue his interests in music and the arts. On the road, he practiced guitar and languages. Back home, he and his wife visited museums on weekends and, on vacations, traveled, looking for art from the rain forests of

South America and Africa. Slowly, they assembled an extensive collection of folk art, specializing in brilliantly colored and patterned feather work.

Though his corporate colleagues often had their noses in the financial pages, Small sensed that he would never be satisfied with just debits and credits. In fact, he claims never to have read *Barron's* or *BusinessWeek* at home. Rather, he devoted his free time exclusively to his family and his hobbies. In terms of reading habits, he preferred Brazilian magazines; *Veja*, the Portuguese-language news weekly, became his favorite. Despite these varied interests, Small quickly developed a reputation within Citicorp as a tough business executive. His direct, no-nonsense approach made him both respected and feared throughout the organization.

Full disclosure: I worked for Small at Citicorp during the early 1970s. From the day I arrived, he revealed a perfunctory management style. Those who performed were rewarded; those who didn't were punished. His special passion was accountability—holding employees to measurable standards.

"My feeling is that you have to make sure that everybody knows what he or she is supposed to do," he says. "If there is anything that I stand for, it is being clear and specific. I believe that one has to be inherently suspicious if things aren't going right. And you have to inspect, not simply expect it. That doesn't mean I'm cynical about the work of close colleagues. But I know when things aren't on plan, usually something is not working right."

Initially, Small's insistence on measurable standards—or "deliverables"—was confounding and smacked of micromanagement. But slowly, staffers discovered that once his system was in place, clarity invariably led to improved performance. And with it came greater autonomy. As Bob Bailey, a key lieutenant of Small's at Citicorp and, more recently, at the Smithsonian, puts it, "Larry will trade information for freedom. If he knows what's going on, you will get more and more freedom." Bailey calls his time at the bank "the most productive and fun period of my life." Small was disciplined, but not dispassionate. Clearly, his concept of applying tight, then loose, controls contributed to Citicorp's rapid growth in the 1970s and 1980s.

Small's focus on details and his financial acumen did not go unnoticed. In 1985, he was promoted to vice chairman and head of the powerful executive committee. Six years later, when it became apparent that he was not going to become chairman of the company, he began contemplating retirement to pursue his varied interests. However, California real estate investor Eli Broad informed Small that he had submitted his name to lead Fannie Mae, the nation's largest provider of funds for home mortgages. The chief executive officer, James A. Johnson, was a man with enormous political and strategic abilities but with little experience running an operating business. The company needed a co-leader: a president and chief operating officer with skills in finance, personnel, systems, and operations. By every standard, Small fit the slot perfectly. In nearly three decades at Citicorp, he had dealt with everything from Third World debt and oil shocks to terrorist attacks on overseas branches. "So when Jim Johnson asked me to take over the business side of Fannie Mae, it looked like it'd be fun," he recalls.

In 1991, Small joined the world's largest non-bank financial services company, best known for "showing America a new way home." He commuted from New York to Washington for almost two years, riding the shuttle more than three hundred times, because he didn't want to disrupt his son's high school education. Eventually, the New Yorkers moved and settled into a spacious house in fashionable Massachusetts Heights in northwest Washington.

A freelance translator, Sandra Small worked as a Spanish-English interpreter in the federal court system (a position she continues to hold), while her husband managed Fannie Mae's day-to-day affairs. In the process, they raised two children: a son, now a lawyer who clerks for a federal judge in New York and plays professional guitar, and a daughter who studies art in Chicago.

As chief troubleshooter for the politically connected powerhouse, Small encountered a world quite different from that of his former employer. "Fannie Mae was a much narrower organization," he says. "It didn't really have the breadth and global scope of Citicorp. But it was much, much deeper. That is, there was a requirement at Fannie Mae to really dig in to a particular topic. Hence, everybody in the organization had to be a subject-matter expert, particularly when it came to the securement and purchase of home mortgages in the United States. In that respect, Fannie Mae's people were brainier than those at Citicorp, where the premium was on the generalist, the jack-of-all-trades."

In this more focused but less urbane environment, Small brought his "you-are-what-you-measure" philosophy to bear. Holding employees strictly accountable for results, Fannie Mae's "Mr. Inside" met the organization's goal of buying $1 trillion in home loans in six years. "You couldn't slip something past Larry Small," vice president David Jeffers told *Forbes*. "If there was ever a force in nature opposite of inertia, it's him." Franklin D. Raines, who succeeded James Johnson as chairman, agrees: "He can operationalize aspirations. We aspired to be a leader in diversity, and Larry says, 'That's great. Now let's get about doing it. Let's measure, let's make sure people's compensation is tied to it.' He made the aspirations into reality."

For almost nine years, Small acted quickly and decisively, helping to transform the huge federally chartered mortgage entity into a more efficient, well-oiled financial machine. "It's fair to say Larry Small's management of the company led to its high performance," says Karen Shaw Petrou, president of ISD/Shaw, a Washington financial consulting firm. With its exemption from local taxes, low borrowing costs, and lofty profits, Fannie Mae was able to pay its executives handsomely. In 1998, Small earned $4.25 million in salary and performance bonuses. While at Fannie Mae, he continued to practice his guitar-plucking skills, often performing in the off-hours at local hospitals and institutions.

Karen M. Jones, senior director of community relations at Washington Home and Hospice, remembers one afternoon when Small played flamenco for Alzheimer's patients for more than an hour. "They were mesmerized," she says. "When he finished, one of the older women remarked, 'I thought I'd never hear Segovia in person.' Everyone—including Mr. Small—allowed her to enjoy her momentary brush with celebrity."

In their free time, the traveling virtuoso and his wife scoured the Washington area for a place to display their ever-expanding collection of tribal art. Because there was a lack of loft space with high ceilings, the couple settled on converting a two-bedroom apartment near their home. They hired the architectural team of Theodore Adamstein and Olvia Demetriou to transform the apartment's 2,500 square feet into a private gallery. The setting, which houses a wondrous assortment of feather headdresses, masks, ceremonial costumes, and other artifacts, won an American Institute of Architects award for design and was featured in *Architectural Digest*.

In 1998 Small, at age fifty-seven, was planning to retire in three years "and devote my life to music, art, and languages." But, he says, "I flunked retirement before I even signed up." Serendipity struck again when the family's feather collection took Small in a new and exciting direction. That fall, the couple sent out a holiday card to a thousand business and personal friends. The card featured an Amazonian feather piece from their collection and carried the inscription "May 1999 find you with a feather in your cap. Happy holidays from the Smalls."

In February 1999, Washington attorney and Smithsonian regent Wesley S. Williams Jr. was at home contemplating the search for a replacement for Secretary I. Michael Heyman, who had announced his retirement earlier that year. Glancing at the mantle over the fireplace, Williams spotted the Smalls' holiday card. Bells went off. Williams turned to his wife, Karen, an attorney and board member at Fannie Mae, and asked, "What about Larry? He's not only a good money man; he likes the arts and sciences, collects all sorts of ethnographic material, speaks several languages [Spanish, Portuguese, and French], knows his way around Washington, and has served on some impressive boards [Brown University, Morehouse College, Citicorp,

Paramount Communications, Marriott International, Chubb Corporation, the U.S. Holocaust Memorial Museum, the National Building Museum, the Spanish Repertory Theatre, and the Joffrey Ballet]."

Mrs. Williams agreed wholeheartedly. Over lunch a few days later, Wesley Williams asked Small what he thought. "You can't really be serious!" Small answered. "Look at the kind of people you've had in the past. Ten people have had the job over the last 153 years, and all ten of them have come from the academic community, and nine have been scientists."

Flattered though Small was, the self-described "Wall Street Philistine" felt that leading the venerable institution might be beyond his reach. Small also was reluctant to put himself in play, knowing that any leaks could jeopardize his effectiveness at Fannie Mae. Yet, out of courtesy to Williams, he agreed to be part of a panel of management specialists to advise the search committee on what to look for in Heyman's successor. Several months passed as the committee sifted through more than 250 résumés. To Small's astonishment, "the committee called back and said they were interested in my candidacy," although some wondered whether the financier would take a 90 percent pay cut—from more than $4 million at Fannie Mae, to $330,000—to head the Smithsonian.

> ### REINVENT YOURSELF
> "I AM PERFECTLY FINE WITH REDUCING MY SALARY. THIS IS MUCH MORE EXCITING THAN A WELL-EXECUTED DEBIT."

Small accepted the offer, saying, "I am perfectly fine with reducing my salary. This is much more exciting than a well-executed debit." For thirty-five years, the busy executive had made it a point to get all his work done during the week so he and his wife could spend weekends visiting museums. "Now," he beamed, "I will get to do it during the week. To be in a position where a good deal of the areas of focus of this institution constitute my hobbies—anthropology, art, language— couldn't be more exciting."

As for his limited academic and scientific credentials, he concedes, "It's like landing the job of chief justice without ever going to law school." Small's dream job also fulfilled the wishes of the organization's seventeen-person governing body, which wanted someone with management moxie rather than academic pedigree. What the first banker and only second nonscientist to be named secretary of the Smithsonian brought to the table was "the ability to manage a large, complex institution," says regent Williams, who chaired the search committee with former senator Howard Baker. "Larry is described by many who have worked with him as being one of the finest managers in America."

Barber Conable Jr., head of the regents' executive committee and a former president of the World Bank, also cheered the new hire, pointing out that Small was chosen unanimously, "which has not always been so in the past. It's hard to imagine a better person to lead the Smithsonian into the next millennium. His vision of the future, his vision of the changes going on in American society and how they impact our great icon of a cultural institution, are inspiring."

Despite the kudos, some Smithsonian insiders—and outsiders—opposed Small's selection. Some questioned his ability to court corporate and individual donors, as well as Congress, which supplies 70 percent of the museum's operating funds. And money was a serious problem. Many of the institution's twenty-seven museums and research units were in sad shape, with leaky roofs, peeling paint, and structural deficiencies that routine maintenance could not keep up with. Funds were also needed to revamp aging exhibits in existing displays, complete the finishing touches on two new museums, and expand the Smithsonian's reach via state-of-the-art technology and museum loans. Critics were reminded that Small's predecessor, Heyman, had fallen short of his fund-raising goals, forcing the institution to tap into its endowment. Could the new chief do any better?

Others doubted Small's ability to survive Washington's notorious infighting. The Smithsonian, as landlord of some of the most visibly placed buildings in the country, finds itself in the public eye at all levels of decision making. And then there were the academics who wondered whether an outsider could understand the culture of this erudite organization. They fretted that the hard-nosed business executive might focus too much on the bottom line—donor totals, attendance levels, and the like—and that his appointment might accelerate the Smithsonian's commercialization or "Disneyfication." Worse yet, a number of staffers feared his well-known penchant for accountability, almost a foreign concept in the cozy institution.

Small had his work cut out for him. But Edward Able, president and chief executive officer of the American Association of Museums, predicted that the incoming director could expect a honeymoon period. "Whenever there is a new head of a major institution like the Smithsonian, there is an opportunity for that person in the beginning to do some things and achieve some objectives that are not always available to a long-sitting chief," he told the *Pittsburgh Post-Gazette.*

Barely had Small received the symbolic brass key from Chief Justice Rehnquist when he began to make his mark on the Smithsonian. In his inaugural address, he set two major goals: making the museum complex more accessible to all Americans and directing its considerable scientific resources to a few select areas where the Smithsonian could shine. "Our job is to gain the attention of an entirely new segment of the population, Americans who have never heard of the Smithsonian," he said. "We must increase our affiliation with local institutions by lending many more items from our collections. We must send out traveling exhibitions. We must exploit the power of electronic outreach."

To make the institution more accessible, Small pledged to increase resources for its Internet site (www.si.edu), which was getting three million visits a month. "Technology is transforming the American public's view of what constitutes a satisfactory or recreational experience," he said. "And it is challenging the traditional approach to reinventing exhibits and publishing magazines. We must make technology a faithful ally."

To increase public awareness of the institution's little-noted scientific prowess, Small argued, "Science at the Smithsonian is too much of a mystery to the outside world. If Americans want to understand the origins of life on earth, if Americans want to unlock the secrets of the Earth's rain forests, and if Americans want to contemplate the future of the universe, they will have to know what's going on at the Smithsonian, because that's where the best work of nature is being done. We are committed that Americans get to know about it, and get to know about it in plain English."

Besides promoting attendance and research, Small introduced tougher standards for the institution: "The Smithsonian has grown to a size that demands adherence to the same principles of management that today guide other large and complex enterprises." Moments after his inauguration, Small also said he would not reconsider a controversial decision by Secretary Heyman to reallocate space in the

> ### KNOW THY EMPLOYER
>
> "IF AMERICANS WANT TO CONTEMPLATE THE FUTURE OF THE UNIVERSE, THEY WILL HAVE TO KNOW WHAT'S GOING ON AT THE SMITHSONIAN, BECAUSE THAT'S WHERE THE BEST WORK OF NATURE IS BEING DONE."

Old Patent Office Building between the National Portrait Gallery and the National Museum of American Art. Portrait Gallery officials had complained that the Museum of American Art would gain twice as much exhibition space, as well as a new main entrance. In making his decision, which prompted the resignation of longtime Portrait Gallery director Alan Fern, Small issued a gag order forbidding staff members to talk about it. "I am not aware of any organization where the individuals who are down at lower levels of the hierarchy are authorized to speak for the institution," he said on his first day on the job. The Smithsonian shake-up had begun.

Responding to public outrage, Small also rejected a plan to create an exhibit of the stuffed remains of the National Zoo's beloved panda Hsing-Hsing. Instead, he negotiated a deal with China to bring two giant pandas—a male and a female—to the zoo at a price tag of $1 million a year for ten years. "I'm a panda lover," Small says. "Conserving them highlights the importance of preserving their environment."

Besides saving endangered species, tapping the federal coffers was high on Small's agenda. In one of his earliest moves as secretary, he warned Congress that current funding levels were inadequate and that the old 1995 estimate of $500 million to repair and restore the institution's facilities was not enough. "The great dilemma of our buildings is nothing more—and nothing less—than time," he says. "Our buildings are too shabby and unworthy of the treasures they contain. And, frankly, it's our own fault, because the institution has not lobbied for enough money. People in Congress should be excited about the need to fund better facilities. I would like to see these buildings shine." (Subsequent studies have proven Small right. Current estimates are that the Smithsonian will need $1.5 billion to mend and modernize its buildings.)

Small voiced what many visitors have been grumbling about for years: America's museums have been booming, but the Smithsonian has remained tired and frayed. As he put it, the mouths of museum visitors should be open in awe of the wonderful exhibitions they are seeing, not in dismay at the condition of the buildings: "Americans should not have to wonder why their treasures are housed in buildings that seem to be falling apart," he says. "Instead they should marvel at the grandeur of the spaces and at the objects that are the icons of our history."

His pitch for funds impressed lawmakers. Rep. Ralph Regula, a member of the Smithsonian's board of regents and chairman of the House subcommittee overseeing its budget, echoed Small's efforts to target more money for renovation and restoration of the institution's century-old buildings. "We tend to neglect maintenance; it's not so glamorous," said Regula. "It's more fun to build a new building or start a new program. But I am a big believer in taking care of buildings and programs we've already got."

The Smithsonian's new ringmaster wasn't content to wait for the feds. In April 2000, he announced a bold initiative to spruce up the nation's attic. Rather than relying on the traditional capital campaign, Small began looking for donations from a few generous millionaires to restore the museum complex to its former grandeur. By devoting a "huge amount" of his time to targeted fund-raising, Small hoped to come up with $1 billion. "We are seeing a time when Americans who have been very successful in the economic world are willing to put back in larger and larger numbers," says the veteran art collector. "I think you'll see a larger percentage of money come from a smaller percentage of people—but in very large amounts."

Donors had already begun to surface after Small's appointment was announced in September 1999. Steven Udvar-Hazy, a Hungarian American businessman, donated $60 million for the massive 700,000-square-foot National Air and Space Museum at Dulles Airport. The revamp, which Small believes will be "wildly successful," will house the largest and most recent spacecraft and airplanes in the museum's collection. Also in 1999, the National Museum of American History reported a $10 million gift from fashion designer Ralph Lauren for the rehabilitation of the Star-Spangled Banner. "Americans want it preserved, not restored," Small said of the project. "It's not meant to re-create what something would look like. We're meant to be the steward of treasures as they are—and to safeguard their authenticity."

Then, in September 2000, Kenneth E. Behring, former owner of the Seattle Seahawks, announced his eye-popping $80 million donation to the Smithsonian's National Museum of American History. The gift, believed to be the largest cash donation ever made to an American museum, will be used to refurbish and update existing exhibits. "I've lived the American dream," the wealthy real estate developer told *USA Today*. "And I hope this gift will allow the museum to create an atmosphere where when [visitors] come out, they'll be able to stand a little taller, a little prouder." The seventy-two-year-old entrepreneur "is showing the way," says Small. "People should take advantage of this opportunity to revitalize this 154-year-old institution."

Fund-raising emerged as one of Small's strong suits. In his first nine months, he shattered all previous records for private giving. In 1999, individual donations totaled $147 million; the next year, they rose to approximately $200 million. Besides tapping business moguls and the federal government for funds, Small saw a vast potential in developing productive partnerships with other museums around the country. He estimated that there were 8,500 to 10,000 museums in the United States; yet only 23 participated in the Smithsonian's "Affiliations" program, begun by Heyman in 1997.

Under this arrangement, affiliates display their own collections, with supplements from the Smithsonian. To become affiliates, they pay a one-time, $2,500 processing fee, as well as the costs of packing, shipping, insuring, and installing loaned objects. The partnership accomplishes several objectives: First, it gets the museum's artifacts out of storage and off the mall. "We have 142 million items in the Smithsonian collections," says Small. "Yet fewer than 2 percent are on display. If things can't be seen by the American public, what good are they? In the future, you'll see a lot more arrangements with local institutions throughout the United States."

Second, the program strengthens the Smithsonian's unquestioned role as the keeper of authentic American history. "You can't invent something of George Washington's or Thomas Jefferson's," says Small. "You either have it or you don't." Invariably, the Smithsonian has it. By making its massive collections more accessible, the institution certifies its standing as the ultimate repository of American culture.

Third, unlocking the dusty vaults and shipping artifacts exhibits to museums around the country demonstrates the Smithsonian's educational and cultural value to the nation—a message that is not lost on Congress. "If government sees us doing more where the constituents of elected officials are voting, they are going to be helpful to us," says

Small. "At the same time, if our privately supported affiliates become more attractive, they will get more from the private sector. It's a complete win-win proposition."

During his first year, Small accelerated the outreach effort. Among others, he joined forces with the Museum of American Financial History, founded in 1988 to put Wall Street's history on display. "It makes all the sense in the world," he told the *Wall Street Journal*, "to be involved in an institution that is focused on capital markets, on how Americans dealt with finance, how the society has produced an economy that is unequal in terms of vibrancy, size, importance, solidity, than anywhere else in the world."

Under Small's direction, the Smithsonian signed up a record sixty-five institutions in 2000, and attendance at the affiliated museums jumped by as much as 37 percent because of loaned Smithsonian collections. In related initiatives, Small wants to see where its 2.1 million subscribers to *Smithsonian* magazine live and to export exhibits to their hometowns. Fulfilling an earlier promise, he also vows to reach out to all Americans via cyberspace. "We clearly are in an age when the use of the Internet and the ability to create what is known as the virtual museum are increasing at an exponential pace," he told *Washington Flyer* magazine.

Small believes that putting a business slant on the historic institution will pay off. Museums compete for people's leisure time. So museums have to find ways to make themselves attractive and interesting, particularly to the younger generation. Revenue from gift shops, catalog sales, and admission to IMAX movies adds to the institution's bounty. Yet Small is "dead set against" charging entrance fees because most of the visitors are taxpaying Americans. A congressionally mandated study also found that ending free entrance to the national museums would lose more than it would generate.

As for "Disneyfication" of the Smithsonian, it's not in Small's game plan. "I do think people like the Disney Company have figured out ways to make [visitor] experiences very compelling," he says. "And we can learn from their approach. But we will never be put in the position of endorsing products. The one thing the Smithsonian conveys is the stewardship of America's treasures. And that's not something we're going to commercialize."

In the days leading up to the start of his new job, Small had lengthy conversations with a wide variety of employees, scholars, and curators about the Smithsonian's role in the twenty-first century. He concluded that the institution's university-like structure was too decentralized. With only the undersecretary and provost reporting to the top, Small concluded "That's not managing. That's presiding."

Only three weeks into the job, he restructured the organization into five divisions whose directors report to him, and phased out scientific divisions deemed neither productive nor distinctive. In addition, he appointed Sheila P. Burke, former top aide to former Senator Robert Dole, as the new undersecretary for American museums, programs, and national outreach. Although Small's plan to reorganize around "natural connections and common priorities" roiled some of the institution's 6,500 staff members, the reactions were generally positive. "The plan he has is very impressive, as is the great speed with which he's putting it in place," said Milo C. Beach, then director of the Smithsonian's Arthur M. Sackler and Freer galleries. "It shows he understands the Smithsonian and its problems very well."

KNOW THY EMPLOYER

"THE ONE THING THE SMITHSONIAN CONVEYS IS THE STEWARDSHIP OF AMERICA'S TREASURES. AND THAT'S NOT SOMETHING WE'RE GOING TO COMMERCIALIZE."

In the months following the reorganization, Small continued his sessions with employees to learn as much as he could about the institution's history, collections, and people. In the spring of 2000, he supplemented these meetings with weekly breakfasts with staffers ranging from security guards to scholars. He also launched his infamous measurement system.

"What we want to get done can't be squishy," Small warned his co-workers. "One of my responsibilities is to help people get the best out of themselves, whatever way I can." Insisting on "transparency of information," the new secretary upgraded the institution's outdated financial and management information systems. These changes were "exactly what was needed here," says Bob Bailey, the ex-Citibanker whom Small coaxed out of retirement to serve as undersecretary of finance and administration. "To leverage the Smithsonian name requires more centralized direction and coordination. And no one's better at doing that than Larry."

Small also commissioned the first-ever survey of employee attitudes in May 2000. The results indicated a workforce that is highly committed to the institution and extremely proud of what the Smithsonian represents. For example, nearly eight in ten want to be part of the organization and would recommend it to others as a place to work.

> ### MAINTAIN A MAVERICK MIND-SET
> "WHAT WE WANT TO GET DONE CAN'T BE SQUISHY. ONE OF MY RESPONSIBILITIES IS TO HELP PEOPLE GET THE BEST OUT OF THEMSELVES, WHATEVER WAY I CAN."

However, a large number of employees perceive the current leadership to be insensitive to their needs. In fairness, the survey was probably conducted too early to serve as an accurate referendum on the new administration. "I'm pleased to see the commitment of employees to the institution today and for the future," says Small. "But clearly there is a challenge for management to provide employees with stimulating working conditions and to communicate better with them."

Does his being a nonacademic negatively affect Small's leadership? Small says, "It hasn't been an issue. On the one hand, I don't purport to be a specialist in anything they [Smithsonian's scientists and scholars] do. On the other hand, I doubt that there are any of them who can play flamenco guitar as well as I do. There's probably only a handful who know as much about Amazonian tribal art as I do. And when it comes to running a large, complex organization, none of them has had anything like the experience I have. So I'm not as good as they are in what they do—and they're probably not as good as I am in what I do."

Nonetheless, despite his "unequivocal commitment to scientific excellence," the nonscientist has been criticized for some of his bold initiatives. The aforementioned Milo Beach, an early supporter of Small, left the museum in a huff in 2001 because it was "being run as a business rather than as a cultural institution." Also, after an uproar from scientists and conservationists, Small reversed his earlier decision to close the Smithsonian's wildlife and conservation center in Front Royal, Virginia. In addition, he found himself on the opposite side of the Senate Appropriations Committee, which, in June 2001, voted to keep open the Center for Materials Research and Education in Maryland. In "making relics of old ways," the museum's activist secretary undoubtedly ruffles some feathers. Yet he enjoys strong support from his board of directors, which—among other things—approved his recent game plan to provide a "new strategic direction" for science.

NEVER STOP LEARNING

"I FIND A PIECE OF MUSIC I WANT TO LEARN AND IF IT TAKES EIGHT YEARS, I'LL BE PLAYING IT UNTIL I GET IT. I LOSE MYSELF IN IT. I'VE BEEN DOING IT NOW FOR FORTY YEARS."

Exhorting Smithsonian staffers to be more business-like by day, Small returns to his musical interests in the evening. His "night job" helps him escape the rigors of work. "I don't practice, I play," he says, reminding us that the guitar and his other avocations "haven't been passing fancies." With the discipline and orderliness he brings to his professional life, Small strives for musical perfection, playing notes over and over until they sound and feel just right.

"I'm not working toward any particular goal," he says. "I find a piece of music I want to learn and if it takes eight years, I'll be playing it until I get it. I lose myself in it. I've been doing it now for forty years. It's part of my life and something that I really have to do to feel okay. I have no purpose other than self-expression."

People often ask how Small finds time to nurture his many sides. But time expands when you are passionate enough about something.

Small tends to get by with little sleep. Normally, he nods off around 2:00 A.M. and gets up five or six hours later, though he admits he's "not especially productive in the wee hours."

Over sixty years ago, Wallace Stevens captured Small's odyssey in "The Man with the Blue Guitar":

> *The man bent over his guitar,*
> *A shearsman of sorts. The day was green.*
> *They said, "You have a blue guitar.*
> *You do not play things as they are."*
> *The man replied, "Things as they are*
> *Are changed upon the blue guitar."*

Smithsonian secretary, banker, musician, collector—none of this was what Small had in mind at Brown. But, as "Blue Guitar" suggests, things change. From his discovery of Carlos Montoya came a love of music and languages. This, in turn, introduced him to the world of international finance. Travel led to a deep interest in tribal art. And the feathered card brought him to the Smithsonian, which he describes as "the best thing I've ever done."

"Had it not been for that card, nobody would have sought me out," Small admits. "It just goes to show how accidental life can be. It's often simply a stroke of fortune, of unusual twists and turns." As with other multifaceted individuals, Small's travels are not entirely accidental. "He is always growing himself," says his wife of thirty-four years. "He's always in process."

LISTEN TO YOUR HEART

"MY ADVICE TO OTHERS INTERESTED IN A DOUBLE LIFE IS DO IT! DO WHATEVER MAKES YOU HAPPY."

In the age of specialists, we often criticize those who do more than one thing well as if they are at fault. "The term *overachiever* is often used to suggest we shouldn't be so ambitious," writes pianist and *New York Times* art critic Michael Kimmelman.

Yet Larry Small's varied achievements are a tribute to the elasticity of the human potential. Constantly "in process," he made it to the top echelons of the profit and nonprofit worlds. Though he may not have the artistic impact of Montoya or Segovia, he can never be accused of squandering his talent. "I've done what I've done in terms of my many interests outside of my institutional life because I felt I had to do it," says Small. "I couldn't exist happily without doing these things. So my advice to others interested in a double life is DO IT! Do whatever makes you happy."

8

Jim Wolfensohn
Banker to the World

*The delight of opening a new pursuit
imparts the novelty of youth even to old age.*

—BENJAMIN DISRAELI, BRITISH PRIME MINISTER

*Minding the World Bank often puts
Wolfensohn at center stage.*

*H*e has seemingly had more lives than the proverbial cat. Seven years ago, Sir James D. Wolfensohn reinvented himself once again as the ninth president of the World Bank. In his current life, he faces the Herculean task of tackling poverty and environmental degradation on a global scale.

The Australian-born naturalized American came to the world's largest public-lending organization with an impressive curriculum vitae: Wolfensohn's past lives include Olympic fencer, Australian Air Force flying officer, expert cellist, Wall Street guru, and arts baron. He was nominated to the World Bank position by his friend Bill Clinton. He has been a regular dinner companion of Federal Reserve chairman Alan Greenspan, IBM chairman Louis Gerstner, and the Kennedy and Rockefeller clans (whom he has advised for years). Whether fly-fishing with Vice President Dick Cheney or playing tennis with Washington insider Vernon Jordan, Wolfensohn has made networking an art form. He often flies the world's movers and shakers on his private jet to his favorite getaway—a Cesar Pelli–designed mansion in Jackson Hole, Wyoming. The self-made millionaire sees no inconsistency in rubbing shoulders with the rich and famous while raising living standards for the world's poor.

> **AIM HIGH**
>
> "IT IS AN OBLIGATION TO THE NEXT GENERATION TO LEAVE THEM A BETTER WORLD—A WORLD OF EQUITY, A WORLD OF PEACE, A WORLD OF SECURITY."

In an age of faceless apparatchiks, Wolfensohn is both colorful and charismatic. With entrée to leading government and business officials, he passionately preaches the merits of foreign aid and market-based economic solutions. At age sixty-seven, the stocky senior statesman constantly reminds his powerful friends that eradicating global poverty isn't simply about economics. "It is an obligation based on shared moral and social values," he says. "It is an obligation to the next generation to leave them a better world—a world of equity, a world of peace, a world of security."

Wolfensohn's engaging smile and direct speech help him connect with people around the world. Since becoming head of the World Bank in 1995, he has traveled to more than a hundred countries—from Ethiopia to Pakistan to Indonesia—to gain first-hand knowledge of the needs of the planet's 4.5 billion poor. Most observers consider him to be the most intelligent and dynamic head of the bank since Robert S. McNamara in the 1960s. Some insiders complain of arrogance and isolation from reality, but those familiar with the organization's entrenched bureaucracy and pernicious resistance to change accept that it takes someone of Wolfensohn's feistiness and strength of character to effect meaningful reform.

> **MAINTAIN A MAVERICK MIND-SET**
> "IF YOU ARE CHANGING THE STATUS QUO, WHATEVER MOVE YOU MAKE IS DISRUPTING SOMETHING ELSE."

Now in the middle of his second term, Wolfensohn concedes that the transition from running his own investment bank to overseeing the fifty-seven-year-old World Bank has not been easy. "Being in public life is bloody hard," he says. "If you are changing the status quo, whatever move you make is disrupting something else." But, frustrations aside, Wolfensohn is convinced that, this time, he has found his true métier; he asserts, "I have a passionate belief in this organization. We can make a difference between peace and war. We can make a difference between poverty and a fair life for all people. My duties here are far, far more important than my time in the private sector."

Born in Sydney on December 1, 1933, Wolfensohn was raised by British immigrants to Australia. His father, a small-business consultant, and his mother, a musician, encouraged a love for arts, music, and education. "There wasn't a lot of material success," he recalls. "But there was a lot of intellectual strength and encouragement." Reaching out to others was another family trait that would stay with him. Though of modest means, the Wolfensohns actively helped Jewish refugees settle in what Australian writer Donald Horn called "the Lucky Country."

An indifferent student, Wolfensohn graduated from Sydney University with degrees in music and economics in 1954 and, in 1956, in law. While at the university, he managed a stint with the Royal Australian Air Force. He also took up fencing and made the Australian National Team. In 1956, he fenced in the Melbourne Olympic Games and, in 1958, at the world championships, where he captained the national team. After he graduated, he began to practice law with Sydney-based Allen Allen & Hemsley.

Bored with wills and trusts, Wolfensohn left Sydney in 1957 for Harvard Business School. He arrived in Cambridge with three hundred dollars for two years of study. "I was too stupid to know how poor I actually was," he says. With a friend, he set up Teddy's Laundry Service and began delivering clean clothes to executives attending Harvard's Advanced Management Program. Every week, he would dip into the proceeds for twenty-five-cent tickets to Boston Symphony Orchestra rehearsals, where he met his future wife, Elaine, who was studying French literature at nearby Wellesley College. Eventually, the couple would have three children: Sara, a concert pianist; Naomi, a lawyer; and Adam, a composer, sound designer, and graduate student in forestry at Yale.

After graduation from Harvard and a brief stint in New York with Rheem International, Wolfensohn returned home in 1963 for a career in investment banking. For the next few years, he toiled at two Sydney merchant banks and became a managing director at Darling and Co. Seeking greater challenges, Wolfensohn again left Australia, in 1967, for London and the venerable Schroder group. There he ascended the intricate hierarchy that shapes British investment banking and reached the number-two position as executive deputy chairman.

However, the brilliant but brash Aussie found himself frustrated by the "more constrictive" rigidities of the British class system. After losing the race to the chairmanship, he departed the U.K. for the "limitless possibilities and total openness" of the United States, whose immigrant heritage and egalitarian values mirrored those of his homeland.

In 1977, Wolfensohn joined the corporate finance group of Salomon Brothers in New York, where he held a series of senior management positions and helped transform the distinguished trading firm into an investment-banking powerhouse. He also engineered the bailout of Chrysler Corporation by the U.S. government. His Chrysler play caught the eye of World Bank president McNamara. Rumored to be on the short list as McNamara's successor, Wolfensohn became a U.S. citizen to better qualify for the job. (Every president, by tradition, has been an American because the United States is the biggest shareholder.) When he was passed over for the job in 1981, he started his own firm, James D. Wolfensohn, Inc.

From its Lexington Avenue headquarters, the investment-banking boutique doled out advice to more than thirty major multinational companies and governments. Specializing in complex mergers and acquisitions, it represented blue-chip clients, including American Express, Du Pont, Daimler-Benz, Ford Motor Company, and Hong Kong & Shanghai Banking Corporation. In addition, Prime Minister Lee Kuan Yew hired the firm for advice in setting up an investment management structure for the Singapore government. During the 1980s and early 1990s, Wolfensohn & Co. handled between $8 billion and $10 billion a year and ranked as the world's seventh-largest adviser on takeovers.

Between deals, Wolfensohn involved himself in a wide variety of cultural and volunteer activities. He found time to serve on the boards of the Rockefeller Foundation, the Brookings Institution, the Institute for Advanced Study, the Business Council for Sustainable Development, the Population Council, and the International Federation of Multiple

Sclerosis Societies. In addition, he saw to it that his bank donated 20 percent of its annual profits to charity—a standard unmatched by any of its peers. Wolfensohn also set up his own foundation, which works in the environment, community development, and medical research and supports promising artists, musicians, and fencers.

Besides being a social progressive, the international financier continued to nurture his musical instincts. Though he studied piano as a child, he longed to learn the cello. When his good friend, the late Jacqueline du Pré, became ill with multiple sclerosis, Wolfensohn, then forty-two, asked her to train him in the instrument. Under her tutelage, he became, in his own words, "a competent amateur," mastering the works of Mozart, Brahms, Beethoven, and others. On his fiftieth birthday, he performed at Carnegie Hall with his friends Isaac Stern, Vladimir Ashkenazy, and Daniel Barenboim (du Pré's husband). His accompanist was his daughter, Sara. To this day, he keeps a Guarnerius cello nearby, although work pressures have limited his practice time.

According to Wolfensohn's wife, Elaine, his investment banking side permitted him to develop his artistic side: "I'm not sure if one would have happened without the other," she told the *Christian Science Monitor*. Perhaps a more obvious link between his business and musical interests was his mission to persuade wealthy people and companies to part with their cash for his favorite causes. In addition to performing full-time duties at his company, Wolfensohn took on the chairmanship of Carnegie Hall and led a rebuilding program to restore the financially troubled arts mecca to its former grandeur. Later, he applied the same dedication to Washington's then-struggling John F. Kennedy Center for the Performing Arts, where he also served as chairman. In 1995, Queen Elizabeth II knighted him for his contributions to the art world.

"You have to have a worthwhile dream," he says, explaining his philanthropic success. "You have to have an appeal which, on its face, grabs the person whom you're asking for money. It should, of course, grab you first."

Whether he was picking other people's pocketbooks or their brains, Wolfensohn's star was on the ascent. As evidence of his ever-widening influence, Wolfensohn convinced Paul A. Volker, the former chairman of the Federal Reserve Bank, to become chairman of his investment bank. In 1996, after Wolfensohn had joined the World Bank, Volker sold the company to Bankers Trust for $210 million. Wolfensohn's stake was an estimated $50 million, of which a large part went to his charitable foundation. At the time, James D. Wolfensohn Inc. had more than 140 employees in New York, London, Tokyo, and Moscow, as well as an investment banking partnership with Fuji Bank of Japan and Lord Rothschild of Britain.

The banker's transition from Wall Street to Washington began in March 1995, when he was nominated by President Clinton to run the World Bank. "James Wolfensohn has already had an extraordinary career in finance and public service, spanning four decades and three continents," said the president of his nominee's double lives. "The deep respect Jim already enjoys will allow him to serve as a forceful advocate for the Bank and development issues." Among those heralding Wolfensohn's nomination was Robert Hormats, vice chairman of Goldman Sachs International Inc. and a former official in the Carter and Reagan administrations. He called Wolfensohn "a Renaissance man, with extremely good judgment and great integrity, and a superb candidate for the job."

Founded in 1944 at the United Nations Monetary and Financial Conference in Bretton Woods, New Hampshire, the World Bank—its proper name is the International Bank for Reconstruction and Development—was established to help war-torn European countries rebuild their economies and infrastructures. Over the years, its scope gradually expanded to focus on helping the world's poor. Owned by

SELL YOURSELF

"YOU HAVE TO HAVE A WORTHWHILE DREAM. YOU HAVE TO HAVE AN APPEAL WHICH, ON ITS FACE, GRABS THE PERSON WHOM YOU'RE ASKING FOR MONEY. IT SHOULD, OF COURSE, GRAB YOU FIRST."

more than 180 member countries, the bank provides nearly $30 billion in loans annually for development aid. From fighting corruption in Poland to purifying drinking water in Morocco, it attempts to reduce poverty by offering sustainable economic growth to those in need. And many are in need: Despite unprecedented global wealth, almost half of the planet's population—roughly 3 billion people—still live on less than $2 a day. And 1.2 billion live on less than $1 a day, barely surviving.

Headquartered on H Street in Washington, the World Bank gets most of its money by tapping international capital markets. It sells low-interest, AAA-rated bonds backed by its member nations. It then lends the proceeds at slightly higher rates to the governments of relatively successful Third World countries: Malaysia, Brazil, Chile, and others. As a result, many of the institution's activities pay for themselves. However, the bank also offers loans (about $6 billion a year) to truly impoverished nations. These high-risk, long-term loans invariably require contributions from wealthier shareholders, including the United States.

For some time, critics have blasted the World Bank for all sorts of things. It has been blamed for being both too lenient and too Scrooge-like. But invariably the finger-pointing turns to the agency's huge bureaucracy, considered too inefficient to help poor countries grow rich. Long dominated by desk-bound bureaucrats, the bank has been largely immune to change. Of its ten thousand employees, more than half work at the head office, two blocks west of the White House. These highly paid civil servants represent 140 nationalities of client countries—and cannot be fired or reassigned easily.

On June 1, 1995, Wolfensohn became the World Bank's ninth president. Like Larry Small, his cross-town buddy at the Smithsonian, he took a whopping pay cut—from several million dollars to $250,000 a year. Still, he described his new position as "a chance of a lifetime," saying that he "came with the best motives in the world: To be a great contributor to world peace and stability."

From his office on the top floor of the bank's thirteen-story complex, Wolfensohn began his biggest challenge. Though aware of the institution's tarnished image, he discovered that the World Bank was in real danger of obliteration. Critics on the left described it as irrelevant, charging it with deepening, instead of eradicating, poverty. They accused the bank of being insensitive to environmental concerns, captivated by free-market dogma, and a puppet for big multinational corporations. Skeptics on the right called the bank a crutch for corrupt, weak-willed, inefficient governments and demanded greater transparency and focus, with greater emphasis on market-oriented initiatives. But both sides agreed on one thing: The World Bank needed a massive overhaul, not tinkering at the edges.

These charges were not lost on the U.S. Congress, which controls the purse strings for the bank and its fellow agency, the International Monetary Fund (IMF). Over the years, various congressional committees have recommended either outright abolition or a dramatic scaling back of both institutions. Given the steady stream of criticism, it is perhaps no surprise that the United States is the stingiest rich nation. America's foreign aid decreased roughly 8 percent in the 1990s. Today, the average citizen pays just $35 dollars in taxes each year to aid overseas interests.

In his first term in office, Wolfensohn went to great lengths to woo U.S. lawmakers. He reminded them that support for the beleaguered organization was simply not optional. "Whether you like it or not," he said, "we're part of the world. We have important economic ties. Four million American jobs depend on exports to developing countries. One-half of the growth of our own GNP and 40 percent of the growth in world trade depends on developing countries." But he also cautioned congressional leaders to think beyond economic self-interest. "We have a deep interest in terms of the environment, in terms of global stability, in terms of migration," he explained. "We have many interconnected issues. Environment, humanity, peace, and stability—those are the real issues."

The politically savvy chief seemed to mollify the traditionally hostile Congress. No doubt his bravura in taking on an organizational culture described as "notoriously inefficient, inward-looking, and highbrow" helped. Wolfensohn promised that the bank would no longer "be arrogant, haughty, or defensive. It will be open. It will be ready to learn. And it will be at the disposal of clients."

In the old days, the World Bank favored funding huge infrastructure projects—highways, dams, power plants—whatever their impact. Now staffers were instructed to worry less about loan volume and more about "putting a smile on a child's face." In the future, the incoming chief insisted, "the World Bank must be based on results, not process. To do that, we need to be more decentralized, creative, and entrepreneurial—in effect, to think and operate more like a private-sector business."

Recognizing that, for years, the bank had been pouring money down a rat hole, Wolfensohn demanded that loan officers pay greater attention to whether projects succeeded or failed. In defense of his staff, the financier says the bank's people don't work any less hard than those in the private sector, just differently. "But the thing I am trying to bring from Wall Street is to get people to feel a sense of accountability and a sense of client orientation," he says.

Wolfensohn decentralized the institution, shipping two thousand staffers from their desk jobs in Washington to borrowing countries in the field. He hired more hands-on employees, such as engineers. He set up new reporting systems, with a faster track for loan approvals. Besides streamlining the bureaucracy and speeding up decision making, he established a six-week management training program, including two weeks at Harvard Business School. Participants were then sent abroad to live in a village to get a real sense of the poverty they were dealing with. To inject greater meritocracy into the system, Wolfensohn also insisted that promotions be based on performance: namely, how well a lending officer's projects worked out over time.

In addition, he sharpened the bank's focus on alleviating poverty. "The issue in the old days was getting projects to the board for approval," he says. "Getting them implemented effectively today, rather than just getting the approval of colleagues, is going to solve the problems of poverty, inequality, and social justice." Instead of lending primarily for infrastructure projects, the leaner, more responsive organization has shifted to smaller-scale, well-integrated projects that are "economically sustainable, environmentally benign, and embraced by the people they are purported to help." Under the new Comprehensive Development Framework (CDF), the accent is on reforms that balance economics with social, human, and physical needs.

Wolfensohn rejects the notion that this broad-based, holistic approach to foreign aid is "squishy" and therefore difficult to assess. To bolster the CDF, he has called for "a new framework to evaluate the macroeconomic performance of each country—a framework that considers the progressing structural reforms necessary for long-term growth, that includes human and social accounting, and that deals with the status of women, rural development, indigenous people, and progress in infrastructure."

With its attention now on country-driven, community-based projects, the World Bank has also begun to conduct a wider dialogue with the development community. A top priority was to improve coordination with other multilateral and bilateral agencies and nongovernmental organizations. "They're all important," says Wolfensohn. "You have to think of them as a totality to get the job done." The bank has partnered with environmentalists to save the Amazon rain forest, joined forces with internal revenue agencies to offer advice on effective tax collection systems, and teamed up with activists to create protected areas for indigenous people. By 2000, more than 70 percent of the World Bank's projects involved the active participation of other organizations—up from less than half at the time of Wolfensohn's appointment five years earlier.

Fighting for greater transparency and improved corporate governance were other key components of the bank's revised attack on world poverty. Opaque financial reporting, lack of independent oversight, and inadequate minority-shareholder rights had caused economic woes in many Third World countries. Wolfensohn pressed for more visible financial systems, with tighter supervision and control. But to do this, he points out, "You have to train supervisors, you have to have systems, and you have to train bankers to respond and to be transparent in what they are doing."

Tougher yet was dealing with the so-called cancer of corruption. "At the core of the incidence of poverty is the issue of equity," Wolfensohn notes. "And at the core of the issue of equity is the issue of corruption." Since 1996, the bank has introduced more than six hundred anticorruption programs and initiatives in almost a hundred countries.

Attacking despots is never easy. "It's a human challenge," says Wolfensohn. "It's a task of building social systems, of putting the right structures in place." Recalling the bank's earlier ties to the Ceausescu, Nyerere, and Marcos regimes, he readily admits that there are risks to lending to leaders in some developing countries. Nevertheless, he claims that you need an individual to make the program work. "There is no getting around the fact that you are backing the jockey as well as the policy," he says.

Part of the bank's revamped lending strategy also includes providing more opportunities for the poor themselves, empowering them politically, and pushing countries to meet the needs of all their citizens. This means tackling the vested interests of economic elites that, for years, have had undue influence on policies, regulations, and laws. Given his private-sector roots, Wolfensohn aggressively champions free-market solutions as the desired path to uplifting the world's poor. By and large, open-market economies tend to nurture a better-educated workforce, more efficient transportation and communications infrastructures, lower taxes, and more honest governments. So, whenever possible, the bank advocates relying on the private sector and giving business a fair shake.

Building prosperity is a two-way street. Wolfensohn reminded his corporate colleagues that economic development "requires a private

SEEK COMPATIBLE GOALS

SINCE WOLFENSOHN'S ARRIVAL, THE BANK HAS
FORMED A GLOBAL COMMUNICATIONS NETWORK
LINKING WASHINGTON WITH POLITICIANS AND
BUSINESS EXECUTIVES IN CLIENT COUNTRIES.

sector that is prepared to bear its responsibility and not just take off and run for the hills—or it will create the very problems that we're all seeking to avoid." Tapping business's leading-edge technologies was one way to stimulate the desired private-sector participation.

During one of his field visits, Wolfensohn observed Indians in the jungles of Brazil using satellites to communicate with villages hundreds of miles away. "Even though they couldn't read," he noted, "they could run a satellite." The possible uses of technology seemed limitless. Hence, the World Bank leader has implored his staffers, "If we don't deal with the technology gap quickly, developing countries will fall further behind. But if we move quickly enough, we have a chance of helping them catch up."

Since Wolfensohn's arrival, the bank has formed a global communications network linking Washington with politicians and business executives in client countries. It has connected students and teachers in four hundred secondary schools in the Third World via satellite and created a virtual university in fourteen African countries. With distance-learning facilities around the world, the institution is now running five hundred video conferences a month. The World Bank has also set up the Global Development Gateway, an initiative aimed at disseminating knowledge for development using high-tech industries, and it recently joined forces with Softbank, a Japanese tech-industry force, to create a $200 million fund aimed at incubating Internet-related businesses in emerging countries. "Communications technology gives us the tool for true participation," says Wolfensohn. "This is leveling the playing field. And this is true equity."

Sidestepping the protests of political conservatives, Wolfensohn has also encouraged debt reduction and looser loan requirements.

Over the years, the bank had been criticized for its "conditionality"—that is, the steps that countries are required to take before receiving financial aid. Frequently, this meant that Third World clients had to slash government spending, consumer subsidies, trade barriers, and other programs

that interfered with debt payments. In the future, Wolfensohn has promised there will be fewer strings attached as well as less meddling and micromanagement. "We will continue conditionality," he insisted. "But we will streamline it and focus on fundamental principles." In 1996, the World Bank, with the IMF, adopted the first comprehensive debt-relief program for heavily indebted poor countries. So far, the bank has forgiven nearly $11 billion in loans. The result for the forty targeted borrowing nations has been astonishing. Mozambique, for instance, has seen nearly 75 percent of its debt written off.

Assessing his first term in office, Wolfensohn claimed that the bank had turned the corner. "More and more developing countries are keeping their side of the bargain," he said. In 1995, 34 percent of the bank's projects were at risk. In 2000, that figure was down to about 15 percent. The institution also became more transparent, now disclosing over 85 percent of its country assistance strategies. These improvements translated into billions of dollars of more effective lending.

After six years in office, the president seemed genuinely pleased with the bank's turnaround. "We have a lot of problems," he conceded. "But we've made a lot of progress." Decidedly discordant, however, were several long-term employees, who found their boss's aggressive behavior less than refreshing. Though open and approachable, Wolfensohn can be brusque. He speaks his mind, does not suffer fools easily, and neither temporizes nor sugarcoats issues. For those long accustomed to less forceful leaders, the adjustment was difficult, sometimes painful.

Some detractors called the Wolfensohn regime "management by terror and verbal abuse." The *National Journal* described him as a "short-fused charmer" and his first term as "exhilarating . . . but rocky." Wolfensohn had always inspired intense loyalty among those who worked closely with him, so the criticism touched an unexpected nerve. The outspoken Aussie promised to muffle any future tirades. "I was too much in a hurry and teed off with my inability to get things done," he confessed. "I used to blow up very quickly, more than I should. I have made a conscious effort to modulate my behavior."

The World Bank's governing board members expressed every confidence in Wolfensohn. On June 1, 2000, they unanimously elected him to a second five-year term, only the third president to be so honored. The Wall Street veteran responded immediately, recommitting himself to narrowing the gap between the rhetoric and realities of economic development. However, a new series of shock waves began to rock the organization in ways that only recently have come into focus.

Entering the new millennium, unfettered capitalism came under attack. Despite the fact that five out of six countries have voluntarily accepted market principles, a backlash against globalization—the growing interdependence of all nations—made strange bedfellows of the right and the left. From protectionists to human-rights activists to nationalists, vocal anti-globalization protesters hit the streets of Seattle, Washington, Prague, and New York. These angry demonstrators argued that instead of opening up the world economy, globalization was actually hurting countries: They were not being helped by liberalized trade and investment. It was time, protesters demanded, to reassess the behavior of world lending institutions and their favored friends, the big multinational corporations.

As the backlash against globalization gained steam, the World Bank found it increasingly difficult to convince its opponents of the

AIM HIGH

"WE CANNOT TURN OUR BACK ON GLOBALIZATION. WE MUST WORK TOGETHER TO HARNESS [ITS] BENEFITS TO DELIVER PROSPERITY TO THE MANY, NOT JUST THE FEW."

positive effects of a more interconnected world economy. "The curious thing is that the people who are our critics are using globalization— the thing they are criticizing—as one of their major tools," Wolfensohn said in an interview at the United Nations. At a time when the world was changing at a dizzying rate, he also warned that it would be folly to dismiss this growing movement. "We cannot turn our back on globalization," he said. "We must work together to harness [its] benefits to deliver prosperity to the many, not just the few. Our challenge is to make globalization an instrument of opportunity and inclusion—not of fear and insecurity."

However, fear and insecurity also seemed to permeate World Bank headquarters. After returning from a visit to India in January 2001, Wolfensohn was criticized by bank employees for low morale in Washington. One internal memorandum, leaked to the press, described the boss as "quick to rebuke and humiliate managers, often in open meetings. Managers at all levels live under fear." Some anonymous critics called him "a follower of fads," including being gripped by Internet fever; others chided him for refusing to share power by not appointing a second-in-command. Rallying back, the straight-talking secretary said that "mistrust and a lack of team spirit seemed pervasive." He regretted the Washington "malaise," caused, in his opinion, by a few disloyal and uncommitted subordinates.

John McArthur, Wolfensohn's lifelong friend, former Harvard Business School dean, and a consultant to the bank, speculated on the reasons for the squabbling: "Jim's gotten into things up to his elbows throughout life. He's intellectually honest and courageous, and when he sees something that he thinks is wrong, he weighs it and tries to change it and, from his point of view, to improve it." Most insiders and outsiders appreciate his derring-do. He "did the big, necessary

> **DELIVER DAILY**
>
> "QUITE APART FROM SOCIAL VALUES, WE NEED TO STAND FOR SOMETHING. WE NEED TO PROVIDE MORAL VALUES AND LEADERSHIP. AND WE MUST COMMIT OURSELVES FOR THE LONG HAUL."

things right," says J. Bradford DeLong, economics professor at the University of California at Berkeley.

"Bureaucracy is the death of achievement," Einstein once wrote. In causing a cultural quake at the bank, Wolfensohn gets high marks. "We are not just another bureaucracy," he often tells his staff. "We're an organization that has phenomenal responsibility. And it's a human responsibility that is real, present, and deep."

Some might regard his remarks as Pollyannaish. But for Wolfensohn, it is not a contradiction to be both a banker and an idealist. He is "totally absorbed" in his most recent turnaround effort, and his enthusiasm remains undimmed. He knows that halting the slide of poverty takes discipline and commitment. "Quite apart from social values, we need to stand for something," he says. "We need to provide moral values and leadership. And we must commit ourselves for the long haul."

> **LISTEN TO YOUR HEART**
>
> "I'D LIKE TO THINK THAT I MADE A DIFFERENCE ON A HUMAN SCALE IN THE FIGHT AGAINST POVERTY, THAT I MADE A CONTRIBUTION TO WORLD PEACE."

The man who moved from the private to the public sector means business. On his way to becoming one of the world's most influential men, he raised the bar in every venue through his remarkable ability to orchestrate effective change.

Reflecting on the aftermath of September 11th, Wolfensohn believes that unless we combat poverty, further terrorism and dissent are likely. "We are all here to work for humanity and to fight against poverty with passion," he says. "But to overcome poverty, passion is not enough. We must act, and act effectively now!"

Is he thinking about what legacy he hopes to leave? When we last talked, he said, "I'd like to think that I made a difference on a human scale in the fight against poverty, that I made a contribution to world peace."

9

José Rizal

Filipino Firebrand

I have glimpsed a little light, and I believe
I should show it to my countrymen.

—José Rizal

*His nation's hero, José Rizal was a
physician, poet, novelist, sculptor, and more.*

6:45 A.M.
December 30, 1898
Luneta, Manila, Spanish Philippines

Since the predawn hours, thousands of Europeans have been gathering to witness the execution of Dr. José Rizal, sentenced to death by a Spanish military court for the crimes of rebellion and sedition. Dressed in their best finery, the eager onlookers are in a festive mood. Tensions are running high in the capital city, however, and extra security forces are on hand to quash any disturbances from Filipino bystanders.

Only thirty minutes ago, Rizal married his sweetheart, Josephine Bracken, in the sinister confines of Fort Santiago. But there will be no wedding march today. In a few minutes, Rizal will meet his maker. With his hands bound behind his back, the alleged traitor will leave his prison cell for the short walk to the Luneta, the famous public park overlooking Manila Bay.

As the first rays of dawn seep through the night fog, drums announce Rizal's arrival. Accompanied by a military escort and two Jesuit priests, the slight-statured, fine-boned man strides past the whispering trees and murmuring surf, exuding the magnetism of a national hero. Impeccably attired in a black suit, white shirt and tie, black shoes and derby hat, Rizal shows no fear. Quietly, he makes his way through the densely packed crowd. His understated dignity belies his mere thirty-five years and countless hardships. As beloved as Rizal is to the Philippine masses, he is equally abhorred by his Spanish masters.

The procession comes to a halt. Under orders from the Crown, Rizal's own countrymen must perform the execution. Behind the six-man firing squad stand Spanish soldiers ready to dispense with any Filipino who shrinks from the task. Rizal asks to face his executioners. "Impossible," says the lieutenant in charge. "My orders are to shoot you in the back." Rizal then requests that his captors shoot him through the heart. "Also impossible," repeats the officer. "Such a favor is only granted to men of rank. You will be shot in the back."

Refusing to be blindfolded or to kneel, the condemned man pivots to face the sea, the island of Corregidor and Bataan's blue mountains in the distance. At the last minute, a Spanish military surgeon asks to feel his pulse, which is surprisingly normal.

"Consomatum est!"—It is finished!—Rizal cries, in a voice audible to everyone in attendance. A hail of bullets strikes him, twisting his body around so his face points toward the sun. At 7:03 A.M., the Messiah of the Philippines lies dead.

Vivas erupt from the Spaniards. "Hurrah for Spain!" they cheer. In the rear ranks Filipinos whisper, "Hurrah for the Philippine Republic and death to Spain." As morning burns into midday, their exhortations grow louder and more insistent. There will be no more fealty to Madrid, and life in the Spanish colony will never be the same.

> **DEFINE SUCCESS IN YOUR OWN TERMS**
> "WHAT IS DEATH TO ME? I HAVE SOWN THE SEEDS. OTHERS WILL REAP."

Rizal's executioners wrongly assumed that by silencing one man, they could kill the spirit of insurrection. Instead, they created a martyr whose loss convinced his countrymen that there was no alternative to independence from Spain. "What is death to me?" Rizal had once warned his captors. "I have sown the seeds. Others will reap."

Spurred on by his death, Filipinos from all parts of the vast seven-thousand-island archipelago took up the call to arms. Within hours, the first national revolution in Asia had begun. Two years later, three centuries of harsh Spanish rule would end.

José Rizal, a contemporary of Gandhi and Sun Yat-sen, is recognized as the greatest Filipino who ever lived. In his multiple lives, he was more than a patriot; he was also a novelist, poet, painter, sculptor, scientist, educator, and surgeon, as well as an expert swordsman and crack marksman. Having traveled extensively in Europe, America, and Asia, Rizal mastered twenty-two languages, including Spanish, English, German, French, Chinese, Japanese, Hebrew, Greek, and various local dialects. To truly appreciate the fullness of his life, it is crucial to understand the Philippines of that time.

At Rizal's birth, the Philippine Islands had long been an integral part of Spain. The Portuguese explorer Ferdinand Magellan, in the service of Spain, sailed to the islands in 1521 and named them for Prince Philip, later Philip II. Subsequent expeditions conquered large parts of the country, gradually pushing Moslem and Hindu elements to the southern islands of Mindanao and Sulu. On June 3, 1571, the Spaniards declared the bamboo-barricaded village of Manila a Spanish city, giving it the name "Distinguished and Ever Loyal City."

Spain's conquest of the country was motivated by the lure of treasure and by religious zeal. Missionaries accompanied the *conquistadors* to the Philippines and worked feverishly to pacify and convert the natives or "indios" (as Filipinos were contemptuously called after the old and mistaken belief that Magellan had discovered India). For the first two hundred years, economic

AIM HIGH

MORE THAN A PATRIOT, HE WAS ALSO A NOVELIST, POET, PAINTER, SCULPTOR, SCIENTIST, EDUCATOR, AND SURGEON.

development was through the galleon trade in which Manila served as the middleman between Mexico and China. Silver from Mexico was exchanged for silks and other precious wares from China and shipped on galleons built of fine Philippine timber. But, by the early nineteenth century, agricultural exports—tobacco and indigo, later sugar and abaca—dominated commerce, making land the primary factor of production.

The Spanish ran this semi-feudal agrarian system from Manila, in what often represented the union of church and state at its worst. The pressures of colonizing the New World and its remoteness made the Philippines a relatively unpopular posting. Though Spaniards often represented one-fifth or more of the population of their South American colonies, in the Philippines their ranks never exceeded 1 percent, with the vast majority congregated in Manila. To conquer the islands' far reaches, government officials depended on a network of parish priests, who were often the only Spaniards in the area. These missionaries dealt directly with the indios. They learned the languages and dialects, governed through them, and were in effect the mayors of the barrios. Operating with little formal supervision, they controlled the countryside with an iron fist. Among other things, this "friarocracy" was responsible for education and health, tax collection, and reporting seditious behavior to the central government. For their efforts, many priests received *encomiendas*, or land grants, from the Crown. These grants, initially intended to be of limited duration, became the permanent booty of the padres, many of whom amassed enormous tracts of choice farmland.

The Catholic Church had a monopoly on education. The friars consistently resisted Madrid's directives that free public education and Spanish language instruction be made available to indios. They felt that an educated native was a dangerous native—someone who might not blindly accept the church's teachings. Therefore, only those Filipino intellectuals in Manila learned Spanish. And, because no one could be appointed to public office without fluency in the language, there were no locals in responsible positions in the central government.

More damning was the Spanish soul-savers' open contempt for Filipinos, who were looked on as immature children and sinful wards. Consider the racist comments of one priest: "They are at one and the same time mischievous and humble; forward and villainous, but devious cowards; full of compassion, but cruel. In these natives, the virtues and their opposite vices are joined like brothers. It is only in what is deceitful that they show no contradictions; for when they lie, no one knows."

Church and state, in tandem, "belonged to a community that had established itself as superior in power and morals over the colonialized natives," writes historian Onofre Corpuz. "The Spanish occupation rested, and lasted, on this equilibrium." Subjugated and humiliated, Filipinos had been reduced to impotence. Still, the seeds of a revolt had been planted indiscriminately by years of ruthless oppression. A successful revolution, however, requires a champion.

José Protacio Rizal Mercado y Alfonso Realonda was born on June 19, 1861, in the small town of Calamba in rice and sugar-rich Laguna province, about forty miles from Manila. His father was a relatively prosperous landowner and sugar planter of Chinese-Filipino descent. His mother, one of the most highly educated women in the Philippines at that time, exerted a powerful influence on her son's intellectual development. It might be said that Rizal inherited dignity and self-respect from his father, literary and artistic skills from his mother, and courageous idealism from both of them.

One of eleven children, José was sickly and undersized, and had an unusually large head. At his baptism, the local priest warned his parents to be especially protective lest the baby fall down and hit his head against anything. "Take good care of José," he said. "Some day he will be a great man."

In no time, the family recognized that their delicate child was exceptionally gifted. By age four, he was writing sentences and poems in Tagalog, his native language, as well as in Spanish. In his parents' extensive library of more than a thousand books, he found a home within a home and also developed a lifelong interest in indigenous plants and animals. During his study breaks, he could often be found sketching and modeling in clay and wood.

By the time he was seven, Rizal had exhausted the teaching capacities of his mother and a private tutor. His parents dispatched him to the Calamba School, but after a few weeks, his instructors conceded that they could no longer cope with their pupil's educational needs. After another stint of home schooling, he was sent to a more challenging school at Biñan, a larger town about eight miles from Calamba, where Rizal boarded with relatives. There his love for languages soared. He began to pen more and more verses in Tagalog and wrote a short comedy that was much admired.

For the first time, the prodigy witnessed Spanish hostility and recognized that indios like himself were not treated as equals. "We saw unrestrained force, violence, and other excesses committed by those who were entrusted with keeping the public peace," he wrote. If a native failed to salute a soldier, he would be whipped. One evening, Rizal was throttled by one of the *guardia civil* because he failed to properly recognize the soldier. When he complained to higher authorities, the youngster was told his appeal was futile. "You see, we are, after all, Spaniards," they boasted.

In his earliest known revolutionary comment, the nine-year-old wrote a poem on the need to officially recognize the Tagalog language:

> *Our tongue was like others,*
> *Having alphabet and letters of its own;*
> *But these, like the small lake craft exposed*
> *To the monsoon's fury, were wrecked*
> *Long ago in the night of time.*

Rizal's bold words showed incredible maturity for his age and represented what would become his lifelong commitment to rekindling Philippine pride.

A year later, Rizal witnessed an incident that strengthened his resolve against the Spaniards. His mother had been unjustly accused of trying to poison her cousin's wife. Without evidence or formal hearing, the blameless woman was imprisoned at Santa Cruz, the provincial capital, where she remained for two and a half years. The friars simply wanted to humiliate this well-respected, highly educated indio.

Another traumatic event brought the Rizals under the church's watchful eye. On January 20, 1872, two hundred Filipino soldiers on the island of Cavite attacked and killed several Spanish soldiers. The alleged instigators were three Filipino priests—Fathers José Burgos,

Mariano Gomez, and Jacinto Zamora—who were arrested and later beheaded at the Luneta. Father Burgos had been a teacher and close friend of Rizal's brother Paciano, and Rizal had often heard the two men talk about the need for reforms in their country.

These episodes had a profound effect on the family. To shield young José from possible retaliation by local authorities, the Rizals sent him to Manila to begin his studies at Ateneo Municipal, the most prominent school in the country. After only a month, the precocious eleven-year-old stood at the head of his class. Despite his small size, everyone called him "emperor." "There seemed to be no limit to the number of things he could do," writes his biographer Austin Coates. "His talents showed principally in scholastic work, poetry, painting, and sculpture, and he excelled in all of them." At age fifteen, Rizal graduated with a bachelor of arts with the highest honors and grades, which have never been surpassed by any Ateneo student. "Good-bye, beautiful unforgettable period of my life!" he wrote. "Farewell, my lost childhood!"

The teenager next took his extraordinary intellectual gifts to the University of Santo Tomás, founded in 1611 and then the foremost center of learning in Asia. His mother had strongly opposed any further study. Despite her own educational credentials, she knew that her son represented the one thing the Spaniards hated and feared most: a capable, proud indio. "Don't send him to Manila!" she begged. "He knows enough. If he goes on to learn more, it will lead to his being beheaded."

Ignoring his mother's protestations, Rizal enrolled at Santo Tomás in June 1877. Although his primary interest was literature, he decided to study medicine, which, along with law and the priesthood, was open to Filipinos. What perhaps influenced his decision most was his hope that, as a physician, he might some day be able to cure his mother's growing blindness.

Rizal demonstrated remarkable resolve in balancing his various interests. As Coates explains, "Each week he allowed so much time for the study of each of his subjects, so much time for his creative work—

poetry, sculpting, and sketching—so much time for the literary and other associations he belonged to, so much time for sleeping and eating, physical exercise and social relaxation, and above all, so much time for reading, thinking (often accompanied by doing something manual), and correspondence."

Because he was bold enough to talk about *patria*—the fatherland—Rizal often found himself censured by the faculty. Indios, he was told, did not have a fatherland, but merely a country; only Spaniards had a fatherland. Yet, the student activist persisted. When he was eighteen, his poem "To the Filipino Youth" won first prize in a public competition organized by the Literacy Society of Manila. Here he wrote that young Filipinos were the "fair hope" of their "motherland." It was the first time anyone had publicly enunciated the concept of the Philippines as a nation distinct from Spain. The following year, his allegory, *The Council of the Gods*, won first prize in a competition open to Spanish and indios. However, when the Spanish judges learned that a Filipino had surpassed one of their own, they reversed their decision, awarding Rizal second place. That same year, his operetta, *On the Banks of the Pasig*, was produced and staged at Ateneo Theatre. A year later, at age twenty, Rizal the sculptor received first prize for his wax model designed for the centennial of the Royal Economic Society of Friends of the Country. His interest in sculpture never waned. (Unfortunately, the ravages of World War II destroyed many of his pieces. What few objects remain include images of saints, a likeness of a favorite professor, and an unfinished bust of his father.)

> **FOCUS, FOCUS, FOCUS**
>
> "EACH WEEK HE ALLOWED SO MUCH TIME FOR THE STUDY OF EACH OF HIS SUBJECTS, SO MUCH TIME FOR HIS CREATIVE WORK—POETRY, SCULPTING, AND SKETCHING—SO MUCH TIME FOR THE LITERARY AND OTHER ASSOCIATIONS HE BELONGED TO," WROTE AUSTIN COATES.

The outspoken indio's triumphs brought increasing scrutiny from the Manila hierarchy. His every success swung at the foundations of Spanish rule. Fortunately, Rizal was not oblivious to the significance of his achievements or the accompanying danger. In May 1882, the boy wonder became a boy wanderer. Rizal secretly fled the

Philippines for Europe, with funds furnished by a brother and with a cousin's passport. After arriving in Barcelona, the twenty-one-year-old proceeded to Madrid, where, in November 1882, he enrolled at Central University for the most formative period in his life.

At the university, Rizal studied medicine, philosophy, and letters. He also took lessons in German, English, arts, and fencing and developed into an expert swordsman. He won first prize in a Greek contest, leading one professor to remark that Rizal was the smartest student he had ever encountered. Like Churchill, Rizal was a steadfast memorizer. Every evening before bed, he would study five difficult words in a foreign language. His goal was to master at least one new language every year.

"There are ten factors for success," he later explained. "One is work; the other nine are more work." To be sure, his schedule left him little leisure. "His time was carefully budgeted to the last minute, with every activity of the day allotted its share of the schedule and its appointed hour," writes biographer Asunción López Bantug. "One wonders if he simply stopped eating or writing when the time for eating or writing had run out!" To keep himself from falling asleep during his studies, he tied a weight to his wrist, which plunged his hand into a basin of cold water and awakened him when he nodded off.

During his precious spare time, Rizal associated with Filipino émigrés who shared his liberal ideas about the future of their country. They noted the freedoms that Spanish citizens enjoyed compared to the oppression of their compatriots back home. In June 1884, Rizal was asked to speak on behalf of two Filipino artists who had won a national competition in Madrid. Although, again like Churchill, he had a lisp and feared speaking extemporaneously, he practiced diligently and, at the Restaurant Inglis, gave the most important speech of his life.

A new dawn was breaking in the Philippines, he said. Filipinos were just as good as Spaniards, and the Crown must change its ways in dealing with its Asian colony. The chief enemy of reform was not Mother Spain, which was going through a profound revolution, but the friars who held his country in political and economic paralysis.

The speech, the most defiant ever by an indio, was widely covered in Spain and the Philippines. In its wake, Rizal became the chief spokesman of expatriate Filipinos. He began to write a passionate novel exposing the evil of the friars' rule. Written in Spanish, *Noli Me Tangere—Touch Me Not*—would be comparable in effect to Harriet Beecher Stowe's *Uncle Tom's Cabin*.

In 1885, Rizal received his doctorate in medicine and his *licenciado* in philosophy and letters. "At last I am a physician," he wrote his family. With his degrees in hand, he set off for Paris to study under Dr. Louis de Wecker, the most famous ophthalmologist in Europe. An innovator in eye surgery, de Wecker attracted patients from around the world. Every day, the new intern learned "something new—a disease or an operation." But after only six months, Rizal concluded: "I know how to perform all the operations." From Paris, it was on to Heidelberg, a major center for advanced ophthalmic research. Studying under Vienna-trained Professor Otto Becker, he worked on a variety of projects, including some of the earliest work on the effects of enzymes on vision enhancement. Next, he left Heidelberg for Berlin, where he met some of Europe's eminent scientists. Displaying an astute knowledge of science, history, and philosophy, he was sponsored for membership in Berlin's erudite Ethnological and Anthropological Societies—a rare tribute for a young Asian doctor who had made no major scientific contributions.

In June 1886, Rizal finished his *Noli Me Tangere* in Berlin. Several months later, he sailed home from Marseilles. Now twenty-five, he arrived in Manila unsure of the reactions his writings would evoke. Although Spanish authorities and the Church were outraged and attempted to block its sale, the book was an instant hit. On orders of the governor-general, the *guardia civil* escorted the controversial author in his travels about the country. But Rizal spent most of his time in his hometown of Calamba. There he set up a medical practice. The "German doctor," as he was called, operated successfully on a host of patients who thought they would never see again. When he was not practicing medicine, he sketched, painted, wrote, and continued to sculpt. However, Rizal and his family were the subjects of frequent government attack, and his homecoming was short-lived. Now officially labeled a *filibustero*—a rebel—Rizal was a marked man. "My family would not let me eat outside the house for fear someone would poison me," he wrote. "I left my country to give peace to my relatives."

On February 3, 1888, after only five months in the Philippines, he departed for Europe via Japan, Hong Kong, and the United States. That spring, he edited Antonio de Morga's *Sucesos de las Islas Filipinas*, a seventeenth-century work in which the former supreme court judge and acting governor-general provided evidence that the islands' early inhabitants had established a worthy civilization prior to the arrival of the Spaniards. Simultaneously, the young doctor started work on a second novel, the sequel to *Noli Me Tangere* and, in his free time, completed several highly regarded pieces of sculpture.

While in Europe, Rizal organized the Propaganda Movement of Filipino expatriates and edited a biweekly newspaper, *La Solaridad*, in which he exposed injustices of the Spanish regime. In one of his most prescient essays, *The Philippines a Century Hence*, he warned of a rising national consciousness. He ended his essay with an urgent appeal: "Spain! Have we to say one day to the Philippines that you are deaf to her ills and that if she wants to be saved she should redeem herself alone?" For the first time, Rizal foretold the possibility of a future Philippines separate from Spain. His subsequent articles called for his country's representation in the Cortes (the Spanish parliament), replacement of Spanish friars by Filipino priests, creation of a secular public school system, freedom of assembly and speech, and equality of Filipinos and Spaniards.

In August 1890, Rizal finished his second novel, *El Filibusterismo—The Rebellious One*—which was later published in Belgium. More strident than his first book, it implied that armed revolution might be the only way to effect social change. The author dedicated the novel to the three Filipino priests who had been executed in the aftermath of the Cavite uprising. *Fili*, as it is popularly known, established Rizal as the ideological father of his country, and his two novels are often referred to as the bible of Philippine nationalism.

But his activism was not without costs. On the continent, Rizal was saddened to learn that his family was suffering because of his defiance. On the orders of the governor-general, his parents, brother, and in-laws lost their land, and several family members were exiled to islands in the south. "My happy days are over," Rizal wrote. "I am a burden to my family."

However, the courageous reformer concluded that he could not spark his nation while living abroad. "The battlefield is the Philippines," he declared. On October 18, 1891, he said good-bye to Europe, which he called "the land of liberty." To prepare for his return home, he spent several months in Hong Kong, where he practiced ophthalmology. There, now called the "Spanish doctor," he built a solid clientele as his reputation spread throughout the British colony. Against the advice of family and friends, Rizal petitioned the Spanish consulate in Hong Kong to reenter the Philippines. Permission was granted. However, the official immediately cabled the governor-general in Manila: "The rat is in the trap."

LISTEN TO YOUR HEART

"NOBODY KNOWS WHAT TAKES PLACE IN MY HEART. I KNOW MY COUNTRY'S FUTURE DEPENDS IN SOME WAY UPON ME.... WHATEVER MY FATE, I SHALL DIE BLESSING HER AND WISHING FOR HER THE DAWN OF HER REDEMPTION."

Rizal fully understood the risks of his second return home. "I know that almost everybody is opposed, but nobody knows what takes place in my heart," he wrote one of his friends. "I know my country's future depends in some way upon me. I have always loved my unfortunate country. Whatever my fate, I shall die blessing her and wishing for her the dawn of her redemption."

After his arrival in Manila, on June 26, 1892, he traveled through the provinces. Despite the watchful eyes of the government, Rizal founded *La Liga Filipina*, a nonviolent mutual-aid society aimed at unifying indios. His efforts were reformist, not separatist, but in the eyes of Spanish officials and friars, advocating reform was tantamount to sedition. In early July, Rizal was arrested and banished to the remote town of Dapitan on the southern island of Mindanao.

For the next four years, Rizal was exiled in one of the most desolate places on Earth. "The town is sad, truly sad," he wrote his family. One of his major poems, "Me Retiro," described the contrasts of his isolation:

Thus pass the days in my obscure retreat,
exiled from the world where I lived;
in my singular fortune I marvel at Providence;
cobblestone abandoned to moss, I draw breath
only to distinguish before all men the world I possess within me.

To fight off depression, Rizal put his talents to use. As enterprising as ever, he founded a school for local children and a hospital that attracted patients from near and far, including his mother, who underwent successful cataract surgery on her right eye. With his own funds, he developed a successful plantation, growing pineapples, mangos, coconuts, bananas, and coffee. He donated money for the town's water system and had the town plaza lighted. To keep his mind active, he communicated regularly with leading ethnologists, botanists, and zoologists in Europe. Continuing his scientific research, he collected previously unidentified flora and fauna. He discovered three rare animal species—a frog, a beetle, and a lizard—all of which are named after him: *rizali*. Working with his hands, he carved numerous pieces, including "Prometheus Bound" and "Science Triumphant over Death." His bust of a former Ateneo professor, crafted from memory, would be awarded a gold medal at the St. Louis Exposition in 1904.

"Keep on advancing," Rizal wrote to a relative. "Learn, learn, and think much about what you learn. Life is a very serious matter. It goes well only for those who have intelligence and heart."

Rizal's heartstrings would be tugged when one day George Taufer, a former patient in Hong Kong, arrived in the hope of recovering his sight. With him was his petite, eighteen-year-old adopted daughter, Josephine Bracken. Rizal and Josephine fell in love and became engaged. However, the church refused to perform a marriage unless Rizal offered a series of political retractions. He refused, and the lovers lived in Dapitan as common-law husband and wife.

Events changed toward the end of August 1896 when indios launched the Philippine Revolution. Rizal had repeatedly warned his countrymen to reject an armed uprising in favor of peaceful reform. The prospects of a victorious revolution were an "absolute impossibility," he wrote. "I abhor its criminal methods and disclaim any part in it, pitying from the bottom of my heart the unwary who have been deceived into taking part in it."

Despite the hostilities, Governor-General Ramón Blanco allowed Rizal to leave the country for Europe in early September. However, a few weeks later, Blanco—apparently forced by Madrid—reversed himself and ordered the ship's captain to place Rizal under arrest and return him to Manila. Dismayed by the broken trust of the Spanish, the prisoner wrote in his diary that he had never plotted against the Crown. Adding a prayer to God, he penned, "Thy will be done, I am all too ready to obey it!"

Rizal returned to Manila in shackles on November 3 and was confined to a Fort Santiago dungeon. On December 26, a military court found him guilty on fabricated charges of promoting a revolution and cited him as "the principal organizer and living soul of the Filipino insurrection." Two days later, he was sentenced to death.

During his final days, Rizal was placed on suicide watch. The Spanish guards permitted only female relatives to visit him. Even his weeping mother was not allowed to embrace her son. In tears, she held out her hand, which he kissed. Rizal gave his few remaining possessions—a chair, a handkerchief, a belt, and a chain—to various relatives. He told his sisters that his alcohol burner would be sent to them, and that they would find something in it.

After the family left his cell, an official presented them with the lamp. That evening, the sisters took it apart and discovered a small, folded piece of paper. On it, their brother had written what was to be his most famous poem, "Mi Ultima Adiós"—"My Last Farewell." Considered a masterpiece of nineteenth-century Spanish verse, this soul-searching piece describes his hope that, in death, he would give life to his beloved nation. It reads in part:

> **MAINTAIN A MAVERICK MIND-SET**
>
> "I ABHOR [REVOLUTION'S] CRIMINAL METHODS AND DISCLAIM ANY PART IN IT, PITYING FROM THE BOTTOM OF MY HEART THE UNWARY WHO HAVE BEEN DECEIVED INTO TAKING PART IN IT."

Farewell, beloved Fatherland,
thou sunny clime of ours,
Pearl of the Orient Ocean, our
lost Paradise!

For thee my life I give, nor
mourn its saddened hours;
And were't more bright, strewn
less with thorns and more with
flowers,

For thee I would give it, a
welcome sacrifice.

In the hours before his execution, Rizal changed his mind about peaceful reform. "If there remains no other hope than to seek our ruin in war, when the Filipinos shall prefer to die rather than endure miseries any longer," they should choose war. In effect, the former pacifist praised his countrymen for answering the call to arms.

After Rizal's death, the Philippines came alive. Indios from all over the islands were united. For the first time, nationalism became the common rallying cry of the eight million inhabitants of the diverse island nation. "The last vestiges of Filipino public support vital to the maintenance of the Spanish position fell away," writes Austin Coates. "Spanish rule was doomed, [and] Spain erected her own sepulcher in advance of the demise."

The Philippine Revolution, then six months old, began to gather momentum. Led by General Emilio Aguinaldo, the insurgents obtained numerous victories against the Spanish, especially in the outlying provinces. Rebel outbreaks continued sporadically and became increasingly serious. However, the introduction of another country stalled the Philippine quest for nationhood.

In April 1898, following the sinking of the battleship *Maine* in Havana harbor, the United States declared war on Spain. To protect the country's commercial and military interests, President William McKinley ordered Commodore George Dewey to lead his squadron of six vessels from Hong Kong to Manila. On May 1, 1898, the sixty-year-old admiral defeated the Spanish fleet in the Battle of Manila Bay without a single American casualty. Overwhelmed by U.S. ground troops and Filipino rebels, Spain surrendered on August 13. The United States, however, was not about to forfeit its newly acquired Asian gem. Despite American assurances to the contrary, Philippine independence was not in the cards. In fact, General Aguinaldo was not even invited to the Paris peace talks that

AIM HIGH

"IN THE PHILIPPINE ISLANDS THE AMERICAN GOVERNMENT HAS TRIED, AND IS TRYING, TO CARRY OUT EXACTLY WHAT THE GREATEST GENIUS AND MOST REVERED PATRIOT EVER KNOWN IN THE PHILIPPINES, JOSÉ RIZAL, STEADFASTLY ADVOCATED," WROTE PRESIDENT THEODORE ROOSEVELT.

would determine the fate of his country. In December 1898, the Philippines was declared a U.S. territory.

For the next two years, Aguinaldo led the fight—which came to be known, inappropriately, as the Philippine Insurrection—against American forces. The long, drawn-out war was characterized by well-publicized atrocities on both sides. By the end, more than 200,000 Filipinos had died at the hands of American soldiers. In April 1901, Aguinaldo surrendered to U.S. authorities. With the "insurrection" quelled, the Philippines became an American possession.

Colonialism under the Americans was far more compassionate than it had been under the Spanish. And the newcomers quickly came to appreciate the immense esteem in which Rizal was held by his countrymen. In April 1903, President Theodore Roosevelt went so far as to say, "In the Philippine Islands the American government has tried, and is trying, to carry out exactly what the greatest genius and most revered patriot ever known in the Philippines, José Rizal, steadfastly advocated."

America's half-century of rule over the Philippines would end—appropriately enough—on July 4, 1946. The ceremony took place on the Luneta in war-ravaged Manila. President Harry Truman's special emissary read the proclamation of independence before the statue of José Rizal.

7:00 *A.M.*
December 30, 2001
Luneta, Manila, Republic of the Philippines

President Gloria Macapagal-Arroyo, government dignitaries, and descendants of José Rizal gather at the Luneta to celebrate the anniversary of the martyrdom of the national hero. Earlier, the official entourage had retraced Rizal's footsteps from Fort Santiago to the execution site. The president raises the flag to half-staff and places a wreath at the Rizal Mausoleum, which contains the patriot's ashes. Every year, the national holiday reminds Filipinos of this great man's many accomplishments. Patriotic prayers and songs echo throughout the countryside. Cars and buses toot their horns gleefully. Some people line the streets; others flock to shrines housing Rizal memorabilia in Calamba, Fort Santiago, and elsewhere.

Today, the Philippines remains a young nation. Its democratic institutions are still fragile, the rule of law exists more in theory than in practice, vested interests control a scandal-weary populace, and terrorism abounds. Clearly, the republic faces enormous challenges.

Despite their country's tarnished image, Filipinos continue to be strengthened by Rizal's remarkable legacy. "Although the first truly notable political figure of modern Asia, he dealt in politics only out of necessity," writes Austin Coates. "At heart he was a scholar and artist." Rizal's multiple lives, including his literary and artistic works, are a source of immense national pride. His countrymen and women are constantly reminded that Rizal stayed focused on obtaining his country's independence.

Rizal's burial instructions reflect his modest nature: "Bury me in the ground, and set me a tombstone and a cross," he requested shortly before his death. "My name, the date of my birth, and that of my death. Nothing more. If besides you wish to surround my tomb with a railing, that may be done. [But] no anniversaries." Rizal believed that it was better to honor a good person in life than in death.

Against his wishes, Filipinos commemorate José Rizal and the anniversary of his death to this day. In honoring him, they also honor present and future generations of men and women who, like the famous leader, devote themselves to the betterment of others.

10

Tom Lynch

Sonnets to Die For

I'm not scared of dying.
    I just don't want to be there
when it happens.

—WOODY ALLEN

*In his mortician's garb, Tom Lynch
takes a break from writing sonnets.*

Thomas Lynch buries a couple of hundred people a year. He also pens highly acclaimed poems and essays. Possibly the nation's most celebrated funeral director, Lynch is the author of three collections of poems (*Skating with Heather Grace, Grimalkin & Other Poems,* and *Still Life in Milford*) and two books of essays. *The Undertaking* won an American Book Award and was a finalist for the National Book Award. His most recent work, *Bodies in Motion and at Rest,* is a further exploration of the relations between the "literary and mortuary arts." Lynch popularized undertaking long before HBO's *Six Feet Under* was even contemplated.

Hailed as a cross between Garrison Keillor and William Butler Yeats, the small-town mortician has been published in the *New Yorker*, the *Paris Review, Harper's*, the *New York Times*, the *Washington Post*, and the *London Review of Books*. His unconventional ruminations on how we regard life and death have made him a media favorite. Quizzical and gently cantankerous, Lynch regularly serves up comments on death, dying, and the vagaries of human nature. No doubt you've heard him on National Public Radio, the BBC, or CNN offering his insights on Dr. Jack Kevorkian's lethal injections, the public's right to view Timothy McVeigh's execution, or what happens when the rules of the death ritual are broken, as they were at a crematory in Nobel, Georgia.

Yet for all his celebrity, the populist poet shows special allegiance to his day job in Milford, Michigan, population six thousand. Undertaker, mortician, funeral director—he prefers the latter term.

"On the one hand, we're appreciated, and on the other, held in contempt," explains Lynch. "People are glad to have someone to call when there's a dead body on the floor; otherwise, they don't want to get too close to us." Lynch maintains a positive perspective on a profession the world needs but scorns. "I really like being a funeral director," he says proudly. "If you're a teacher, you really have to wonder if you have an impact on people's lives. As a funeral director, we know immediately if we've been a force for good in the lives of the families we serve. They not only pay us, but they also thank us."

Lynch has a corner on the market. He is the only undertaker in Milford, a picturesque village nestled in the Huron Valley. Old neighborhoods of Victorian-style wooden houses built in the late nineteenth century dominate the community. Lynch & Sons, Funeral Directors, occupies an eleven-thousand-square-foot gingerbread house on the corner of Liberty Boulevard and First Street, not far from the Oak Grove Cemetery.

In his airy office on the second floor, the bearded, bespectacled fifty-two-year-old chats easily with visitors, pointing out evidence of his juxtaposed lives. His university degree in mortuary science and Michigan mortician's license share a wall with framed poems of W. H. Auden and Matthew Sweeney. Copies of *Mortuary Management* and the *American Funeral Director* mingle with works by Kipling, Yeats, and Dickinson.

> ### SEEK COMPATIBLE GOALS
> "BEING A WRITER HELPS ME BE A BETTER FUNERAL DIRECTOR BECAUSE IT MAKE ME THINK IN LANGUAGE ABOUT WHAT I DO. . . . AND BY THE SAME TOKEN, HAVING TO DEAL WITH PEOPLE AT A VERY DIFFICULT INTERSECTION IN THEIR FAMILY HISTORY GIVES ME A RICH SET OF RESOURCES TO DRAW UPON FOR WRITING."

"Poetry and funerals have much in common," says Lynch. "Each tries to address unspeakable things: great love, great loss, great hope, great pain, great wonder. There is something about language that helps us manage events that might otherwise overwhelm us." Poems and funerals are all about form and pattern. "The arrangement of flowers and homages, casseroles and sympathies; the arrangement of images and idioms, words on a page—it is all the same."

Some of the similarities are even more concrete. Both professions have a fondness for black, irregular hours, "free drink, and horizontal bodies." Because the two activities have so much in common, Lynch earnestly believes his time in the basement embalming room contributes to his literary success. "Being a writer helps me be a better funeral director because it makes me think in language about what I do and with whom I do it," says the soft-spoken mortician, who has embalmed, buried, or cremated six thousand bodies. "And by the same token, having to deal with people at a very difficult intersection in their family history gives me a rich set of resources to draw upon for writing."

Lynch wears the badges of his double lives proudly. His occupational identity remains central to his writing, and he is reminded constantly of the words of his friend and fellow poet Seamus Heaney: "Poetry is what we do to break bread with the dead."

Traditionally, bards have come from all walks of life. Mariners to musicians, bishops to blacksmiths have crafted rhymes, songs, and tales passed down through generations. Businessman Alfred Nobel, the inventor of dynamite who endowed the well-known prize, wrote satirical verse. During his twenty-five-year diplomatic career, Mexico's Octavio Paz wrote lyrical poetry that won him one of Nobel's prizes. Czech President Vaclav Havel discovered that looking at the world with a poet's eye prepared him for public office. And, as we've seen throughout, the corporate world can be an excellent companion to the Muse.

Musing and managing present similar challenges and risks. Both require discipline and structure. But in writing verse, relationships don't fall together obviously or as a matter of habit. They require nonlinear thinking. As Robert Frost put it, "Poetry is the one permissible way of saying one thing and meaning another."

Given an opportunity for self-expression, poets are sprouting across the country. Alice Quinn, director of the three-thousand-member Poetry Society of America, reports that "there's an explosion of interest in poetry right now. Poems are a major source of spiritual nourishment for millions of people every day." From cowboy poets to fisher poets, the annual People's Poetry Gathering brings together occupational bards of all sorts—morticians included. At last year's weekend-long jamboree, Lynch gave a midnight reading at Manhattan's Marble Cemetery.

"Anyone can [write poetry]," says Robert Haas, poet laureate of the United States from 1995 to 1997 and two-time winner of the National Book Award. "Anyone who has grown up in a culture and listened to its rhymes and sung its songs and listened to its speech knows how to write poetry. The material of poetry is the stream of language that is constantly going on in our heads. It's very low-tech." Frost agreed: "No poet really has to invent, only to record." But, Haas warns us, to master the Muse one must be "open-eyed."

Lynch, if anything, is a good listener and observer. "Poetry is a kind of communion," he writes, "the chore of ordinary talk made sacramental by attention to what is memorable, transcendent, permanent in the language. It is the common tongue by which the species remains connected to the past and bears witness to the future." His writings represent the fusion of ideas and firsthand images about our mortality. He treats his poetry and prose as mosaics fashioned out of passages collected from personal experience.

Engagement is the heart of any poem. Few people write better than Lynch about life-and-death issues in small-town America. His work is rooted in the authentic details of the world around him and what poet-physician William Carlos Williams called the "exceptional truth of ordinary people." The places and characters of his Midwestern childhood are remembered fondly and with stunning clarity: the de-

> **TAKE ONE STEP AT A TIME**
>
> "ANYONE CAN [WRITE POETRY]," SAYS ROBERT HAAS. "ANYONE WHO HAS GROWN UP IN A CULTURE AND LISTENED TO ITS RHYMES AND SUNG ITS SONGS AND LISTENED TO ITS SPEECH KNOWS HOW TO WRITE POETRY."

spondent charm of his hometown cemetery, the Irish priest who taught him Latin hymns, his father's fishing lessons, his first love, and his first signs of incipient alcoholism. His writings take stock of everything, including the great losses that furthered his education.

Yet for all his rural roots, Lynch is not content to be another Garrison Keillor. Despite his Lake Wobegon sensibility, the Michigan mortician wants his poems to be understood in the way Archibald

McLeish referred to verse: "A poem," McLeish wrote in *Ars Poetica* in 1926, "should not mean but be." Indeed, Lynch is far more than a regional writer. The trials of mankind that he poignantly portrays are universal: marriage, divorce, abortion, childrearing, and aging.

Poet and painter William Blake once said that an artist "must create a system . . . or be enslaved by another man's." Applying his wit, verbal fluency, and fertile imagination, Lynch found a voice, at once plainspoken and potent, that captures readers. With hearse humor, he makes lyrical connections between the words he writes and the trade he practices. "Caskets and condoms serve well as late-century emblems of sex and death, how it is we come and go," he writes in *Bodies in Motion and at Rest*. "Practically speaking, one size fits all, but existentially they border on the voids between human being and human ceasing to be."

This poet is in love with words—but not blindly. Many poets babble. Not Lynch. "Poetry is the diamond of speech," he asserts reverently. Like those of Yeats, Auden, and Stevens, his verses are like spoken language. They are sparse, informal, and proselike. He has no room for the flowery, romantic topics of a Hart Crane or the arid, pessimistic incantations of a T. S. Eliot. And forget dreary, desiccated couplets and onomatopoeia. His poems come in short, punchy sentences that reflect the stability of a person comfortable in his own skin.

No doubt Lynch's dark humor springs from his Gaelic roots. His paternal great-grandfather migrated to Michigan in the 1890s from Moveen West, a tiny hamlet close to the mouth of the Shannon River. Lynch's father, Edward, joined the U.S. Marines in World War II. As a light machine gunner, he saw action in the South Pacific, surviving, on one occasion, nine banzai charges. After the war, he returned home to marry his childhood sweetheart, Rosemary O'Hara.

As a youngster, Edward Lynch had observed a relative being prepared for burial. Beyond the pungent sights and smells, he was impressed by how the local funeral director was able to offer distraught family members comfort. An undertaker, he reckoned, was someone who stood with the living, confronted death, and pledged to do whatever could be done about it. At the end of the war, Edward enrolled in mortuary school. After graduation, he and his wife settled in Birmingham, Michigan, where they proceeded to build a practice and raise a family.

In no time, area residents noticed that the senior Lynch had a special knack for helping bereaved families resolve their grief. "He cared about those people, their strengths and weaknesses, and their opinions," recalls his son. "And the community sensed his caring." Over the intervening years, he became the funeral director of choice for the surrounding communities. His single-office mortuary expanded to four locations, and Lynch & Sons became a thriving family business.

"My father was a funeral director, and three of my five brothers are funeral directors; two of my three sisters work pre-need and bookkeeping in one of the four funeral homes that bear our name, our father's name," says Lynch of the present operation. "It's an odd arithmetic—a kind of family farm, working the back forty of the emotional register, our livelihood depending on the deaths of others in the way that medicos depend on sickness, lawyers on crime, the clergy on the fear of God."

While growing up, Lynch had great difficulty explaining what his dad did for a living. He figured it had to do with digging deep holes and burying bodies. However, over time, he watched the skill with which his father comforted the survivors. And Father Kenny, his parish priest, told him that one must "celebrate" a funeral—in effect, boost the spirits of those in pain. The advice gave Lynch a sense of how being a funeral director was "a way to minister."

In neighboring Wisconsin, another famous writer, James Bradley, was coming to grips with the role of his war-hero father as a small-town mortician. "Funeral directors were not merely selling a commodity," he wrote in *Flags of Our Fathers*. "Other than the clergy, they were the ones most intimately in touch with the townspeople in their times of sorrow and need." These "respected, dignified men of service," he added, were not mere embalmers, but were more akin to "a diplomat, a psychiatrist, a psychologist, a counselor."

Lynch observed these same virtues in his father. But he noticed that funeral directors, in the process of giving care to others in difficult times, often became chronic worriers. Edward Lynch saw peril in everything; danger was always at hand. "In every football game, he saw the ruptured spleen, the death by drowning in every backyard pool, leukemia in every bruise, broken necks in trampolines, the deadly pox or fever in every rash or bug bite," his son recalls. "His fear was genuine and not unfounded." Fortunately, Mrs. Lynch buffered her husband's fearfulness. A staunch Irish Catholic, the mother of nine relied on God's protection. "[She] believed in the assignment of guardian angels whose job it was to keep us all out of harm's way," writes Lynch.

NEVER STOP LEARNING

"WE'D LOVE TO THROW AN IDEA OUT AND ARGUE IT TO DEATH. WORDS WERE IMPORTANT TO US AND WE WOULD NEVER SAY TALK WAS CHEAP. TALK WAS WHAT WE DID."

Both parents constantly reminded the children of their roots. "We were well aware of being Irish," Lynch remembers. "It accounted for such things as temper—whenever we'd lose our tempers, it was because we were Irish." A gift for gab was another ancestral trait. "Our dinner tables were full of contention and argument," he says. "We'd love to throw an idea out and argue it to death. Words were important to us and we would never say talk was cheap. Talk was what we did."

Through his mother's prayers and Latin studies, the youngster developed a love for words. Bookish and unathletic, Lynch attended Catholic schools, thinking that he wanted to be a teacher. After high school, he enrolled in Oakland University in nearby Rochester, while working part-time at the family funeral parlor. Professor and poet Michael Heffernan taught him the inventiveness and effervescence of well-crafted rhymes and meters. Besides Homer, Virgil, and Shakespeare, Lynch studied Walt Whitman, Wallace Stevens, and his favorite, W. B. Yeats.

Lynch graduated from college in 1969. The Vietnam War was at its zenith. Earlier, he had registered for the new lottery-assigned draft—"the Nixon lotto," as it was called. Typically, any number below 150 guaranteed a tour of duty in Vietnam, which, to Lynch, was "as synonymous with death as cancer was." Fortunately, his number was 254.

"I was spared," he recalls. "I had a future. I wanted to be a poet. I had discovered Yeats. I wanted to be Simon and Garfunkel. I could play the guitar. I briefly considered teaching. I thought that getting my license as a funeral director would not be a bad thing, in case I didn't get a record contract or a Pulitzer. I was utterly preoccupied with the first-person singular."

Full of himself, yet unsure of the future, Lynch felt driven by curiosity about his Irish roots and his affection for Yeats. For years, the mantra at Sunday dinners had been "Don't forget Tommy and Nora Lynch (Tom's great-uncle and great-aunt) of Moveen West County Clare on the banks of the River Shannon." In 1970, in the dead of winter, the twenty-one-year-old arrived at Shannon Airport with a hundred dollars in his pocket. He promptly departed for the southwestern coast of the country, purportedly strewn with places where fairies hide. The coarsely fecund land meets stiff winds from the sea; the countryside is littered with mortarless stone walls and emerald green fields. In this mystical part of Ireland, the natives are fiercely proud of their Gaelic culture and uncompromising Catholicism.

> **REINVENT YOURSELF**
>
> "I WANTED TO BE A POET. I HAD DISCOVERED YEATS. I WANTED TO BE SIMON AND GARFUNKEL. I COULD PLAY THE GUITAR. I BRIEFLY CONSIDERED TEACHING . . . . I WAS UTTERLY PREOCCUPIED WITH THE FIRST-PERSON SINGULAR."

Arriving at Moveen, the young Yank was greeted warmly by Tommy and Nora Lynch, who welcomed him to the snug ancestral stone cottage. There was no plumbing, phone, furnace, television, or automobile. "All winter we watch the fire," Nora explained to her great-nephew. "All summer we watch the sea."

Lynch found great comfort on the time-chiseled coast. "It was a good life," he remembers. "Nights of song and stories and poetry common in the country in the years before TV." During this first visit to Ireland, Lynch worked as a night porter at the Great Southern Hotel in Killarney. On the weekends, he made for the famous green storefront of Kenny's Bookshop on High Street in Galway—the haunt of many famous Irish poets: Matthew Sweeney, Philip Casey, and Seamus Heaney.

After four months in his adopted homeland, "my life and times began to make sense," Lynch wrote. The prodigal son returned home and completed his studies in mortuary science at Wayne State University. He was now officially one of the sons of Lynch & Sons.

In 1971, Lynch was married in a ceremony he later described as "the public spectacle of private parts: checkbooks and genitals, house wares, fainthearts, all doubts becalmed by kissing aunts." Three years later, the first of his four children was born, and he acquired a funeral parlor in Milford, a quiet hamlet forty miles northwest of Detroit. As his business grew, Lynch began to write verses "in any spare moment." In 1980, with the encouragement of Professor Heffernan, he penned "A Death," inspired by a childhood friend's death at thirty-two from cancer. John Nims, legendary editor of *Poetry* magazine, accepted the piece, and several other Lynch poems on life and death were published the following year.

During those early years, Lynch began to see undertaking and poetry as inseparable parts of his life. Like many of the best poets, Lynch saw parallels between the mundane and the mystical. He discovered that "a good funeral, like a good poem, is driven by voices, images, intellections, and the permanent. It moves us up and back the cognitive and imaginative and emotive register."

LISTEN TO YOUR HEART

AFTER FOUR MONTHS IN HIS ADOPTED HOMELAND, "MY LIFE AND TIMES BEGAN TO MAKE SENSE."

As the largely self-taught poet's reputation grew, so did his funeral business. However, the stresses and strains caused his marriage to crumble. "We agreed on almost nothing—money, religion, the rearing of children," he wrote. "We made beautiful babies and enjoyed doing it, but otherwise we were at odds. I could live with her, but I could live without her too. It seems she thought as much of me."

In 1985, Lynch divorced his wife and was awarded custody of his children, then ten, nine, six, and four. With his first marriage over, Lynch penned "For the Ex-Wife on the Occasion of Her Birthday":

Tumors or loose stools
blood in your urine, oozing from any orifice
the list is endless of those ills I do not pray
befall you.

During this dark period, he characterized his heartbreak as "an invisible affliction. No limp comes with it, no evident scar . . . the heart is broken all the same. The soul festers. The wound untreated can be terminal."

Now a single parent, Lynch rose early every day to prepare breakfast and school lunches for his kids, squeezing in precious time for writing poems. At 9:30 A.M., he headed off to the funeral parlor for a full day of comforting the bereaved. Then it was back home for more family duties. At day's end, he was exhausted, consumed by "low-grade, ever-ready anger at anything that moved." And, like his father, he worried.

The pressures of parenthood, business, and loneliness drove Lynch to drink. He had first developed a taste for alcohol as a teenager. Like his father, who fought and later conquered alcoholism, Lynch became a "garden-variety suburban boozer." Thirteen years ago, he stopped cold turkey and joined the local chapter of Alcoholics Anonymous.

"I was a drunk who didn't drink," he recollects. "Eventually I came to understand that I was more grateful than resentful for the deliverance." With his sobriety came a sea change. Lynch's anger subsided and he gained an acceptance of his middle years. "There is about midlife," he later wrote, "a kind of balance, equilibrium—neither pushed by youth nor shoved by age; we float momentarily released from the gravity of time. We see history and future clearly. We sleep well, dream in all tenses, wake ready and able."

Lynch's newfound peace of mind contributed to his literary output. In 1987, Knopf published his first collection of poems, *Skating with Heather Grace*. Over the next decade, four other books followed. And his love life revived. In 1991, he married Mary Tata, a designer and sculptor, who maintains a studio across the street from the family's place of business. In celebrating the union, Lynch wrote an epithalamium, or marriage poem, entitled "The Nines":

> **LEARN FROM FAILURE**
>
> "I WAS A DRUNK WHO DIDN'T DRINK. EVENTUALLY I CAME TO UNDERSTAND THAT I WAS MORE GRATEFUL THAN RESENTFUL FOR THE DELIVERANCE."

Darling, I reckon maybe thirty years,
given our ages and expectancies.
Barring the tragic or untimely, say,
ten thousand mornings, ten thousand evenings,
please God, ten thousand moistened nights like this,
when, mindless of these vows, our opposites,
nonetheless, attract. Thus, love's subtractions:
the timeliness from ordinary times—
nine thousand, nine hundred, ninety-nine.

His strong second marriage and the maturity of middle age also gave Lynch a better appreciation of the lives of women. Combining seriousness with a tongue-in-cheek style, his terse poem "Aubade" describes the tragedy of spousal abuse:

When he finished hitting her he went
to work. She woke the boys, sent them to school,
then hung herself with a belt she'd bought him
for his birthday. He would never get it.

In "The Riddance," he sympathizes with the wife who has just buried her unworthy husband:

> *. . . she sat in the chill parlor*
> *of her new widowhood*
> *remembering the bruises,*
> *the boozy gropings*
> *and sad truths. And hugging herself*
> *in the quiet she reckoned*
> *the riddance she held there*
> *was a good one.*

In 1990, Lynch's mother died of cancer. After her death, his father began actively courting various women, but the strain on his weak heart got him. In 1992, Edward Lynch died in the arms of a lady friend on Boca Grande Island off the Gulf Coast of Florida. As was the family custom, Lynch and one of his brothers packed a traveling kit of embalming supplies and ventured south. With the cooperation of a local funeral parlor, the two sons dutifully prepared their father's body for burial. "It was something we always promised him," says Lynch, adding that, when he goes, one of his brothers or sons will keep the practice in the family.

With their father in a black three-piece suit, striped tie, wing-tip shoes, and AA medallion around his neck, the Lynches "brought our dead man home. Flew his body back, faxed the obits to local papers, called the priests, the sexton, the florists, and stonecutter." In tribute to their father's twenty-five years of sobriety, they buried him with a bottle of whiskey under each elbow.

Even now, Lynch claims to talk to his parents. "I've never had the sense that they're separate from me." In one poem, he describes his father's ghost appearing before him:

> *He lets me hold him, hug him*
> *weep some, wake repaired again,*

says he'll take my kisses home
to her [his dead mother]

But Lynch is proudest when speaking of his children: Tom, a professional fishing guide; Heather, a law student; Michael, a mortuary science major; and Sean, who works at Lynch & Sons. "They're lovely," he says, adding that each of his kids has taught him to live in different ways. Tom, for instance, the youngster he taught to fish, has turned tables on him. "He rows me down the river, through the deep holes and gravel runs, and shows me what to cast and where to cast it," Lynch wrote in *Bodies in Motion*.

There's a special bond between father and son Sean, both recovering alcoholics. "It hurt so bad to think I cannot save him, protect him, keep him out of harm's way, shield him from pain," Lynch wrote at the time. "What good are fathers if not for these things?" At the time of this writing, Sean has been sober for two years.

Over the years, Lynch returned to Ireland time and again. In 1971, he went back to attend the funeral of great-uncle Tommy, whom Nora outlived by twenty-one years—until just shy of her ninetieth birthday. He subsidized Nora's five trips to the United States, where she was warmly greeted by her American kin. When she died, Lynch inherited the family homestead. The frequency of his visits to Moveen West increased, as did his literary output. Today, the cottage provides a spiritual retreat, which he also makes available to fellow writers, including novelists Mike McCormack, A. L. Kennedy, Philip Casey, and poet Macdara Woods.

When he's not in residence, Lynch keeps in touch: He regularly e-mails and calls his neighbors in West Clare. He subscribes to the *Clare Champion* and reads the *Irish Times* online. Des Kenny of Kenny's Bookshop provides him with a regular flow of reading material on various topics of interest. The Celtic Muse is never far away.

Back home, Lynch takes his double lives seriously. He has followed the same self-imposed regimen throughout his adulthood: Rising at

5 A.M. each day, he writes his sonnets for two or three hours on a keyboard ("I like the clicking and visualization of it all"). Then he repairs to "traffic in leavings, good-byes, final respects."

For this hardworking poet, Lynch & Sons comes first. Like his father before him, Lynch understands the special responsibility to his clientele. "To undertake," he says, "is to bind oneself to the performance of a task, to pledge or promise to get it done." It's about "trust, personal attention, and accountability. If we take care of our customers, the sales will follow."

In this trade, there is no avoiding deadlines. "When the telephone rings at two o'clock in the morning, people expect you to remove the dead body on the floor," he says. "There's no sidestepping that. But no publisher ever told me I'd have to complete a verse by the end of the day." Yet Lynch claims that the business's demands for prompt action have a liberating effect on his writing: "It forces you to get things done."

Poetry and undertaking are both uphill ways to make a living, even in the best of times. Few writers can sustain themselves. The fortunate, like John Updike, live off their novels. But most poets also work in teaching, journalism, or some other field. So, too, for undertakers. The earliest pioneers in the business were usually barbers or carpenters. As the needs of the bereaved increased, their duties expanded. They began to provide caskets, gravestones, flowers, even clothing. Some entrepreneurial undertakers developed their own cemeteries. Even today, what is a full-service industry remains dominated by some twenty thousand small, family-owned enterprises. "We're standard, middle-class folks," Lynch says of his peers, "with most incomes comparable to that of a high school administrator or an associate professor."

Undertaking can be tough on a marriage, as Lynch knows from experience. "There's been no intimacy that hasn't been interrupted by

DELIVER DAILY

LYNCH TAKES HIS DOUBLE LIVES SERIOUSLY. RISING AT 5 A.M. EACH DAY, HE WRITES HIS SONNETS FOR TWO OR THREE HOURS ON A KEYBOARD.

a death in this town," he says. Funeral directors spend an average of fourteen hours a day dealing with deaths, some the most gut-wrenching tragedies imaginable: murder, suicide, and ravaging illnesses. "There are times when it is overwhelming," says Lynch. "At the end of the work day, we often seek to retreat into our own private world. It's hard to be a great conversationalist at home." No wonder the attrition rate for funeral directors in the United States is roughly 50 percent.

Even more troublesome to Lynch is the way Americans have come to deny not only the dead but also the grieving process. Anthropologist Margaret Mead spotted this trend decades ago. "Mourning has become unfashionable in the United States," she wrote in the postwar period. "The bereaved are supposed to pull themselves together as quickly as possible and to reweave the torn fabric of life. We do not allow for the weeks and months during which a loss is realized."

Lynch agrees. "Too often, Americans isolate death from the rest of life," he laments. "It's now seen as a big mistake, something that someone should be liable for. If we can't blame the undertaker or doctor, we'll blame the dead guy. We've come to regard death as an embarrassment, the aged as a problem." He contends that a society's attitude toward the living can be judged by the way it treats the dead. The United States has developed a predilection for convenience, including pre-need and package deals. "There's this hopeful fantasy that by pre-arranging the funeral, one might be able to pre-feel the feelings," he writes in *The Undertaking*. "You now get a jump on the anger and the fear and helplessness. It's as modern as planned parenthood and prenuptial agreements and as useless, however tidy it may be about the finances, when it comes to the feelings involved."

Also, Lynch frets about the growing consolidation of funeral businesses. Every year, hundreds of small parlors are gobbled up by large, publicly traded corporations. Lynch fears that corporate moguls are making a life event a retail one. "You can buy a casket off the Internet or buy plans for a self-built 'coffin table' or one that doubles as a bookshelf until you 'need' it," he says. "There's a push for 'do-it-yourself' funerals—

as if grief were ever anything but." The personal services offered are in sharp decline. "The funeral used to be a thing given by the living to the dead. Now it is by the dead to the living. We're going to save time and money, the bother of the funeral. You won't have to take a day off from work—just use your Gold Card and disappear!"

When it comes to living and dying, Lynch is capable of delivering satire reminiscent of Jonathan Swift. In one essay, he sarcastically speculates on what it would be like to build a combination golf course/graveyard or "golfatorium." A golf course could be built over gravesites and then be surrounded by elegant, expensive homes. "The combination of golf and good grieving seems a natural, each divisible by the requirement for a large tract of green grass, a concentration of holes and the need for someone to carry the bags—caddies or pallbearers."

The poet-undertaker always brings us back to the gravesite. He reminds us that fulfilling our responsibilities to the dead puts us in touch with our humanity. Good funerals press our faces up against the fact that we are mortal. "Grief is the tax we pay on our attachments," he writes. Hence, rather than sedate or dull the pain when those attachments are broken, we should be "open to grief: deregulated, unplanned, unruly, potentially embarrassing grief."

Lynch rejects the requests of those who tell their relatives to "just throw me in a box and throw me in a hole" as futile attempts to avoid the consequences of dying. The living have to live with your death, he tells them: you don't. For similar reasons, he advocates seeking closure in dealing with death. "It is why we drag rivers and comb plane wrecks and bomb sites," he says quietly. "It is why MIA is more painful that DOA. Knowing is better than not knowing."

"But do we really need proof?" Lynch is often asked. "Yes," he answers. He describes the brutal rape and murder of a teenage girl in sleepy Milford several years ago. After a five-month search, the killer was apprehended and led the police to the shallow grave where he had buried the girl. The remains were taken to Lynch & Sons. Against the wishes of family, friends, the clergy, and the medical examiner, the mother insisted that the decaying remains of her daughter be prepared for viewing. Lynch agreed and worked on the bits and pieces as best he could. When he presented them to the grief-stricken woman, the tearful mother exclaimed, "She's beautiful!" The woman found

closure in seeing the body. "She was asserting the longstanding right of the living to declare the dead dead," explains Lynch.

"The dead can't tell the living how to feel," he adds. "The newly dead are not debris or remnants. They are hatchlings of a new reality that bear our names and dates, our images and likenesses. It is wise to treat such new things tenderly, carefully, with honor."

Lynch is a man of contrasts. To fellow poets, he is a freethinking soul whose work is respected throughout the English-speaking world. To locals, he is the town undertaker, a modest man who dislikes pomp and ceremony.

"Tom Lynch epitomizes 'the Common Man,'" says Pastor John Harris of the Milford Presbyterian Church, located two blocks from the funeral parlor. "Frankly, most people around here—the people he has coffee with every morning at the Coney Island Restaurant or his fellow Rotarians—probably haven't read any of his stuff. And if they did, they probably couldn't figure it out. But they just don't care, because they like and respect him so much."

Lynch's genius, of course, is the ability to explain death in a positive way. "He's an extraordinary theologian," says Harris. "His Christian faith is always on display." Other townsfolk praise his unusual compassion and generosity over the years: free burial services, caskets, and counseling troubled youths.

A former president of the local Chamber of Commerce, Lynch also gets high marks for transforming this once unabashedly provincial township into a more interesting and diverse community. Twelve years ago, he convinced area residents that poetry and art could enrich their lives. As a charter member of the Village Arts Association, he nurtured Poetry Art Night, which brings together artists, poets, and musicians in an annual weeklong competition that attracts hundreds of visitors.

> **DEFINE SUCCESS IN YOUR OWN TERMS**
>
> HIS FORMULA FOR SUCCESS IS TO READ, THEN WRITE, THEN WRITE SOME MORE.

"His efforts have ignited an energy and spirit of creativeness throughout the entire region," says Suzanne Haskew, an accomplished artist who oversees the Arts Association. "Things have snowballed beyond belief. It's amazing what an influence one person can have on a community."

Lynch seems equally enamored of his adopted home. "It's a good place to raise families and to bury them," he quips. In his verse "Still Life in Milford," he writes,

I have steady work, a circle of friends
and lunch on Thursdays with the Rotary.
I have a wife, unspeakably beautiful,
a daughter and three sons, a cat, a car,
good credit, taxes and mortgage payments
and certain duties here. Notably,
when folks get horizontal, breathless, still:
life in Milford ends. They call. I send a car.

With three books under contract, the prize-winning author will continue to focus on poetry and essays. He eschews novel writing as "the day labor of literature. It requires far too much discipline." He doesn't rule out a novella or a series of short stories, but poetry—"the mother's milk of literature"—remains his first love.

"To love poetry is to study it," wrote Robert Frost, who often squeezed in his sonnets between jobs ranging from mill laborer to newspaper writer. Lynch also believes you can't write seriously without reading the greats in that peculiar way that all writers read, attentive to the particularities—in his words, "the acoustics"—of language. His formula for success is to read, then write, then write some more.

That is not to say the writing process comes easily. Carl Sandburg spent a day or more seeking just the right word or phrase. James Merrill often wrote thirty or forty drafts of a poem. Lynch devotes countless hours attempting to match rhyme with reason. "I agonize over every sentence," he admits. "That's the fun of it."

Lynch is in great demand as a speaker at undertakers' conventions. A gathering of morticians might sound like a somber affair, but they are, by and large, a cheerful lot, sharing the concerns of most small-business people. Of course, they were not happy when Jessica Mitford's *The American Way of Death* savagely portrayed those in their profession as a group of sanctimonious con men who exploit the bereaved at the moment of their greatest weakness. Lynch lashed out at muckraker Mitford in a torrent of op-ed articles.

"She just got it wrong," he says. "Her basic premise was that when someone you love dies, you are in a very bad bargaining position—which of course is true. It's the same when you have a gallbladder burst—you can't go shopping for a surgeon. When you have a dead body on the floor, you *are* in a bad bargaining position. But it's ludicrous to call every undertaker a crook."

Lynch's fiery defense of the trade has made him an industry hero, and the self-described "Buddy Holly of mortuary conventions" is busy on the speakers' circuit. "After years of psycho-babblers and marketing gurus dispensing warm fuzzies and motivationals," Lynch reckons, "a reading and book signing by 'a poet and author and one of our own' has a certain panache."

Even his fellow poets agree he's "odd." On literary tours, his writer friends invariably come around to the fact that their colleague is a mortician. How is it, they want to know, that someone who writes sonnets can also embalm, sell a casket, drive a hearse, and greet mourners at the door? Why isn't he teaching graduate students something meaningful about dactyls and pentameters at the university?

To both camps, Lynch's vocations take on a special fascination. Mixing burials with sonnets has clearly enhanced his life, and he encourages anyone interested in straddling two worlds: "Just do it!

I never thought that being a funeral director disqualified me from being a writer—and vice versa."

As for yet another life beyond undertaking and poetry, Lynch says he envies those with a well-tuned artistic sense. "I love music and art, but I really don't get it," he admits. Literature, however, is different. "When it comes to language, I *do* get it." For now, the musing mortician will continue to report from the front—a front we may not want to know about. But Lynch knows that whistling past the graveyard sells better than going in.

11

A Life
Within *a* Life

Life is a promise; fulfill it.

—MOTHER TERESA

*N*o one is happy all his life long," wrote Greek philosopher Euripides. Today, untold numbers of people are living Thoreau's "lives of quiet desperation," without the drive to shift gears. Yet, *anyone* can break through life's narrow boundaries, not just the few who seem to soar effortlessly. But where does one begin?

As expressed in *South Pacific*, "If you don't have a dream, how you gonna have a dream come true?" The starting point, in philosopher Joseph Campbell's words, is to "follow your bliss." As Harvard psychologist Erik Erikson reminded us, happiness depends on equal doses of work, love, and play. Increasingly, people are starting to associate happiness with double lives. But choreographing those lives takes courage—the courage to change. It may mean sacrificing money and security for the pursuit of lifelong passions. "Think of yourself as between trapezes when you've let go of one rope but haven't grabbed on to the next," says Gail Blanke, president of Lifedesigns, a New York–based counseling firm. "The space is scary but also thrilling."

It's also important to remember that a double life is a journey—not a destination—requiring continuous rediscovery, with many stops and starts along the way. What have we learned about incorporating our passions into our daily lives by looking at these versatile personalities? The following sections explore the twenty keys to a successful double life, exemplified by the individuals profiled in this book.

1. LISTEN TO YOUR HEART

An old Chinese proverb says happiness depends on something to work on, something to hope for, and someone to love. To craft a second identity, your heart must be in it. As we have seen, a double life demands dedication and energy—nothing less.

Begin with an inspired obsession that won't go away. What matters most to you? Fame? Fortune? Material possessions? Self-expression? Helping others? How strong is that hidden dream? Truman Capote was once asked in an interview, "Why do you write?" He answered, "The serious artist, like Proust, is like an object caught by a huge wave and swept to shore. He's obsessed by his material; it's like a venom in his blood and art is the antidote."

That's the creative urge required for success. But it takes more than just listening to your heart. People pursuing a double life must look at themselves objectively and analyze their strengths and weaknesses. They must also encourage full and frank feedback from their confidants.

2. Define Success in Your Own Terms

Success is one of the most seductive lures imaginable. And yet much of the time we allow the terms of success to be determined by others. Albert Einstein had priceless counsel on this matter: "Try not to become a success," he said, "but rather try to become a man of value."

Make sure you're doing exactly what you really want to do. Michelangelo's father disapproved of his son's artistic ambition and tried to beat it out of him. He equated sculpture with stonemasonry, a humiliating trade for someone whose family, although impoverished, claimed noble lineage. Undeterred, Michelangelo followed his passion, and his persistence led to great achievements as a sculptor and painter.

Look at what control you have over your destiny. Ask yourself, "Is there something in my heart I know I want to be doing?" If the answer is "yes," find a way to make it happen. Don't let the fears that risks generate keep you jogging in place.

Wise people find avocations that they love and do well. They find people and causes they can believe in and serve with all their hearts and minds. They give their love and their energy to projects that improve people's lives, not diminish them. They find ways to savor all of life, not just the rewards of work. They define success in their own terms.

3. Aim High

"Not failure, but low aim, is a crime," wrote poet, critic, and diplomat James Russell Lowell. Swim in bigger ponds. Set giant goals. Construct a grand vision of where you want to go and how you'll get there. You don't have to be superhuman to lead a double life. But you do have to imagine both your goal and how you will get there.

Link your goals to life's big picture. "I've learned that the happiest people are those who lose themselves in something bigger," says ninety-five-year-old Rose Resnick, author of *Dare to Dream*. Blinded in early childhood, Resnick became a concert pianist and, at seventy-four, earned a doctorate in education. She founded the Rose Resnick Lighthouse for the Blind and Visually Impaired in San Francisco in the 1950s and later cofounded Enchanted Hills Camp, the first California-based summer camp for blind and deaf children.

"When you are caught up in other people's problems, your own are easier to hear," she wrote. "Dare to dream. Without dreams there would be no discovery, no invention, no trip to the moon. The challenge, the reaching out, the exploration, lifts us out of everyday, well-trodden paths into fresh fields of endeavor and fulfillment."

Resnick's lofty ambitions led her to shift from music to education to establish agencies that give blind people an opportunity to shape their destinies and achieve personal independence.

4. Take One Step at a Time

According to the Chinese proverb, "a journey of a thousand miles begins with a single step." Live life incrementally: Define your goal and break it down into manageable steps. By working on your second life one step at a time, each achievement will build confidence and create momentum. Self-confidence, in turn, enhances performance and your skills will grow exponentially. Learning develops much like a coral reef—layer on layer of your new interest will compress into a solid base.

But don't lose sight of your main goal by focusing too much on intermediate objectives. Mary Wayte Bradburne, a two-time Olympian with gold, silver, and bronze medals to her credit, says, "I've seen so many athletes spend four years trying to make the Olympic team rather than trying to win a gold medal. After they make the team at the trials, there's a letdown. But if they focus from the start on winning the gold medal, their preparation is much higher. Making the team simply becomes part of the process."

5. DELIVER DAILY

Recall Larry Small's devotion to flamenco guitar. Despite exhausting work and travel demands, he practices fifteen minutes to two hours every day—and has done so for the past forty years. Nothing gets in the way.

Singer Tony Bennett, seventy-five, paints every day. "Backstage, in hotel rooms, in limos," he says. "Whatever is in front of me—city streets, nature scenes, a vase of flowers. I always keep my sketchbook handy." As testimony to his artistic prowess, the legendary crooner's works are on display nationally.

Richard Jenrette, seventy-two, cofounder of the securities firm Donaldson, Lufkin & Jenrette Inc. and former chairman and CEO of The Equitable Cos., finds that keeping a daily diary not only energizes him but also forces him to focus on his multiple interests. Besides his business and academic pursuits (trusteeships at the Duke Endowment and Harvard), Jenrette maintains another active life buying and restoring dozens of historic houses, from St. Croix to South Carolina. He starts each day the night before, writing lists of business and other activities he hopes to accomplish.

"When I read the diary every six months, I emerge with a great feeling of catharsis," says Jenrette. "I've squeezed what there is out of it, and I'm ready to launch into a new period. Daily note taking allows you to see where you're making progress and to shore up your weaknesses."

Make it a practice every day to mark priorities—work, family, outside interests—on your calendar. Periodically reevaluate your progress in shaping a second life. For each goal you didn't reach, ask yourself, "Did I not get it done because I changed my mind about its importance, or was it too lofty?" When you're satisfied, establish new goals.

6. LEARN FROM FAILURE

Fear of failure is one of the most paralyzing forces than can seize the human spirit. It constricts people's visions of futures that are theirs for the taking.

Crises, when confronted directly, provide opportunities to improve. "Never confuse a single defeat with a final defeat," wrote F. Scott Fitzgerald, who received more than 120 rejection slips for short stories before his best-selling *This Side of Paradise* was published in 1920. "The anger of rejection motivated me to keep going," he recalled. For him, rejection was like grains of sand for oysters. By reacting positively, he often wrote sixteen hours a day, turning out up to eight thousand words.

Olympic gymnastics champion Mary Lou Retton also refuses to accept failure, "because it implies you've reached the end of an enterprise. You've given something a try, and it hasn't worked out." Learning is an ongoing process, and "part of learning means trying again and again until you get the results you're looking for."

"Erase the word 'failure' from your vocabulary," she says. "No case is ever truly closed, [and] no challenge is ever over." Cultivating optimism enabled Retton to move beyond gymnastics to a second career as a motivational speaker and author.

Don't equate the occasional setback with defeat. In fact, expect some dry spells in forging another life. It's a rare man or woman who achieves traction right away. Remember Winston Churchill's admonition to Harrow students: "Never give in! Never give in!"

7. IGNORE THE NAYSAYERS

When it comes to shaping a second life, don't listen to second-guessers, says musician-painter Joni Mitchell, who often finds herself vilified by both sides. Still, the singer who paints persists, shedding negative influences from her life.

Pediatric nurse and real estate agent Lindsay Frucci had always been passionate about food and was convinced the world was waiting for her low-fat and fat-free brownies. Many friends and relatives, however, thought her dreams were ridiculous. "I heard a lot of 'That's crazy,'" she recalls. "But that motivated me. There was a part of me that said, 'I'll show you,' but I also set out to do this for *me*, to prove that I could pull off something different when everyone around me said I couldn't."

Now, just five years after their appearance on grocery shelves, Frucci's No Pudge fat-free brownie mixes are a million-dollar business. Looking back on her professional makeover, the forty-nine-year-old mother of two boys says, "There's absolutely nothing wrong with trying and failing. What's wrong is when you don't try."

8. MAINTAIN A MAVERICK MIND-SET

Too often we're unwilling to try something new because we fear the outcome. The more you push the edges of your comfort zone, the easier it gets. By doing so, you can train yourself to deal with the unknown.

Rebels with a cause are willing to let new ideas take root. Most of us rely on a narrow field of expertise to support our ego and self-esteem. But, just as you can't add water to a cup that's already full, you can't add new ideas to a mind that already knows it all. The trick, then, is learning to suspend what you know to discover what you don't know.

Chuck Watson refused to become a prisoner to preexisting ideas. The busy contractor saw value in the scrap heaps at various job sites and transformed bits and pieces into award-winning sculptures.

"Avoid being practical," says management guru Tom Peters. "Instead of the nice familiar two weeks on the beach, take the kids and fly to Asia. Go to Shanghai or Bangkok. See something you have never seen before. Eat strange foods. Listen to alien languages. Notice what people wear and where they spend their time. Explore. See what you find. Or what finds you."

9. Focus, Focus, Focus

Mia Hamm, one of the world's greatest female soccer players, advises us to make life as simple as possible. In her book *Go for the Gold*, she suggested, "Focus on what you know you can do. Know what you're capable of on any given day, what you can count on. Do the simple things well, and then use that confidence to build up the rest of your game. Learn to differentiate between what is truly important and what can be dealt with at another time."

At sixty-one, Pat Williams also knows the value of concentration. The cofounder and senior executive vice president of the Orlando Magic basketball team in the National Basketball Association has run thirteen marathons, written eighteen books and headed up a family that includes nineteen children—fourteen adopted. His secret? "To manage time, you've got to have your values lined up," he says. "Your values have to be written down, constantly reviewed and studied. Patience accomplishes its objective, while hurry speeds it to ruin." Using patience, he advocates taking fifteen minutes every day to work on a new interest.

"Select an important task that you have been wanting to get accomplished," Williams says. "Next, make a commitment to yourself that you will devote just fifteen minutes of every day to your cherished dream, no matter what, come rain or shine." Assuming a six-day week, he reckons you've freed up a whopping seventy-eight hours a year for your second life.

10. Avoid Distractions

Some interruptions are inevitable. But many are just a waste of time. When a distraction arises, quickly evaluate it in terms of its importance to your goals. If it isn't helping your progress, eliminate it.

"To avoid drifting away from your focus, ask yourself at regular intervals, 'Is what I'm doing right now helping me to achieve my goals?'" write Jack Canfield and Mark Victor Hansen, coauthors of the best-selling *Chicken Soup for the Soul* series. "That takes practice," they add. It also means saying no a lot and resisting various pressures to get sidetracked.

For many, noise inhibits creativity. If so, rediscover silence. Turn off the phone and e-mail and unplug the TV and radio.

Doctor-writer-entrepreneur Michael Crichton writes in a sparsely furnished room late at night or early in the morning because "I'm very sensitive to outside influences, so I prefer to work where and when the world is quiet." Maya Angelou secreted herself in a hotel room for days and weeks of concentrated isolation while she worked on her autobiographical tales. Richard Russo wrote his first novels in the secluded corners of cafes. E. B. White wrote in his Maine boathouse, while Kent Haruf prefers the coal room in the basement of his house in southern Illinois.

For anyone working at home, it's important to tell family members not to interrupt you. "Wear a baseball hat as a visual signal" that you're working says Bonnie Russell, cofounder of an online expert-referral company. Whatever the technique, carve out some space and time.

11. Never Stop Learning

In the New Economy, the demarcation between education and career is being blurred to the point of obliteration. Invariably, new experiences provide new insights that open up new horizons. Keep reading and learning new things. To ensure his novels' credibility, Michael Crichton has studied quantum mechanics, genetics engineering, chaos theory, medieval European history, international economics, fractal geometry, and airline deregulation, to name a few subjects. For his science-based thriller *Timeline*, he read more than two hundred books.

Columnist George F. Will also credits his consumption of books in all forms with laying the groundwork for his success. "You have to be interested in the world, not just the political world," he says. "I don't think I'm doing a good job unless a third of my stories are outside of 'the news.'" As further proof of his desire to maintain balance, the longtime baseball fanatic enjoys a second life as an adviser or board member for the San Diego Padres, the Baltimore Orioles, and the Little League Foundation.

Build your capabilities through lifelong learning, and the opportunities will come. The key is to maintain curiosity and passion for new information and experiences throughout life. People with a "Field of Dreams" mentality open the door to interesting opportunities and ultimately to success.

12. Plan and Persevere

Keep your technical skills sharp. The more competence you develop, the more you are able to transfer those attributes to your new life. Remember, learning is evolutionary.

John Milton, the blind poet, would wake up in the middle of the night and compose more than a hundred lines in his head. In the morning, he would dictate the lines to a nephew. Milton kept up this routine for more than a decade in writing the twelve books of *Paradise Lost*.

After spending more than five years preparing for the ascent, New Zealand adventurer Sir Edmund Hillary and climbing companion Tenzing Norgay scaled the world's highest peak, Mount Everest, on May 29, 1953.

During the climb, Hillary, then thirty-three, recalled, "each night, when I went to bed, I'd let my mind dwell on the likely things that [might] happen the next day, and think out carefully the sorts of decisions that might be necessary to make." With proper planning and perseverance, Hillary said, "You can extend yourself far more than you ever believed."

13. Build a Brain Trust

Connections are invaluable. Develop a cadre of knowledgeable people—mentors, peers, and friends—you can consult in nurturing a double life. Soliciting feedback is the best way to find out if your dreams and your strategies for reaching them are realistic.

"Lean on someone you trust," says management expert Stephen Covey. "Good colleagues and mentors give you honest feedback about your failings. People who don't provide unearned praise will shake you out of your comfort zone. If you don't see the big picture, they can help you frame it."

But don't expect any one person—a spouse, a professor, a boss, or a friend—to give you all the support and encouragement necessary. Cast a wide net. Assemble a team to help you achieve your dreams. Benjamin Franklin, the ultimate networker, found something of interest in all sorts of people. By the end of his life, at age eighty-four, his circle had become huge. About eighteen thousand people—more than half of Philadelphia's population—attended his funeral.

Besides talking to people in and outside your fields of interest, get wired. The Internet is a tremendous tool to help you jumpstart a second life. It seems no avocation is so obscure that it isn't discussed on the Web. Interested in the arts? Try www.wetcanvas.com. Writing: www.writingclasses.com. Aviation: www.av8rgs.com. My favorite—the search engine www.askjeeves.com—allows users to simply type in a question and then directs them to sites that have information on the subject.

14. Recharge Your Creativity

"Curiosity is one of the most permanent and certain characteristics of a vigorous intellect," said Samuel Johnson. Multitalented people are intellectually interested, alert, and adaptable. In their leisure, they read, explore new places, and engage their senses. For example, Florida senator Bob Graham has long employed "Work Days" to experience the lives of his constituents. Over the years, he's been a citrus packer, a firefighter, and even an actor.

Always seek freshness. Change your physical setting: Go outside. Walk. Jog. Stand up instead of sitting down. Turn on the music. Physically and intellectually turbocharge your thinking.

One of the simplest ways to boost creativity is to broaden your knowledge base. Try random reading. Pick up whatever you notice— *Modern Maturity* to your child's *Weekly Reader*—and read it. Create opportunities to talk about, think about, and advance yourself into the future.

The more diverse your experiences are, the better the prospects for unleashing your creative juices. "If you're writing your first symphony, and you've never heard any music other than symphonies by Beethoven, your style will probably be limited," writes Roger Epstein, author of *The Big Book of Creativity Games*.

Virtuoso cellist Yo-Yo Ma will try anything once. He's played tangos on his cello—as well as bluegrass, jazz, and traditional Chinese songs.

With each new musical type, he gets a chance to meet a whole new audience—in effect, to shape a new life. "It's not the road always traveled," says Ma. "It's the road *never* traveled that you have to find."

15. REINVENT YOURSELF

Cultivate the art of making yourself up as you go along. The process of rediscovery will expand your world. As Jean-Jacques Rousseau once put it, "The world of reality has its limits; the world of imagination is boundless."

Don't draw lines that limit what you are or are not. Doing so may eliminate novel invitations and the chance of switching gears. Don't edit out choices or become pigeonholed. Do be on a continuous hunt for what you love, what you do well, and what just piques your curiosity.

"When I sit down in the morning to write," says Marcia Emery, author of *The Intuitive Healer*, "I feel so happy, so in my glory. In my younger years, I was a dancer. At thirty-five, I started painting as well as dancing. In my forties, dancing was no longer that practical and painting seemed cumbersome. But writing was a wonderful outlet. It's as if one of my talents got transmitted into another—and writing waltzed right in!"

16. SELL YOURSELF

In shaping a double life, often it's *who* you know that counts. Successful people endeavor to raise their profile. After all, recognition is an important avenue to gain a competitive advantage in your new field. Don't be a hermit. Be proactive and keep pitching.

Go to professional meetings, attend workshops, accept speaking engagements, publish articles. These activities can boost your second life and afford you valuable exposure. The Internet opens another way to get the word out; try these Web sites: TalentMarket.Monster.com, FreeAgent.com, and Guru.com.

Some people do great work without seeking publicity. But for most of us, self-promotion helps.

17. KNOW THY EMPLOYER

After searching your soul, you have decided to explore some options. But is your boss ready to let you? Every enterprise has a distinctive culture, a set of shared assumptions that governs how it operates. An organization that goes by the book may not welcome your attempts to explore new horizons. Failure to recognize the unwritten rules can lead to frustration and unnecessary opposition.

Some organizations are supportive initially but become uneasy as employees begin to live their second lives more fully. Recognize that you'll need at least the tacit support of the person at the top.

In the best of all possible worlds, the enterprise will wholeheartedly support your outside interests. But even when given the green light, first serve the organization. Sony's Norio Ohga understood this. Despite top management's blessing to "wear two hats," he soon realized that pursuing his musical dreams would detract from his performance on the job. So, Ohga put his second life on hold until, at age sixty, he felt comfortable pursuing it.

18. SEEK COMPATIBLE GOALS

As a corollary, avoid goals that compete for time and energy. If you're working extra hours to earn a promotion at work and trying to write the Great American Novel at night, chances are you will not succeed. One goal may compromise the other.

"You might come home too tired to do your best work on the novel," says Cord Cooper, who reports on career trends for *Investor's Business Daily*. "Or you could wind up less efficient at work due to late nights at the word processor."

The moral: Make sure your goals are in sync.

19. Savor Serendipity

Double lives are often happy accidents. Winston Churchill discovered painting while watching his sister-in-law splash away, and Ron Kent was introduced to wood turning after receiving a second-hand lathe at Christmas.

Every area of our lives and relationships is a potential source of creativity. Interaction with those outside our professions often inspires new ideas, as when a scientist points to an idea that came from a conversation with a child. Ideas, sociologist Max Weber observed, "come when we do not expect them, and not when we are brooding and searching at our desk." Rather, they come when we are "smoking a cigar on the sofa or taking a walk on a slowly ascending street."

Astronomer and science writer Carl Sagan once said, "I can attribute whatever success I have enjoyed to the fact that I was, since childhood, passionately interested in the possibility of planetary exploration and extraterrestrial life. Had I been born fifty years earlier, I would have had no opportunity to pursue this interest in any serious way. Had I been born fifty years later, the discoveries would all have been made. While some degree of skill is no doubt required, my experience is that success is very largely a matter of luck."

Double lives are often fortuitous. They are matters of coincidence and timing and are therefore largely serendipitous—another reason to make yourself up as you go along.

20. Start Now

It may be best, or easier, to start planning for a double life at an early age, but it's never too late. You may feel you have all sorts of reasons to hold back: "I'm too young to know anything"; "I'm too busy"; or "I'm too old to begin a new adventure." Don't let procrastination, excuses, or regrets steal your dreams.

"Don't live a deferred life plan," says Mark Albion, a former Harvard Business School professor, who now runs You & Co., a career management firm in Dover, Massachusetts. "Go for the whole thing, now! It's never too late to be what we could have been, to seek a newer world." Twelve years ago, he traded in a lucrative teaching and consulting career to live a more philanthropic, spiritually enriching life. His mission today is to help people discover their true passion and build a life around it. "If you work from the inside out on what kind of person you want to be," says Albion, "the material stuff takes care of itself."

Reflecting on his accomplishments, Pulitzer Prize winner James Michener commented, "I haven't wasted my life." With more than forty books to his credit, the acclaimed novelist and historian found little to regret. "One of the truths about my work is that the books are there," he said. "I don't have to say, 'I might have done this or that.' There they are—I did it!"

Don't just dream—do something. Set in motion a chain of activities that will channel your feelings of restlessness. Remember Shakespeare's words in *Julius Caesar*:

> *There is a tide in the affairs of men,*
> *which taken at the flood leads to fortune;*
> *omitted, all the voyage of life is bound in*
> *shallows and in misery.*
> *On such a full sea are we now afloat:*
> *We must take the current when it serves or*
> *lose our ventures.*

To be sure, a double life is not for everyone. It's hard to imagine Donald Trump or Sumner Redstone ever taking their eyes off the corporate ball. "It takes a mad genius to reach some goals," says *New York Times* columnist Daniel Akst. "The world would be a lot poorer without people willing to throw themselves heart and soul into what they're doing." Indeed, the old-fashioned image of the successful man or woman was that of the compulsive workaholic—in former times, who could fault John D. Rockefeller or George Patton for their obsessions? But even their contemporaries sometimes criticized such tunnel vision. Henry Ford, for instance, was mystified by those who turned their backs on self-discovery and experimentation. "Life, as I see it, is not a location, but a journey," he wrote. "Everything is in flux and meant to be. We may live at the same number of the street, but it is never the same person who lives there."

The lesson of the people in this book is that lifestyles can—and should—be elastic. As we proceed through the new millennium, this message is gaining momentum. People today want to lead an examined life and explore a broader sweep of interests. Avoiding the confines of traditional careers, they are on an emotional jailbreak—embarking on a spiritual quest to expand their lives and benefit from their passions.

Get a life—a double life! As Willy Loman put it in *Death of a Salesman*, "A man can't go out the way he came in. He has got to add up to something."

Notes

Unless otherwise indicated, quotations are from interviews with the author. The following references, in chapter sequence, complement those interviews.

Preface

xiii   President Kennedy's well-remembered axiom was rendered in the immediate aftermath of the 1962 Bay of Pigs invasion in Cuba.

xiii   Frank Kermode and Joan Richardson (eds.), *Wallace Stevens: Collected Poetry and Prose* (New York: Library of America, 1997).

xiv   Mitch Albom, *Tuesdays with Morrie* (New York: Doubleday, 1997), p. 43; see also Sandra Riley, "A Tuesday with Mitch," *Hermes*, Fall 2001, pp. 11–15.

Chapter 1: The Case for a Double Life

3   "Jacques Cousteau: Lord of the Depths," *TIME* 100, special issue, October 25, 1999, p. 190.

4–5   Michael J. Bandler, "Ron Bass," *America West*, February 1999, p. 122.

8   For more on Schott's double life, see Richard Phalon, "The Freudian Speculator," *Forbes*, February 26, 1996, p. 128.

9   John Grisham, "The Rise of the Legal Thriller: Why Lawyers Are Throwing the Books at Us," *New York Times Book Review*, October 18, 1992, p. 33.

10   The Exec-U-Net poll is reported in "Figuratively Speaking," *Across the Board*, June 2000, p.15; see also Karin Schill Rives, "Americans Are Tired, Overworked and Stressed Out," *Honolulu Star-Bulletin*, July 30, 2001, p. D1.

10   Stephen Kern is quoted in Warren Bennis, "The Future Has No Shelf Life" (paper presented at "A Festschrift to Celebrate Warren Bennis," Marina del Ray, Calif., May 6, 2000).

10   Sue Shellenbarger, "The Tomorrow Trap," *Wall Street Journal*, December 17, 1999, p. W1; "Give Me a Break!" *Wall Street Journal*, May 5, 2000, p. W4; and "The American Way of Work (More!) May Be Easing Up," *Wall Street Journal*, January 1, 2000, p. B1.

10–11   Kurt Vonnegut is quoted in Paul Sullivan, "Soul Man Is a Most Becoming Champion," *Financial Times*, June 24–25, 2000, p. 3.

11   John W. Gardner, *Self-Renewal: The Individual and the Innovative Society* Rev. ed. (New York: W. W. Norton, 1995), p. 7.

11   Alan Wolfe," The Pursuit of Autonomy," *New York Times Magazine*, May 7, 2000, p. 54.

11   Alexis de Tocqueville is quoted in Richard Powers, "America Dreaming," ibid., p. 67.

12   For more polling information, see Peter Benesh, "Sept. 11 Attack Forged Patriotic Togetherness, Shared National Goals," *Investor's Business Daily*, November 26, 2001, p. A1; see also Terry Jones, "Optimism Hits a New 2001 High in the Face of Heavy Job Losses," *Investor's Business Daily*, December 11, 2001, p. A1.

12   Powers, "America Dreaming," p. 67.

12   Michael Lewis, "The Artist in the Gray Flannel Pajamas," *New York Times Magazine*, March 5, 2000, p. 48.

12   Peter F. Drucker, "Managing Oneself," *Harvard Business Review*, March–April 1999; see also Peter F. Drucker, *Management Challenges for the 21st Century* (New York: HarperCollins, 1999).

13   Gail Sheehy is quoted in Joelle Delbourgo (ed.), *New Passages: Mapping Your Life Across Time* (New York: Ballantine Books, 1996).

13   Martin Groder, "For Ages . . . Humans Lived 40 to 50 Years, Science Has Added Another 30 to 50 Years," *Bottom Line*, July 1, 2000, p. 9.

14   For more on the relationship between mental challenges and cognition, see Tara Parker-Pope, "Help Combat Senility: Learn a Language, Read a Good Book," *Wall Street Journal*, November 23, 2001, p. B1.

14   Robert Otterbourg, "Time to Retread," *Kiplinger's*, April 2000, p. 102.

14   Ed Koch is quoted in ibid., p. 103.

14   Paul Bowles is quoted in Christopher Sawyer-Laucanno, *An Invisible Spectator: A Biography of Paul Bowles* (New York: Weiderfeld & Nicolson, 1989), p. 62.

15   Julia Cameron is quoted in Tom Pickens, "Jump-starting the Creative Spirit," *Creative Living*, Summer 1998, p. 12; see also Karen Campbell, "Shouldn't I be doing . . . more painting?" *Christian Science Monitor*, August 17, 1999, p. 17.

15   Douglas Lees is quoted in Laura R. Walbert, "Using Music to Forget a Hard Day's Work," *New York Times*, August 22, 1999, p. 23.

15   Enzo Guggliuzza is quoted in Catherine Saint-Louis, "What They Were Thinking," *New York Times Magazine*, June 25, 2000, p. 24.

15   Abraham Zaleznik is quoted in Myron Magnet, "You Don't Have to Be a Workaholic," *Fortune*, August 9, 1993, pp. 66–67.

16   The Wellesley College study and related quote are from Pepper Schwartz, "Some People with Multiple Roles Are Blessedly Stressed," *New York Times*, November 17, 1994, p. B1.

16   Andrè Gide is cited in Douglas S. Looney, "What We Learn from Sports," *Christian Science Monitor*, November 19, 1999, p. 11.

16   Ethan Canin is quoted in Robin Pogrebin, "Theme in a Book and a Life: Choosing the Risky Path," *New York Times*, November 10, 1998, p. C2; see also Joanne Kaufman, "Doctor, Author, Hunk All Rolled into One," *Wall Street Journal*, March 22, 1994, p. A12.

16   John Heckathorn, "Success Eludes Most People. But It Seems to Pursue Gardner McKay," *Honolulu*, January 1999, p. 14.

16   Kenneth Clark is quoted in Michael J. Gelb, *How to Think Like Leonardo da Vinci* (New York: Delacorte Press, 1998), p. 50.

17   J. William Grimes is quoted in Bill Meyers, "Start-up Fever Rages Through Doctor-Inventor," *USA Today*, January 19, 1999, p. 5B; see also Amy Alexander, "Going from M.D. to CEO," *Investor's Business Daily*, November 14, 2001, p. A6.

17   David McCullough, *John Adams* (New York: Simon & Schuster, 2001); see also "Morning People," *US Airways Attaché*, September 1998, p. 16.

17   James Cramer is quoted in Gary Strauss, "Wall Street's Pied Piper of Capitalism," *USA Today*, December 2, 1997, p. B1.

17–18   David Baldacci is quoted in Katy Kelly, "Good Reads, Good Times for Write-at-Home Author Baldacci," *USA Today*, December 2, 1998, p. D2.

18   Kristin Lohse Belkin, *Rubens* (London: Phaidon Press, 1998), p. 5; see also Marie-Anne Lescourret, *Rubens: A Double Life* (Chicago: Ivan R. Dee, 1993).

18   Benjamin Franklin is quoted in James Grant, "Healthy, Wealthy, Wise and Much More," *Wall Street Journal*, September 20, 2000, p. A24; see also H. W. Brands, *The First American* (New York: Doubleday, 2000).

19   James Autry is quoted in Nancy Marx Betten, "Business Is the Muse," *New York Times*, July 28, 1991, p. F23.

19   James Patterson, "How I Went from Ad Exec to Novelist," *Los Angeles Times*, November 2, 1998, p. D2; see also James and Melanie Wells, "Adman Turns Page to Pitch Novels," *Los Angeles Times*, November 14, 1997, p. B6.

19   Olaf Olafsson is quoted in Magnet, "You Don't Have to Be," p. 68.

19   Lindsay Hill is quoted in Betsy Wiesendanger, "A Marriage of Art and Commerce," *Journal of Business Strategy*, January/February 1994, *15*(1), p. 62.

20   J. B. Fuqua, "What's Wrong with Today's CEO?" *Chief Executive*, Spring 1987, p. 22; see also J. B. Fuqua, *How I Made My Fortune Using Other People's Money* (Atlanta, Ga.: Longstreet Press, 2001).

21   Louis Auchincloss is quoted in Joanne Kaufman, "Legions of Lawyers Turned Novelists," *Wall Street Journal*, August 1, 1991, p. A10.

21   Hal Lancaster, "Some Busy Employees Are Getting Busier with Parallel Careers," *Wall Street Journal*, August 13, 1996, p. 1.

21   Steve Allen, "Blessings in Disguise," *Creative Living*, Summer 1997, p. 12.

22   James Autry is quoted in "Straddling Worlds," *Across the Board*, November/December 1997, p. 31.

Chapter 2: Winston Churchill

The reference library on Churchill is well stocked. According to the Churchill Center in Washington, D.C., there are approximately 650 biographies, including Martin Gilbert's eight volumes and more than a dozen memoirs that Churchill wrote himself. For more on Churchill, including many quotes, visit www.winstonchurchill.org. See also James C. Humes, *The Wit & Wisdom of Winston Churchill: A Treasury of More Than 1,000 Quotations and Anecdotes* (New York: HarperCollins, 1994). For the sake of convenience, I have cited only his most pithy quotations.

25   William Manchester, *The Last Lion: Winston Spencer Churchill; Visions of Glory: 1874–1932* (Boston: Little, Brown, 1983), and *The Last Lion: Winston Spencer Churchill; Alone: 1932–1940* (Boston: Little, Brown, 1988).

26   Manchester, *Visions of Glory*, p. 125.

26   "Twenty to twenty-five," see John Connell, *Winston Churchill* (London: Longsmans, Green, 1956), p. 15.

27   "The most noteworthy act," see Martin Gilbert, *Churchill: A Life* (New York: Henry Holt, 1991), p. 86.

27   "To improve," see Winston S. Churchill, *Thoughts and Adventures* (London: Thornton Butterworth, 1932), p. 297.

28   "The English language," see Humes, pp. 32–33.

28   "Books in all their variety," ibid., p. 11.

28   Manchester, *Alone*, p. 473.

28   "Writing a long and substantial book," ibid., p. 431.

28   "To begin with it is a toy," see Manchester, *Visions of Glory*, p. 261.

28   Walter Graebner, *My Dear Mister Churchill* (London: Michael Joseph, 1965), p. 69.

28–29 For Bill Deakin's description, see Manchester, *Alone*, p. 7.

29   For "A very hard taskmaster" description, see ibid., p. 433.

29   "No one can ever say," see Manchester, *Alone*, p. 10, and Humes, p. 3.

29–30 "Smoking cigars is like falling in love," see Humes, p. 16.

30   For Churchill's depression, see Manchester, *Visions of Glory*, p. 24.

30   William James is cited in Manchester, *Alone*, p. 203.

30   Sir Ian Jacob is quoted in ibid., p. 622.

30   Maxine Elliot is quoted in ibid., p. 305.

31   "Money, how it melts" see Humes, p. 60; see also Manchester, *Alone*, p. 301.

31   Manchester, *Visions of Glory*, p. 29.

31   "All great things are simple," see "Wisdom to Live By," *Investor's Business Daily*, September 12, 2000, p. A4.

31   "Short words are best," see Humes, p. 32.

31   Robert Blake and William Roger Louis, *Churchill* (New York: W. W. Norton, 1993), p. 4.

31   Sir Isaiah Berlin is cited in ibid., p. 21.

32   "The further backward you can look," see Humes, p. 30.

32   The "a little bit of sugar" remarks are from Lady Mary Soames, *Winston Churchill: His Life As a Painter* (Boston: Houghton Mifflin, 1990), p. 190.

32   "It was my ambition all my life," see Manchester, *Visions of Glory*, p. 31.

32   "Of all the talents bestowed upon man," see Humes, p. 67.

32   Lord Moran, *Churchill: The Struggle for Survival, 1940–1965* (Boston: Houghton Mifflin, 1966), p. 13.

32   "I never had the practice," ibid., pp. 456, 831; see also Blake and Louis, p. 507.

33   Soames, *Winston Churchill: His Life As a Painter*, p. 73.

33   Graebner, p. 65.

33   F. E. Smith is quoted in Manchester, *Visions of Glory*, p. 32.

33   Arthur Balfour is quoted in Manchester, *Alone*, p. 106.

34   Ibid., p. 215.

34   The *Daily Express* description is from Gilbert, p. 139.

34   "I don't know much about oratory," see Moran, p. 13.

34   Manchester, *Visions of Glory*, p. 30.

34–35 The Churchill phrases can be found in Humes, pp. 116–123.

35   " . . . arrested by a silent veto," see Churchill, *Thoughts and Adventures*, p. 307.

35   Lavery's remarks are from ibid., p. 308.

35   Gilbert, p. 322.

35   "Painting came to my rescue," see Churchill, *Thoughts and Adventures*, p. 302.

36   *Painting As a Pastime*, see Churchill, *Thoughts and Adventures*, p. 306.

36   Paul Maze is quoted in Manchester, *Visions of Glory*, p. 500.

36   Walter Sickert is quoted in Soames, *Winston Churchill: His Life As a Painter*, p. 84.

36   Patricia Cromwell, *Jack the Ripper: Case Closed* (New York: Putnam, 2002).

36   For Churchill's battlefield analogy, see Churchill, *Thoughts and Adventures*, p. 309.

36–37 Soames, *Winston Churchill the Painter*, in *Proceedings of the International Churchill Societies*, Vancouver, British Columbia, May 1989, p. 4.

37   For Churchill's color preferences, see Churchill, *Thoughts and Adventures*, p. 313.

37   "A tree doesn't complain," see Humes, p. 69.

37   "Every country where the sun shines," see Churchill, *Thoughts and Adventures*, p. 319; see also Graebner, pp. 73, 90.

38   "Painting is a friend," see Churchill, *Thoughts and Adventures*, p. 302.

38   Soames, *Winston Churchill, His Life As a Painter*, p. 7.

38   Graebner, pp. 77–79.

38   Soames, *Winston Churchill, His Life As a Painter*, p. 8.

38–39 Gilbert, p. 859.

39   "Even at the advanced age of 40!," see Churchill, *Thoughts and Adventures*, p. 305.

39   For Churchill's love of the Atlas Mountains, see Gilbert, p. 738.

39   Soames, *Winston Churchill the Painter*, p. 6, and *Winston Churchill: His Life As a Painter*, p. 118.

39   "When I get to heaven," see Churchill, *Thoughts and Adventures*, p. 313.

40   Ron Cynewulf Robbins, "Churchill As an Artist," n.d., pp. 1–2.

40   Graebner, p. 91.

40   Robert Lewis Taylor, *Winston Churchill: An Informal Study of Greatness* (Garden City, N.Y.: Doubleday, 1952), p. 406.

40   Sir John Rothenstein is quoted in Manchester, *Visions of Glory*, p. 22.

40   Picasso is quoted in Taylor, p. 410.

40–41 Sir John Lavery is quoted in Soames, *Winston Churchill the Painter*, p. 24.

41   Sir Oswald Birley is quoted in Robbins, p. 2.

41	"I am not a great painter," see Churchill, *Thoughts and Adventures*, p. 305.
41	Soames, *Winston Churchill: His Life As a Painter*, p. 167.
41	"Painting is a companion," see Churchill, *Thoughts and Adventures*, p. 302.
41	"Happy are the painters," ibid.
41	"The creation of a hobby," ibid., p. 298.
41	". . . a dangerous breeding ground," see Humes, p. 46.
41	"To be really happy," see Churchill, *Thoughts and Adventures*, p. 298.
41	"The master key" remarks, ibid., p. 297.
41	"The tired parts of the mind," ibid.
42	"A very fair pilot" comment, see Manchester, *Visions of Glory*, p. 446.
42	"The air is an extremely dangerous mistress," see Humes, p. 38.
42	"The vistas of possibility," see Churchill, *Thoughts and Adventures*, p. 313.
42	"Energy of mind," ibid., p. 297; see also Humes, p. 46.
42	Arthur Marder is quoted in Manchester, *Alone*, p. 555.
42	"Difficult to find new interests," see Humes, p. 65.
42–43	Taylor, p. 6.
43	Lady Churchill is cited in John H. Chettle, "Winston Churchill in America," *Smithsonian*, April 2001, p. 90.
43	"Never give in," see Moran, p. 830, and Humes, p. 82.

Chapter 3: Norio Ohga

47	"The unique thing about my life," see John Nathan, *Sony: The Private Life* (Boston: Houghton Mifflin 1999), p. 118; see also Paul Abrahams, "A Conductor Calls Time," *Financial Times*, April 4–5, 1998, p. 7.
48–49	"It's my nature to concentrate," see Nathan, p. 116; see also Mark Kanny, "Sony Chairman Balances Business, Music Worlds," *Pittsburgh Tribune-Review*, February 18, 2000, p.1.
50	Ibuka's assessment of Ohga is from *Genryu* (Tokyo: Sony Corporation, 1996), pp. 50–51, 98–99; see also Nathan, p. 120.
50	"Setting a Refined Tone," *Süddeutsche Zeitung*, June 13, 2000, pp. 1–4.
51	Ibuka's founding prospectus is cited in Jim Collins, "Corporations Will Shape Our Future Values," *USA Today*, September 23, 1999, p. 19A.
51	Akio Morita is quoted in John Kay, "Beating the West at Its Own Game," *Financial Times*, October 13, 1999, p. 25.
52	"At the time it was difficult to obtain a visa," see "Setting a Refined Tone," p. 2.
54	"We want to create a worldwide standard," see *Genryu*, p. 204; see also Nathan, p. 127.
55	The Sony cofounders' independent strategy is discussed in Charles Bickens, "An Inside View of Sony," *Far Eastern Economic Review*, September 9, 1999, pp. 72–73.
56	For Ohga's preference for CD technology, see *Genryu*, pp. 222–232.
57	Ohga's discussion of "fun" is variously reported. See, for example, *Sony Annual Report 1997*, p. 1. For a continuation of that policy under Idei, see *Sony Annual Report 2000*, p. 12.
58	For Ohga's remarks on the music business, see Brent Schlender, "Sony Plays to Win," *Fortune*, May 1, 2000, p. 150; see also *Genryu*, pp. 350–352.
59	For Ohga's explanation of his choice of Idei, see *Genryu*, p. 372; see also Schlender, especially p. 155.
60	Douglas Hughes, "Sony's Ohga Conducts with a Slow, Subtle Hand," *Georgia Straight*, April 22, 1999, p. 2.
60	Ruth Bingham, "Worldly Choirs Tackle 'Ninth,'" *Honolulu Star-Bulletin*, January 18, 1999, p. D5.
60	Tom Todd is quoted in Andrew Druckenbrod and Rona Kobell, "Sony Chief Is No Semi-conductor," *Pittsburgh Post-Gazette*, February 18, 2000, p. 3.

61   Bob Greenberg, "The CEO As Maestro," *Context*, February–March 2000, p. 35; see also *Genryu*, p. 364.

62   "Do it!," see Reiji Asakura, *Revolutionaries at Sony* (New York: McGraw Hill, 2000), p. 37

62   "It was rather good. Very Sony!," ibid., p. 175; see also "Berlin Is the Crossroads of Europe," *Die Welt*, June 14, 2000, pp. 1–2.

62   "Lowering the price," ibid., p. 190.

63   "Beasts with a hundred heads," see Greenberg, p. 34.

63   Ohga's fund-raising remarks are reported in Peter Landers, "Tokyo Philharmonic Has So Much Talent, Everyone's in a Snit," *Wall Street Journal*, July 9, 2000, p. A14.

64   "We have only one life to live," see Paul Abrahams, "Career Choice Is Music to the Ears," *Financial Times*, July 31/August 1, 1999, p. 3.

64   "Like the traveler in Aesop's fable," Norio Ohga, "Perspectives on Japan and the World Economy," address to the Japan Society of Northern California, San Francisco, November 13, 1998, p. 6.

64   "There's not much I haven't done," see Abrahams, p. 3.

Chapter 4: Sally Ride

For more on Sally Ride, see Carolyn Blacknall, *Sally Ride: America's First Woman in Space* (New York: Macmillan, 1984); Karen O'Connor, *Sally Ride and the New Astronauts: Scientists in Space* (New York: Franklin Watts, 1983); Jane Hurwitz and Sue Hurwitz, *Sally Ride: Shooting for the Stars* (New York: Fawcett Columbine, 1989); Mary Virginia Fox, *Women Astronauts Aboard the Shuttle* (New York: Julian Messner, 1984); Carole Ann Camp, *Sally Ride: First American Woman in Space* (Springfield, N.J.: Enslow, 1997); Barbara Kramer, *Sally Ride: A Space Biography* (Springfield, N.J.: Enslow, 1998); and Sally Ride with Susan Okie, *To Space and Back* (New York: Lothrup, Lee & Shepard, 1986).

68   Karen Ride is quoted in Kramer, p. 12.

69   Joyce Ride is quoted in Camp, p. 12.

69   Elizabeth Mommaerts is quoted in ibid., p.15.

71   Ride's conversation with George Abbey is discussed in Kramer, p. 17.

71   For more on the simulator experience, see Camp, p. 36.

73   "There's no sag in zero-g," see "Sally Ride Remembers Troubles of Being First U.S. Woman Astronaut," *Florida Today Space Online*, July 26, 1999, p. 2.

73–74   Ride is quoted in Frederic Golden, "Sally's Joy Ride into the Sky," *TIME*, June 13, 1983, p. 56.

74   George Abbey and Robert Crippen are quoted in ibid., p. 58.

74   Steven Hawley is quoted in Kramer, p. 24.

74   Gloria Steinem is quoted in Camp, p. 45.

75   "All we can see of the trail of fire," see Ride with Okie, p. 17.

75   "The best part of being in space," ibid., p. 29.

76   "The thing I'll remember most about the flight," see Frederic Golden, "Mission Accomplished: Sally Ride and Friends," *TIME*, July 4, 1983, p. 26.

77–78   Ride's assignment and responses are reported in Jonathan Eberhart, "Ride Report: The Going, Not the Goal," *Science News*, August 22, 1987, pp. 117–118; see also Anastasia Toufexis, "Getting NASA Back on Track," *TIME*, August 31, 1987.

78–79   Ride's departure from NASA is reported in Mark Carreau, "Sally Ride Is Leaving NASA After Making Major Contributions," *Houston Chronicle*, September 21, 1987.

79   KidSat and Frank C. Owens's comments are reported in David Graham, "A Satellite for Kids," *Technology Review*, July 1995, p. 18; see also Camp, pp. 91–94.

80   Lou Dobbs's remarks are cited in "Challenger Center for Space Science Education to Honor Former NASA Astronaut and Space.com President Sally Ride," Space.com News Release, August 8, 2000, p. 1.

80–81   Ride's response is cited in "Sally Ride Named President of Space.com," Space.com News Release, August 2000, p. 1; see also Doug Tsuruoka, "Web Space Newest Frontier for First Woman Astronaut," *Investor's Business Daily*, July 21, 2000, p. A4.

82–83   "The baseline commitment," see Tsuruoka, p. A4

83   "It's an enormous logistical effort," ibid.; see also Sally Ride interview transcript in "Challenge the Space Frontier," Scholastic Web Site: teacher.scholastic.com, November 20, 1998.

Chapter 5: Ron Kent and Chuck Watson

87   Ron Kent's double life is also described in Rose Stanek, "Ron Kent: The Stockbroker Who Turns Bowls into Gold," *ALOHA*, January/February 1987, pp. 31–35; Janice Otaguro, "Bowled Over," *Honolulu*, April 1995, p. 20; Susan Hooper, "Woods Man," *House Beautiful*, March 1999, p. 66; and Glenn Adamson, "Ron Kent," *American Craft*, June/July 2000, pp. 42-45.

89   For more on the Kent method, see Marcia Morse, "Wood Vessels Merge Technology," *Honolulu Advertiser*, February 21, 1999, p. E8; Ron Kent, "Turning from Frozen," *Woodturning*, Summer 1991, pp. 15–18; and Ron Kent, "Translucent Norfolk Island Pine Bowls," *Woodturning*, Autumn 1990, pp. 19–22.

90   John Perreault, *Turned Wood Now: Redefining the Lathe-Turned Object* (Tempe: Arizona State University Art Museum, 1997), p.17.

90   Matthew Kangas, "Ron Kent: American Artist in Context," an occasional piece, 1999, p. 3.

91   Igor Stravinsky is quoted in "Music Lessons," *Honolulu Star-Bulletin*, June 28, 1999.

91   Deborah Shinn in quoted in Hooper, p. 66.

91–92   Other woodturners with double lives are described in Perreault, pp. 14–15; Edward Jacobson, *The Art of Turned-Wood Bowls* (New York: E. P. Dutton, 1985), pp. 12–13; and Tran Turner, Matthew Kangas, John Perreault, and Edward S. Cooke Jr., *Expressions in Wood: Masterpieces from the Wornick Collection* (Oakland: Oakland Museum of California, 1996), p. 31.

92   Kent's primary calling as a stockbroker is cited in Otaguro, p. 20; see also Stanek, p. 34.

93   The "imposter syndrome" is cited in Stanek, p. 35.

96   "Engineering and construction make a good base for art," see Murray Engle, "The Art of Laughing at Money," *Honolulu Star-Bulletin*, March 29, 1973, p. F2.

96   Chuck Watson's desire to be an architect is discussed in ibid., p. F1.

97   "Painting was frustrating," see Harry Matte, "The Builder: Sinner or Scapegoat," *Honolulu Star-Bulletin*, October 11, 1973, p. A21.

97   "Few things in nature have pure forms," see Marilyn Wellemeyer, "On Your Own Time: Personal Messages in Man's Oldest Art," *Fortune*, November 1975, p. 76.

98–99   Victor Bergeron is quoted in ibid., p. 80.

99   "I'm sure that if . . . environmentalists," see Matte, "The Builder," p. A21.

100   "Anyone [like Chuck Watson], see Wellemeyer, p. 80.

101   The "lacking in aesthetic quality" criticism is cited in Engle, p. F1.

Chapter 6: Tess Gerritsen

107   "A scalpel is a beautiful thing," see Tess Gerritsen, *Life Support* (New York: Pocket Books, 1997), p. 1.

108   Gerritsen's comments on her Chinese heritage are cited in "A Conversation with Tess Gerritsen," *Pocket Books News*, 1999, p.1.

109   Gerritsen's award-winning short story was "On Choosing the Right Crack Seed," *Honolulu*, December 1983, pp. 56–69.

110   Michele Kremen Bolton is quoted in Jaine Carter and James O. Carter, "Stuck in the Middle," *Boston Herald*, October 2, 2000, p. 44.

111   James Patterson's kudos are from Tess Gerritsen, "New York Times Best Selling Author," www.tessgerritsen.com, August 9, 2000.

112   Gerritsen's romance writing comments are cited in Judy Harrison, "Camden Writer Ventures in ER," *Bangor Daily News*, August 23, 1997, p. 12; see also Gene Williams, "Ex-Doctor Reaps Literary Success . . . ," *Contra Costa Times*, September 14, 1997, p. 2.

112–113 "I first hear their voices," see Williams, p. 2.

114   "Medicine really contributes," see Joanne Lannin, "Just What the Doctor Authored," *Portland Press Herald*, September 5, 1999, p. 1E.

115   "I had a longtime interest in space," see "Tess Gerritsen" (interview), www.ivillage.com, August 8, 2000.

115   *Publishers Weekly* review is cited in *Pocket Books News*, p. 1; see also Katy Kelly, "'Gravity' Pulls Readers in with a Fearful Force," *USA Today*, October 4, 1999, p. 6D.

115–116 Steven King's praise is cited in "Fantastic Fiction," www.fantasticfiction.com., August 7, 2000. See also Alicia Anstead, "Center of Gravity," *Bangor Daily News*, August 14, 1999, p. 4.

116   "When you sell film and television rights," see Harrison, p. 13.

117   Anton Chekhov is quoted in Howard Markel, "Patients Are Discovering 'My Doctor, the Author,'" *New York Times*, August 22, 2000, p. D7; see also Martin Arnold, "Doctors Study the Gory Details," *New York Times*, October 11, 2001, p. E3. Doctors seeking to become writers may contact Seak, Inc., at www.seak.com.

117   Among the best studies of Doyle and his work are John Dickson Carr, *The Life of Sir Arthur Conan Doyle* (New York: Harper & Row, 1949); Don Richard Cox, *Arthur Conan Doyle* (New York: Frederick Ungar, 1985); Charles Higham, *The Adventures of Conan Doyle* (New York: W. W. Norton, 1976); Jacqueline A. Jaffe, *Arthur Conan Doyle* (Boston: Twayne, 1987); Pierre Nordon, *Conan Doyle: A Biography* (New York: Holt, Rinehart and Winston, 1967); and Hesketh Pearson, *Conan Doyle: His Life and Art* (New York: Taplinger, 1977). See also Arthur Conan Doyle, *Sir Arthur Conan Doyle, Memories and Adventures* (Boston: Little, Brown, 1924); Jean Conan Doyle, *Epilogue; Arthur Conan Doyle, The Life of Sir Arthur Conan Doyle* (London: John Murray, 1949); Ira B. Nadel and William W. Fredeman (ed.), *Victorian Novelists after 1885* (Detroit: Gale, 1983); and Tom Huntington, "The Man Who Believed in Fairies," *Smithsonian*, September 1997, pp. 107–144.

117   "I have had a life," see Daniel Stashower, *Teller of Tales* (New York: Henry Holt, 1999), p. 8.

117   "Every kind of human experience," ibid.

117–118 "I never dreamed I could myself produce decent prose," see Arthur Conan Doyle, *Memories and Adventures*, p. 68.

118   Adrian Conan Doyle, *The True Conan Doyle: The Life of the Creator of Sherlock Holmes* (New York: Coward-McCann, 1946), p. 31.

118   "A diversified genius," see Jaffee, p. 128.

118   "My life has been dotted," see Stashower, p. 8.

120   John Stone is quoted in Anita Sharpe, "The Doctor As Poet: John Stone's Theme Is 'Listen to Patients,'" *Wall Street Journal*, March 3, 1998, p. A1.

120   Abraham Verghese is quoted in Craig Wilson, "Doctor Follows Through with Matchless Memoir," *USA Today*, August 17, 1998, p. 2D; see also Markel, p. D7.

120   Ethan Canin is quoted in Joanne Kaufman, "Doctor, Author, Hunk All Rolled into One," *Wall Street Journal*, March 22, 1994, p. A12; see also Robin Pogrebin, "Theme in a Book and a Life: Choosing the Risky Path," *New York Times*, November 10, 1988.

120–121 The Association of American Medical Colleges report is cited in Sara Steindorf, "A novel approach to work," *Christian Science Monitor*, January 29, 2002, p. 16.

121   Robin Cook is quoted in Michael Kaplan, "Terror of Wall Street," *Smart Money*, August

1998, p. 77; see also "The Outbreak Started with Cook," *USA Today*, April 3, 1995, p. 6D.

121   Michael Crichton's "excruciating" description is cited in Jane Gross, "A Time Traveler Is Back, Still Restlessly Studying," *New York Times*, November 11, 1999, p. B1.

121   For Crichton's unique work schedule, see ibid; see also David Kipen, "Crichton's Got a Lot of Explaining to Do," *San Francisco Chronicle*, November 18, 1999, p. E1.

Chapter 7: Larry Small

128   William Rehnquist's remarks are quoted in "Lawrence M. Small Installed As 11th Smithsonian Secretary," Smithsonian Institution press release, January 29, 2000, p. 1.

131   "My feeling is that you have to make sure," see Jacqueline Trescott, "Team Player," *Washington Post*, January 25, 2000, p. C8.

133   David Jeffers is quoted in Adrienne Sanders, "The Guitar-Bank-Museum Career Track," *Forbes*, April 17, 2000, p. 124.

133   Franklin D. Raines is quoted in Jacqueline Trescott, "Smithsonian Picks Banker As New Chief," *Washington Post*, September 14, 1999, p. A1.

133   Karen Shaw Petrou is quoted in Trescott, "Team Player," p. C8.

134   Karen M. Jones, "Larry Small's Compassion," Letters to the Editor, *Washington Post*, January 31, 2000, p. A18.

134   Roland Flamini, "Amazonian Tribal Art: The Head of the Smithsonian's Private Showcase," *Architectural Digest*, December 2000, pp. 124–134; see also Benjamin Forgey, "In Fine Feather," *Washington Post*, January 15, 2000, pp. C1–5.

135   "I am perfectly fine with reducing my salary," see Sanders, p. 124; see also Claudia H. Deutsch, "Top Execs Seek Job with Fulfillment, Pay Cut Optional," *New York Times*, November 20, 2000, p. 26.

135   "Now I will get to . . . ," see Frank Bruni, "Where to Put a Renaissance Man? In the Smithsonian," *New York Times*, September 20, 1999, p. B1.

136   Wesley Williams is quoted in Trescott, "Smithsonian Picks . . . ," p. A10.

136   Barber Conable Jr. is quoted in Irvin Molotsky, "President of Fannie Mae Is to Head Smithsonian," *New York Times*, September 14, 1999, p. B1.

137   Edward Able is quoted in Karen MacPherson, "Smithsonian's New Leader Is Already Leaving His Mark," *Pittsburgh Post-Gazette*, April 16, 2000, p. 4.

137   "Our job is to gain," see Christian Toto, "Smithsonian's Small Has Big Plans for Future," *Washington Times*, January 25, 2000, p. C4.

137–138   "Technology is transforming the American public's view," see "Smithsonian Head Urges Outreach," *Charleston Post & Courier*, January 25, 2000.

138   "Science at the Smithsonian," see Toto, p. C4.

138   "The Smithsonian has grown to a size," ibid.

138   "I am not aware," see Trescott, "Team Player," p. C8.

139   For Small's remarks on the museum's deterioration and lack of maintenance, see Lawrence M. Small, "America's Icons Deserve a Good Home," *Washington Post*, June 26, 2000.

139–140   Ralph Regula is quoted in MacPherson, p. 4.

140–141   Kenneth E. Behring is quoted in Jessie Halladay, "$80M donated to Smithsonian," *USA Today*, September 19, 2000, p. 7B.

141   Small's response is quoted in ibid., p. 1A.

141   "You can't invent something of George Washington's," see Carl Hartman, "National Zoo Raises $8M for Pandas," Associated Press' *Wire*, April 4, 2000, p. 2.

142   The joint venture with the American Museum of American Financial History is discussed in Eric Gibson, "A Bullish Idea: Ticker Tape Joins the Collection," *Wall Street Journal*, January 19, 2001, p. W13.

142   John Greenya, "Washington Insider," *Washington Flyer*, January–February 2000, p. 7.

142–143 Small restated his desire not to Disneyfy the megamuseum in *The News Hour with Jim Lehrer*, Public Broadcasting System, January 25, 2000. Conversely, see Eric Gibson, "The Enronification of a Museum Near," *Wall Street Journal*, February 8, 2002, p. W12.

143   "That's Not Managing," see Sanders, p. 124.

143   Milo C. Beach is quoted in Joanna Shaw-Eagle, "A Major Reorganization Ahead at Smithsonian," *Washington Times*, February 12, 2000.

143–144 "What we want to get done can't be squishy," see Trescott, "Team Player," p. C8.

144   "I'm pleased to see the commitment," see Trescott, "Poll: Smithsonian Staff Feels Loyal but Stuck," *Washington Post*, September 27, 2000, p. C8; see also "SI Survey Shows Pride, Concerns," *The Torch*, October 2000, p. 1.

145   "Unequivocal commitment," see Lawrence M. Small, "Smithsonian Science," *Smithsonian*, June 2001, p. 14.

145   Milo Beach's criticism is cited in Gibson, p. W12.

145   For a discussion of Small's shortcomings, see Elaine Sciolino, "Smithsonian Chief Draws Ire in Making Relics of Old Ways," *New York Times*, April 30, 2001, p. A1.

145   Support for Small's "new strategic direction" is cited in Sue Fleming, "Smithsonian Science Director Resigns," *Honolulu Star-Bulletin*, May 31, 2001, p. A12.

145   Small's musical goals are discussed in P. Michael Kernan, "A Renaissance Man," *Smithsonian*, January 2000, pp. 23–24.

146   "The Man with the Blue Guitar," in *The Collected Poems of Wallace Stevens* (New York: Knopf, 1971), p. 165.

146   Sandra Small is quoted in Trescott, "Team Player," p. C8.

146   Michael Kimmelman, "Finding Bach's Genius in Elasticity," *New York Times*, November 26, 2000, p. E2:30, and "Click Here for Glamour, Drama and Michelangelo," *New York Times*, May 15, 2000, p. E1.

Chapter 8: Jim Wolfensohn

152   "It is an obligation," see James D. Wolfensohn, "Building an Equitable World" (Address to the Board of Governors, Prague, Czech Republic, September 26, 2000, p. 18; see also Wolfensohn's interview on *Pinnacle*, CNN, November 23, 2001.

152   "Being in public life," see "Profile: James Wolfensohn," *Developments*, Fourth Quarter 1998, p. 1.

152   "I have a passionate belief," see Richard W. Stevenson, "The Chief Banker for the Nations at the Bottom of the Heap," *New York Times*, September 14, 1997, p. C13.

153   "I was too stupid," see Louise Sweeney, "Wolfensohn Left Australia for America with Just $300," *Christian Science Monitor*, June 18, 1900, p. 11.

155   Elaine Wolfensohn is quoted in ibid.

155   "You have to have a worthwhile dream," see Louise Sweeney, "An Arts Baron with Panache," *Christian Science Monitor*, June 18, 1990, p. 11.

156   President Clinton is quoted in "James Wolfensohn Selected President of World Bank," *World Bank News*, March 23, 1995, p. 1.

156   Robert Hormats is quoted in Peter Truell, "The Renaissance Banker," *New York Times*, March 13, 1995, p. D2.

157   "A chance of a lifetime," see Peter Hartcher, "James Wolfensohn's Ultimate Challenge," *Australian Financial Review*, March 31, 2000, p. 5.

158   "Whether you like it or not, we're part of the world," see Jim McTague, "It's a New World," *Barron's*, May 25, 1998, p. 28.

158   "We have a deep interest in the environment," see James D. Wolfensohn, "The Other Crisis," *Across the Board*, February 1999, pp. 20–21; see also Stevenson, p. 12.

159   Wolfensohn's desire to make the World Bank's culture less arrogant is cited in McTague, p. 31.

159   "The World Bank must be based on results," see Stevenson, p. 12.

159   "But the thing I am trying to bring from Wall Street," see McTague, p. 31.

160   For Wolfensohn's discussion of the Comprehensive Development Framework, see James D. Wolfensohn, "Learning a Brutal Lesson," *The Banker*, February 1999; see also "Comprehensive Development Framework," Issue Brief, The World Bank, September 2000, pp. 1–4.

161   "You have to train supervisors," see *Proceedings of a World Bank Press Conference*, Washington, D.C., September 30, 1999, p. 9.

161   "At the core of the incidence of poverty," see Wolfensohn, "Building an Equitable World," p. 13.

161–162 Wolfensohn's challenge for greater private-sector involvement is cited in McTague, p. 28; see also Wolfensohn, "The Other Crisis," p. 19.

162   "If we don't deal with the technology gap quickly," see Alexandra Nusbaum, "Bridge to Span Technology Gap," *Financial Times*, February 15, 2000, p. 24; see also Wolfensohn, "The Other Crisis," p. 21.

162   "Communications technology gives us the tool," see Wolfensohn, "Building an Equitable World," p. 12.

163   "We will continue conditionality," ibid., p. 14.

163   "More and more developing countries," ibid., p. 16.

163   "We have a lot of problems," ibid., pp. 12–13; see also James D. Wolfensohn, "Note from the President of the World Bank," Prague, September 28, 2000, p. 11, and Paul Blustein, "Missionary Work," *Washington Post Magazine*, November 10, 1996, pp. 28–29.

164   For detractors' comments, see Stephen Fidler, "Victim or Bully?," *Foreign Policy*, September–October 2001, p.1; see also Nancy Dunne, "Controversial Bank Chief," *Financial Times*, September 24, 1999, p. 5.

164   For "short-fused charmer" comment, see Bruce Stokes, "The Bank's Short-Fused Charmer," *National Journal*, May 27, 2000, p. 1.

164   "I was too much in a hurry," ibid., p. 2; see also Stephen Fidler, "Wolfensohn Set to Serve Second Term," *Financial Times*, September 27, 1999.

165   "The curious thing is that the people who are our critics," see interview with James D. Wolfensohn, *U.N. World Chronicle*, New York, October 25, 2000, p. 3; see also Wolfensohn, "Building an Equitable World," pp. 5–7.

165   The criticism following Wolfensohn's visit to India is reported in Stephen Fidler, "Wolfensohn Stirs Hornet's Nest of Criticism," *Financial Times*, January 31, 2001, p. 6; see also Alan Beattie, "Wolfensohn Has a World of Complaint," *Financial Times*, August 28, 2001, p. 13, and Stephen Fidler, "Who's Minding the Bank?," *Foreign Policy*, September–October 2001.

165   For the "follower of fads" criticism, see Stephen Fidler, "A Benevolent Dictator," *Financial Times*, February 3–4, 2001.

165   For Wolfensohn's rebuttal of his critics, see Stephen Fidler, "World Bank Employees Blame Wolfensohn for Morale Crisis," *Financial Times*, January 3, 2001, p. 4; see also Alan Beattie, "Wolfensohn Blames Low Morale on Cash Freeze," *Financial Times*, April 28–29, 2001, p. 4, and Joseph Kahn, "World Bank's Policy Goals Under Fire," *International Herald Tribune*, September 8–9, 2001, p. 9.

165   John McArthur is quoted in McTague, p. 31.

165–166 J. Bradford DeLong, "Emerging Markets Are Back," *Fortune*, August 14, 2001, p. 46; see also Thomas Plate, "The Bank That Doesn't Get Enough Credit," *Honolulu Advertiser*, May 6, 2001, p. B2.

166   "We are not just another bureaucracy," see Wolfensohn, "Building an Equitable World," p. 2.

166   "Quite apart from social values," see "The CDF: A Structure for Holistic Sustainable Development," The World Bank Group, March 30, 2001, p. 2.

Chapter 9: José Rizal

Among the many excellent sources on Rizal, see José Arcilla, *Rizal and the Emergence of the Philippine Nation* (Manila: Ateneo de Manila, 1961); Fernández Barón, *José Rizal, Filipino Doctor and Patriot* (Manila: Morato, 1981); Austin Coates, *Rizal: Philippine Nationalist and Martyr* (London: Oxford University Press, 1968); Austin Craig, *The Story of José Rizal: The Greatest Man of the Brown Race* (Manila: Philippine Education Co., 1909); Austin Craig (ed.), *Rizal's Own Story of His Life* (Manila: National Book Company, 1918); Leon Ma Guerro, *The First Filipino: A Biography of José Rizal* (Manila: National Historical Commission, 1963); Bernard J. Reines, *A People's Hero: Rizal of the Philippines* (New York: Praeger, 1971); José Rizal, *Selected Essays and Letters of Rizal* (Manila: G. Rangel & Sons, 1964); Geminiano de Ocampo, *Dr. Rizal, Ophthalmic Surgeon* (Manila: Philippine Graphic Arts, 1962); Asuncíon López Bantug, *Lolo José: An Intimate Portrait of Rizal* (Manila: Ministry of Human Settlements, Intramuros Administration, 1982). See also www.rizal.net, dedicated to Rizal watchers.

170	"What is death to me?" see José Rizal, "Mi Utima Adiós."
171	General sources on the Philippines include Murat Halstead, *The Story of the Philippines* (Chicago: Our Possessions Publishing, 1898); Alden Cutshall, *The Philippines: Nation of Islands* (Princeton, N.J.: D. Van Nostrand, 1964); George M. Guthrie (ed.), *Six Perspectives on the Philippines* (Manila: Bookmark, 1968); Onofre D. Corpuz, *The Philippines* (Englewood Cliffs, N.J.: Prentice Hall, 1965).
172	"They are at one and the same time mischievous and humble," see "The Friarocracy," http://memory.loc.gov/frd/cs/phtoc.html.
173	Church and state description is from Corpuz, p. 28.
173	The local priest's comments are cited in Bantug, p. 10, and Coates, p. 9.
174	Rizal's observations are reported in Craig, p. 59, and Bantug, p. 59.
175	Rizal's unlimited potential is described in Coates, p. 35; see also Bantug, p. 21.
175	"Good-bye, beautiful unforgettable period," see Bantug, p. 32.
175	"Don't send him to Manila!" see Coates, p. 40.
175–176	"Each week he allowed so much time," ibid., p. 45.
176	Rizal's feelings about Filipino youth are revealed in ibid., p. 46.
177	"There are ten factors for success," see de Ocampo, p. 111.
177	"His time was carefully budgeted," see Bantug, p. 77.
178	"At last I am a physician" and related medical quotes are from Rizal's letter of June 28, 1884, cited in de Ocampo, p. 108, and Bantug, pp. 80–81.
179	"My family would not let me eat outside the house," see Bantug, p. 109.
179	"Spain! Have we to say one day to the Philippines," see José Rizal, *The Philippines a Century Hence, Escritos Politicos e Historicos, Tomo VII* (Manila: Comision Nacional del Centenario, 1961), p. 163.
180	"My happy days are over," see Bantug, p. 155.
180	"The battlefield is the Philippines," ibid., p. 129.
180	"The rat is in the trap," ibid., p. 157, and Coates, p. 230.
180	"I know that almost everybody is opposed," see Bantug, p. 155.
181	"The town is sad," see Craig, p. 79.
181	"Keep on advancing," ibid., p. 81.
182	Rizal's rejection of revolution is found in ibid., p. 184, and Coates, pp. 287, 299–300.
182	"Thy will be done," see Coates, p. 306.
183–184	"If there remains no other hope" is from "Mi Ultima Adiós"; see Coates, pp. 300, 321.
184	See Coates, p. xix.
185	Theodore Roosevelt is quoted in Eufronio M. Alip, *José Rizal: His Place in World Affairs and Other Essays* (Manila: Alip & Sons, 1961), p. 84.
186	See Coates, p. xxxi.
186	"Bury me in the ground," is from "Mi Ultima Adiós"; see Coates, p. 324.

Chapter 10: Tom Lynch

189–190   "On the one hand we're appreciated," and "I really like being a funeral director," see Dinitia Smith, "Matters of Life and Death," *New York Times*, June 8, 2000, p. B1; see also Thomas Lynch, *The Undertaking* (New York: W. W. Norton, 1997), p. 180.

190   For more on the commonality of poetry and funerals, see Craig Wilson, "They're Poets, and They'll Show It," *USA Today*, March 9, 2001, p. D1, and S. L. Wisenberg, "Being and Not Being," *Chicago Tribune*, July 23, 2000, p. 2; see also Thomas Lynch, *Bodies in Motion and at Rest* (New York: W. W. Norton, 2000), pp. 25, 260, and Kristin Davis, "Six Feet Under," *Managing Kiplinger's*, February 2002, pp. 78–84.

190   "Poetry and funerals have much in common," see Chris Wright, "Dying Words," *Boston Phoenix*, November 20–27, 1997, p. 5; see also Jim Buie, "Last Acts," *Electronic Newsletter*, January 1, 2001.

191   Seamus Heaney is quoted in Lynch, *Bodies in Motion*, pp. 263–264.

191   For more on musing and managing, see Susan Adams, "Why Not a Sonnet?," *Forbes*, May 17, 1999, pp. 344–348, and Mukal Pandya, "They're in a Position to Mix Metaphors with Business," *New York Times*, November 27, 1994, p. F5.

191   Alice Quinn is quoted in Marjorie Coeyman, "To Her, Every Spot Needs a Touch of Poetry," *Christian Science Monitor*, April 3, 2001, p. 17.

192   Robert Haas is quoted in Adams, pp. 345–346.

192   "Poetry is a kind of communion," see Lynch, *Bodies in Motion*, p. 264.

192   For more on William Carlos Williams, see "Words As Image," *The Economist*, March 3, 2001, p. 80.

192–193   Archibald McLeish, *Ars Poetica*, reprinted in www.poets.org, p. 1.

193   William Blake is quoted in Mark Matousek, "Life Force," *Modern Maturity*, May/June 2001, p. 25.

193   See Lynch, *Bodies in Motion*, p. 81.

194   "My father was a funeral director," see Lynch, *The Undertaking*, p. 18.

194   See James Bradley, *Flags of Our Fathers* (New York: Bantam Books, 2000), p. 21.

195   "In every football game, he saw the ruptured spleen," see Lynch, *The Undertaking*, pp. 45–47.

195   "[She] believed in the assignment of guardian angels," ibid., p. 45.

195   For more on Lynch's Irishness, see Brian Fallon, "Lynch Lore," *Dublin Live*, April 21, 2001, and Darina Molloy, "Chapter and Hearse," *Irish America*, April 21, 2001.

195   For more on the family's love of language, see Smith, p. B6, and Molloy, p. 8.

196   "I was spared. I had a future," see Lynch, *The Undertaking*, p. 145.

196   Nora Lynch is quoted in "The Moveen Notebook," in Thomas Lynch, *Still Life in Milford* (New York: W. W. Norton, 1998), p. 58.

197   Lynch's life change is discussed in Fallon, p. 3; see also Lynch, *The Undertaking*, p. 31.

197   "A good funeral, like a good poem," see Lynch, *Bodies in Motion*, p. 257; see also Smith, p. B6.

197–198   "We agreed on almost nothing," ibid., p. 102.

198   "For the Ex-Wife on the Occasion of Her Birthday," ibid., p. 207.

198   Lynch's "heartbreak" comments are from Lynch, *The Undertaking*, p. 64; his anger is highlighted in *Bodies in Motion*, p. 102, and *The Undertaking*, p. 54.

198   For Lynch's inheritance of his father's worrywart tendencies, see Lynch, *The Undertaking*, pp. 50, 53.

198–199   "There is about midlife a kind of balance," ibid., p. 143.

199   See "The Nines," in Lynch, *Still Life in Milford*, p. 125.

199   "Aubade," ibid., p. 130.

200   "The Riddance," ibid., pp. 110–111.

200   "[The Lynches] brought our dead man home," see Lynch, *The Undertaking*, p. 24.

200–201 "He lets me hold him, hug him," see "Kisses," in Lynch, *Still Life in Milford*, p. 38.

201   "He rows me down the river," see "Fish Stories," in Lynch, *Bodies in Motion*, pp. 151–157.

201   "It hurt so bad to think I cannot save him," see Lynch, "The Way We Are" (essay); see also Wisenberg, p. 2.

202   "To undertake is to bind oneself," see Lynch, *The Undertaking*, p. xix; see also Lynch, *Bodies in Motion*, p. 174.

203   Margaret Mead is quoted in Jane E. Brody, "After a Death, Doctors Can Offer Families Healing Help," *New York Times*, May 15, 2001, p. D5.

203   "Too often, Americans isolate death," see Richard Bak, "Working Stiff: Author-Undertaker Thomas Lynch Finds a Greater Purpose in Life and Death," *Detroit News*, August 12, 1997.

203   Lynch's criticism of prearranging funerals is reported in Lynch, *The Undertaking*, p. 186, and Lynch, *Bodies in Motion*, p. 179.

203   Easy casket purchases are described in ibid., p. 90, and Lynch, *The Undertaking*, pp. 184–191.

204   For more on "golfatoriums," see ibid., pp. 84–87; see also Heather Mallick, "Lynch's Understanding of Science," *Jam! Book Reviews*, September 27, 1998, p. 2.

204   "Grief is the tax," see Lynch, *Bodies in Motion*, p. 194; see also Lynch, *The Undertaking*, p. 7.

203–204 The need for closure is discussed in Wright, p. 5; see also Thomas Lynch, "How Mourners Were Betrayed," *New York Times*, February 22, 2002, p. A27, and Somini Sengupta, "Why Disposing of the Dead Matters to the Living," *New York Times*, February 24, 2002, p. WK5.

204   "The dead can't tell the living," see Lynch, *The Undertaking*, p. 198.

206   "Still Life in Milford," in Lynch, *Still Life in Milford*, p. 135.

206   Robert Frost is quoted in Michael Mink, "Poet Robert Frost: Determination and Passion Made Him an American Literary Icon," *Investor's Business Daily*, March 2, 2001, p. A4.

207   See Jessica Mitford, *The American Way of Death* (New York: Simon & Schuster, 1963), and *The American Way of Death Revisited* (New York: Alfred A. Knopf, 1998).

207   "She just got it wrong," see Tom Lynch, "Whistling Past the Graveyard Again—," *San Francisco Chronicle*, August 16, 1998; see also Wright, p. 3.

207   "After years of psycho-babblers," see Lynch, *Bodies in Motion*, p. 256.

Chapter 11: A Life Within a Life

211   Joseph Campbell's "bliss" remarks are variously reported. See, for example, John M. Maher and Dennie Briggs (eds.), *An Open Life: Joseph Campbell in Conversation with Michael Toms* (New York: Harper Perennial, 1990).

211   For more on Erik Erikson's characterization of happiness, see his Pulitzer Prize-winning *Gandhi's Truth: On the Origins of Militant Non-Violence* (New York: W. W. Norton, 1969).

211   Gail Blanke is quoted in Carol Hymowitz, "Learning How to Brave the Next Career Leap When There's No. Job," *Wall Street Journal*, June 26, 2001, p. B1.

212   Truman Capote is quoted in Dennis Palumbo, "News Flash: Writing Is Hard!" *The Writer's Life*, June 1997, p. 16.

212   For Albert Einstein quotes, see Alice Calaprice (ed.), *The Quotable Einstein* (Princeton, N.J.: Princeton University Press, 1966).

213   For James Russell Lowell quotes, see "Creative Quotations from James Russell Lowell" at bemorecreative.com and "Great Quotations by James Russell Lowell" at cybernation.com, 2000.

213   See Rose Resnick, *Dare to Dream: The Rose Resnick Story* (San Francisco: Strawberry Hill Press, 1988); see also Linda Stockman-Vines, "Two Overcomers," *Investor's Business Daily*, April 11, 2000, p. A4.

214   Mary Wayte Bradburne is quoted in Cord Cooper, "From Defeat to Olympic Gold," *Investor's Business Daily*, August 2, 2000, p. A3.

214   Tony Bennett is quoted in John C. Tibbetts, "Tony Bennett," *Fort Lauderdale and Palm Beach*, 2000, p. 15; see also Geraldine Fabricant, "His Heart's in San Francisco, The Money in his Son's Hands," *New York Times*, May 2, 1999, p. C1, and "Walter Scott's Personality Parade," *Parade*, February 6, 2000, p. 2.

214   Richard Jenrette is quoted in Cord Cooper, "Track Your Persistence Daily," *Investor's Business Daily*, January 11, 1999, p. A10; see also "Richard Jenrette's Southern Comfort," *CEO Magazine*, November 2001, p. 15.

215   F. Scott Fitzgerald is quoted in Cord Cooper, "Persistence: The Write Approach," *Investor's Business Daily*, July 10, 2000, p. A4; see also Susan Vaughn, "Writer F. Scott Fitzgerald," *Investor's Business Daily*, February 2, 2000, p. A4.

215   See Mary Lou Retton, *Gateways to Happiness* (New York: Broadway Books, 2000), pp. 127–131; see also John Steinbreden, "After the Career Is Over," *Sky*, October 2000, pp. 114–115.

216   Joni Mitchell's double life is discussed in James Brooke, "Joni Mitchell, Musician, Shows Another Side: Painting," *New York Times*, August 22, 2000, p. B1.

216   Lindsay Frucci is quoted in Linda Stockman-Vines, "Modifying to Innovate," *Investor's Business Daily*, September 23, 1999.

217   Tom Peters is quoted in Anne Fisher, "Tom Peters, Professional Loudmouth," *Fortune*, December 29, 1997, pp. 274–276.

217   See Mia Hamm, *Go for the Gold: A Champion's Guide to Winning in Soccer and in Life* (New York: HarperCollins, 1999), p. 38.

217   Pat Williams is quoted in Amy Reynolds Alexander, "How One Busy Man Focuses His Time," *Investor's Business Daily*, April 19, 2000, p. A4.

218   For more on "focus," see Jack Canfield and Mark Victor Hansen, *Chicken Soup for the Soul* (Deerfield Beach, Fla: Health Communications, 1993); see also Jack Canfield, "Soup Way," *Writer's Digest*, June 2000, p. 29.

218   Michael Crichton is quoted in Jane Gross, "A Time Traveler Is Back, Still Restlessly Studying," *New York Times*, November 24, 1999, p. B1.

218   Bonnie Russell is quoted in Amy Reynolds Alexander, "Stopping Distractions at Work," *Investor's Business Daily*, September 14, 2000, p. A4.

219   George F. Will is quoted in Jonah Keri, "Columnist George F. Will," *Investor's Business Daily*, August 31, 2000, p. A4.

220   Sir Edmund Hillary is quoted in Cord Cooper, "The Power of Preparation," *Investor's Business Daily*, October 4, 1999, p. A4.

220   See Stephen Covey, "Stephen Covey on Recharging Creativity," *USA Weekend*, November 17–19, 2000, p. 10.

221   Bob Graham's "Work Days" are discussed in Neal Santelmann, "How to Burn 10 Million Calories," *Forbes FYI*, September 18, 2000, p. 159.

221   See Robert Epstein, *The Big Book of Creativity Games* (New York: McGraw-Hill, 2000); see also Linda Stockman-Vines, "Unleashing Creative Expression," *Investor's Business Daily*, September 2, 2000, p. A4.

222   Yo-Yo Ma is quoted in Amy Reynolds Alexander, "Cellist Yo-Yo Ma," *Investor's Business Daily*, October 9, 2000, p. A4.

222   See Marcia Emery, *The Intuitive Healer: Assessing Your Inner Physician* (New York: St. Martin's Press, 1999).

223   See Cord Cooper, "Tips for Achieving Goals," *Investor's Business Daily*, July 5, 2000, p. A4.

224 Max Weber is quoted in Mark Gerson, "Who Has the Time to Be Bored?," *USA Today*, August 8, 2000, p. 15A.

224 Carl Sagan is quoted in "The Career Labyrinth," *Executive*, 2 (2), Winter 1976, p. 15.

225 See Mark S. Albion, *Making a Life, Making a Living* (New York: Warner Books, 2000); see also Linda Stockman-Vines, "Deciding What's Important," *Investor's Business Daily*, May 24, 2001.

225 James Michener is quoted in Bob Minzensheimer, "Michener's Legacy for Late Bloomers," *USA Today*, February 4, 1999, p. D7.

225 Brutus's famous quote is from William Shakespeare's *Julius Caesar* (1623); see William and Barbara Rosen (eds.), *The Tragedy of Julius Caesar* (New York: Penguin Putnam, 1998), p. 84.

225 See Daniel Akst, "Workaholics Arise, Now Get Back to Work," *New York Times*, May 6, 2001, p. C3.

226 Henry Ford is quoted in *Bottom Line*, January 1, 1998, p. 2.

226 See Arthur Miller, *Death of a Salesman* (New York: Viking Press, 1949), p. 125.

Index